FRANK SHERWIN
Independent and Unrepentant

Passport photo, taken in 1964, of Frank Sherwin aged 59.

FRANK SHERWIN
Independent and Unrepentant

Edited by
FRANK SHERWIN JR

Foreword by
EUNAN O'HALPIN

IRISH ACADEMIC PRESS
DUBLIN • PORTLAND, OR

First published in 2007 by
IRISH ACADEMIC PRESS
44 Northumberland Road, Dublin 4, Ireland

and in the United States of America by
IRISH ACADEMIC PRESS
c/o ISBS, Suite 300, 920 NE 58th Avenue
Portland, Oregon 97213-3786

Copyright © 2007 Frank Sherwin Jr

Website: **www.iap.ie**

British Library Cataloguing in Publication Data
An entry can be found on request

ISBN 0 7165 2848 7(cloth)
ISBN 978 0 7165 2848 7
ISBN 0 7165 2849 5(paper)
ISBN 978 0 7165 2849 4

Library of Congress Cataloging-in-Publication Data
An entry can be found on request

Typeset in 11pt on 13pt Baskerville by
FiSH Books, Enfield, Middx.
Printed by Biddles, King's Lynn, Norfolk

So never say die... I remain independent and unrepentant in the hope that my past actions will be understood and accepted by a more enlightened public.

Frank Sherwin

CONTENTS

Acknowledgements   xi

Abbreviations   xii

Foreword by Eunan O'Halpin   xiii

Introduction by Frank Sherwin Jr   xv

PART I: FRANK SHERWIN'S POLITICAL HELL

1   Small Beginnings   5

2   The War of Independence and Civil War   12

3   Politics: No place for the lone man   34

4   From the dole to the *Dáil!*   56

5   Politics: The Art of Deception   66

6   *Dáil Éireann* with *Introduction* by Frank Sherwin Jr   77

7   The turnover tax   90

8   Slander in the *Dáil*!   96

9   *The Irish Times* libel action   111

10 Bribery and thuggery   127

11 My world had collapsed   134

12 I saved the country   151

13 My work as councillor and TD   158

PART II: REFLECTIONS BY FRANK SHERWIN ON THE IRELAND OF HIS DAY

14 Mental hospitals are a sorrowful sight   169

15 A reflection on the history of Ireland   173

16 The partition of Ireland   182

17 Travels abroad   189

18 The auction business   197

Postscript   201

Afterword by Frank Sherwin Jr   208

Appendices

   Appendix I: 'Ifs' in Irish history – An essay written by
     Frank Sherwin in 1944   211
   Appendix II: Lost Opportunities – An essay written by
     Frank Sherwin *c.* 1950   217
   Appendix III: Frank Sherwin – An Appreciation by
     Francis J. Feely   220

Bibliography   222

Index   225

Frank Sherwin's story illuminates the ebb and flow of political events during the twentieth century given his involvement in a wide range of causes. He is best remembered for his central role in the turnover tax debates of 1963 and his subsequent pivotal position in the *Dáil* when the fate of the government was at stake. Through his account, we get a closer insight into the events of those dramatic days.

Dr Michael Gallagher, Department of Political Science,
Trinity College Dublin

From poverty to *Dáil Éireann* and from a Free State prison cell to a successful business career, the life of Frank Sherwin was as varied as it was challenging. A quintessential inner city Dubliner and a man whose concern for the poor in Irish society was paramount, he served on the City Council for nineteen years. His name will live on as a result of the Council's decision in 1982 to name a new bridge over the Liffey: The Frank Sherwin Memorial Bridge.

Dr Gerry McElroy, Royal Irish Academy

Frank Sherwin was an authentic Dublin character who for a vital few years exercised great influence in *Dáil Éireann*. He was fearless in fighting for his constituents, was a genuine champion of the underdog and had a very colourful turn of phrase which he used to great advantage in *Dáil* exchanges. He was one of a small number of Independents who made a real impact in the *Dáil* over the years and showed great courage in sticking by the commitment he made to support Seán Lemass through some very difficult years, especially in sustaining the government through the very unpopular turnover tax of the mid-1960s. It was this commitment which ultimately cost him his seat.

Dr Maurice Manning, President of the Irish Human Rights
Commission, former *Dáil* and *Seanad Éireann* deputy
and lecturer of Politics in UCD

Sherwin was intellectually convinced that the [turnover] tax was necessary. He voted for it and the measure was narrowly passed. It cost him his seat in the next election, in 1965 . . . He was a natural politician who, despite his lack of financial resources, still managed to get elected to Dublin Corporation again in 1974 and again in 1979, just two years before his death . . . Some of the most colourful passages in the book concern the fiery times of the early Twenties, the days of the *Fianna*, the Civil War and the early years of the Free State, as it then was. At this time, Sherwin was imprisoned by Free State troops . . . From his teens, Frank Sherwin was clearly a strong-minded individual who would not kow-tow to what he saw as inefficiency or stupidity. Inability to put 'politics' before principles cost him the advantage of being 'in' with the *Fianna Fáil* party from the beginning. But for that fiery and uncompromising streak in his nature, he might have become an established *Fianna Fáil* TD himself. Had that happened, Ireland would have lost one of the mid-century's most colourful fringe politicians but his family would have gained a reliable breadwinner. Despite Frank Sherwin's strong sense of the injustice done to him, he would still not have had it any other way.

'The Sherwin Diaries: A secret revealed'
by Ginnie Kennerley, *The Sunday Press*,
Sunday 8 January 1984, p. 5.

Frank Sherwin and I became both political and personal friends. I recall vividly a dramatic evening in June 1963 when the *Fianna Fáil* government of the day was engaged in a perilous situation in the *Dáil*, legislating for the introduction of a new tax, the Turnover Tax. The defeat of the government was widely forecast but Deputy Frank Sherwin sent for me at an early stage and assured me that he was voting with the government. I was then able to be the bearer of this good news to the *Taoiseach* Seán Lemass who was in the *Dáil* piloting the legislation through the house. Lemass as was his habit merely nodded though his relief must have been immense. As the messenger, having been put in the position of bearing good news, I felt deeply grateful to my friend Frank Sherwin.

Charles J. Haughey,
Sixth *Taoiseach* of the Republic of Ireland

ACKNOWLEDGEMENTS

I would like to thank the following people who were of inestimable assistance throughout the editing of this work: I am very grateful to the staff of the National Library of Ireland for their kindness and relentless assistance; a special thank you to the staff of the Ilac Centre Library, Henry Street Dublin and the staff of the Political Science Department of Trinity College Dublin. I am particularly grateful to the Department's secretary Toni Garcia; to Professor Michael Gallagher, Head of the Department of Irish Politics and to Professor Michael Marsh, Head of the School of Politics. I would especially like to thank the Royal Irish Academy and Dr Gerry McElroy. I wish him well in his production of a *Dictionary of Irish Biography*, due to be published shortly.

I would also like to acknowledge the input of Professor Eunan O'Halpin of the Department of Contemporary History at Trinity College Dublin; to Professor Tom Garvin and Dr Michael Kennedy of the Politics Department at UCD and to the late Proinsias MacAonghusa of RTÉ for his positive encouragement in the 1980s when the future of this project looked dim. I am also grateful to Dr John Bowman of RTÉ for his valued help and suggestions and Dr Maurice Manning, President of the Irish Human Rights Commission, for his assistance and helpful advice. I was particularly pleased with the warm wishes and expressions of goodwill sent by many, including Ginnie Kennerley, former journalist with *The Irish Press* and Frank Feely, former City Manager with Dublin Corporation. I am very grateful to Frank for giving me permission to use his obituary originally written for Frank Sherwin after his death in November 1981. I have used it for the Appendices section of this book. I am most indebted to John Mullally, Origination Manager at Cahill Printers, East Wall and Dr Adrian Kelly, Assistant Editor at Leinster House for their unwavering support and assistance. I would also like to thank Carol Briscoe, Carolyn Cawley of the Pensions Administration Section of the Department of Defence, Barry Condron and Mary Henry of the Central Bank, Joseph Crosbie of Dublin City Council, Tony Gregory, Seán Haughey, Tony Heffernan, Gay Mitchell, Mary O'Rourke, Michael Smith and Tom Stafford for the various ways in which they helped and were of support. On a final note, I feel I must express my deepest gratitude to my niece Elaine Sherwin, for without the unbounded enthusiasm and drive devoted by her, this book would not have taken its final step to the bookshelves. Her involvement, together with that verve that tends to come somewhat easier to one of younger years was invaluable to this endeavour.

ABBREVIATIONS

DPD	Department of Planning and Development
DUTC	Dublin United Tramway Company
EEC	European Economic Community
FAI	Farmers Association of Ireland
GHQ	General Headquarters
GMIT	Galway-Mayo Institute of Technology
ICA	Irish Citizen Army
IRA	Irish Republican Army
IRB	Irish Republican Brotherhood
ITGWU	Irish Transport and General Workers Union
MEP	Member of the European Parliament
NATO	National Association of Tenants' Organisation
NCO	Non-commissioned Officer
NFO	National Farmers Organisation
NPK	National Public Radio
NUDL	National Union of Dock Labourers
O/C	Officer Commanding
PC	Peace Commission
PR	Proportional Representation
RGDATA	Retail, Grocery, Dairy and Allied Trades Association
RIC	Royal Irish Constabulary
RMS	Royal Medical Society
RTC	Regional Technical College
SA	*Sturmabteilung*
SC	Senior Counsel
SS	*Schutzstaffel*
TD	Teachta Dála
YMCA	Young Men's Christian Association

The *Saorstat* Pound was introduced in 1927 under the Currency act of 1972. This was the title of the currency in Ireland which was known as '*punt*' in Irish and 'the Irish pound' in English. Decimalisation was provided for in the Decimal Currency Acts of 1969 and 1970 and formally commenced 15 February 1971.

The table below gives the approximate value of the IR£ in 1930 and 1972.

IR£	Euro	American $	£ Sterling
1930	66.21	84.81	44.68
1972	12.61	15.84	8.62

The table below gives the approximate value in euro of one shilling in the years referred to in this work.

1905	0.06	1945	0.2
1915	0.08	1955	0.28
1925	0.13	1965	0.39
1935	0.11	1971	0.54

FOREWORD

Frank Sherwin's autobiography is a gripping account of a life spent largely in fighting the established political parties in the interests of the ordinary people of Dublin who elected him as a representative at local and national level. Proud of his participation in the civil war, in which he acquired injuries under torture which stayed with him to the end of his days, he had the courage and insight to criticise the thinking and conduct not only of the government but of the anti-treaty republican leadership. His forthright and sometimes abrasive language, and the personality behind it, recalls in some respects another Dublin republican, C.S. 'Todd' Andrews. Like Andrews, Sherwin distinguished between parties and individuals, between people he respected and those, like Constance Markiewicz and Oliver J. Flanagan TD, whom he disliked for good reason.

Frank Sherwin was an uncompromising critic of what he saw as the ineradicable chicanery of party politics in independent Ireland, and a man who understood and accepted the huge cost and effort which independent politicians had to meet in order to secure election and to keep their seats. He valued the freedom which his position as an independent councillor and TD gave him, and unlike many politicians he avoided the safe course of pandering to public whims, e.g. on the turnover tax, even though that sometimes cost him votes. His memoirs reflect his disdain for, and his considerable knowledge of, the dubious arts and contrivances of electoral politics in Ireland and internationally.

Frank Sherwin's personal story is a refreshing counterpoint to prevailing conceptions of what motivates politicians. So far from enriching himself through winning election, participation in politics cost him time and money he could ill afford. He died a poor man, proud that Ireland had done far better out of him than had he out of Ireland.

Few Irish politicians of the civil war generation wrote memoirs of historical and contemporary interest. Frank Sherwin's family are to be congratulated on bringing this authentic, unvarnished, and wide ranging memoir, spanning six decades of its author's engagement with Irish political life, into the public domain.

Professor Eunan O'Halpin
September 2006

INTRODUCTION

Frank Sherwin Jr

In these days of copious rectitude in all things pertaining to the
established order what thoughts tend to come to mind when faced
with the term 'politician'? I might, if I may, mention a few:
'corruption', 'fat brown envelopes', 'very lucrative shady planning
deals', 'jobs for the boys', 'the gravy train', 'endless evasive double
talk', 'feathering your own nest' in all that that entails, 'looking after
number one, first and foremost'; or perhaps 'how soon can I secure
my pension and head off?' Not a pretty picture, is it? However, how
deserved is this unflattering image currently held of the politician?
Sadly, stemming from over fifty years of observation of the hurly burly
that is politics, I would have to say, most of it, if not all of it. I have seen
it in action from those heading off with their inflated pensions to
those feathering their own nests as has been borne out in recent times
by various tribunals etc. and that unsavoury list just mentioned is not
complete by any means.

For instance, I have not mentioned 'the empty promise' the great
ploy of the politician as he enters yet again on the rounds when the
populace is faced with yet a new onslaught of competing pledges. One
political group after another endeavour to outdo its opposite number
in its generosity as they pitch their wares before confused eyes, in
between taking a great interest in your baby etc. Indeed, with a sense
of *déjà-vu* hanging over the whole scene like Scrooge's ghost of
Christmas past, the promised gimmick outdid itself in the late
nineteen-seventies when the family silver was put up for sale at a
knock-down price, when it was a question of power at any price.[1] Not,
mind you, that the big promise of the nineteen-seventies was an empty
promise. No, perish the thought! It was just too blatantly out front not
to be honoured. However, it had a touch of the sleight of hand about
it. It was like going into a store and paying for advertized goods, then
before you leave the store, the goods are repossessed by the store,
while they hang on to your money. How did it work? Well, to procure
the votes, they promised to remove certain levies that weighed heavily
on the shoulders of the Irish citizen, or so they claimed. Did they

honour their promises? Yes, as already mentioned. Mind you, they neglected to mention that they intended to reintroduce them under different names, like 'waste charges' and draconian 'car parking charges', with even more draconian measures if you do not pay etc. Indeed, the motorist was and is probably the biggest victim. Did they get away with it? Yes, of course they did. They laughed all the way back to the *Dáil* with a record number of seats.[2] Won't the voter be wary come the next election? No. The voter's memory doesn't seem to stretch that far. Besides, he'll be too bamboozled with a fresh array of promises, but I think this is where we came in, is it not? Oh, just one more question. Are you saying that the voter could be persuaded to fall for the same trick second time round, I mean will it work? Yes, of course it will. It's been working since democracy was invented. In the light of this little exchange, used mainly for demonstration, I'm tempted to ask: when the ancient Greeks devised the democratic system, did they take into consideration the insidious Machiavellian opportunism that would come to dominate that grand notion?

So what is it all about? Who would want to be a politician under these circumstances? Power, that's what it's about and those that crave power. The opposition front bench of our *Dáil* in particular and those with aspirations in that direction, is where they're to be seen at their most comical. This is especially the case when some red herring is introduced that may bring them closer to power. They jump up and down like the proverbial 'Jack in the Box' to carp and interrupt the opponent across the floor of the *Dáil*, who happens to be the current holder of that coveted prize, i.e. power, who incidentally is no healthier when he is in opposition. This little game is usually saved for the media's presence; otherwise it is considered a waste of effort. It is hoped that this exhibition will see them into the extra comforts of a Mercedes car that happens to come with that power. This, we are assured, will solve their 'Jack in the Box' syndrome.

All of these thoughts came to mind on setting out to write this introduction to my father's autobiography. How, you might ask, did he differ from all of this? That is a fair question, and I will try to answer it. Let me put it this way. No one could ever say that they had bought him, although were he open to such coercion he could have made himself a rich man. Such were the offers at his disposal, either real or fanciful. I saw him in those days (1963) opening envelopes and beginning to read letters, which he would instantly throw into the open fire beside him. Some however managed to escape that fiery end. I came upon a scattering of these when searching though his papers, one of which accused him of accepting £30,000 in exchange for his support of a minority government during the early 1960s.

That's not however from where the offers stemmed, except maybe the fanciful ones, such as the one just mentioned. The minority government took his support and practically abused him for it. No, they were enjoying power and if it is at the goodwill of someone outside of their clique, that's his affair, but let him not think that we will be grateful. Money was never mentioned, or taken, in spite of what was claimed to the contrary by the power-hungry opposition of the time. In fact, nothing was mentioned regarding his support. He was not supporting them for that reason, and had never discussed the matter with them. It must have been one of the best bargains a political party ever got. Generally, there is a shopping list handed to a party seeking support, either from Independents or diminutive parties of four or five members who usually end up as ministers, the party members, that is. An Independent would be overstepping themselves were he or she to make such a demand. Ministerial appointment, the much sought after prize, is the sole prerogative of the party or so it would appear. It was because there had been no talks or deals done in advance that my father was to find himself 'hung out to dry' when his support was no longer needed.

No. It was certainly not from the government that he supported that the offers came. We must look elsewhere for the trail of offers. There will always be those that long to take some of that power from those who appear to have it, as they seek to live out their insidious belief that everything has a price. This however is where the problem lay for those who thought that money could buy my father. Their frustration knew no bounds. 'Why doesn't someone tell this fool the rules of the game? This is politics we are dealing with here, where the laws of the jungle prevail, not some daft idealistic notion of what he calls putting his country first.' Then other tactics were resorted to. It was thought that levelling spurious accusations would destroy his support base and in consequence, his support for a government that he at the time saw as the only feasible alternative. However, should it be thought that he enjoyed what some might have called 'cosying up' to the *Fianna Fáil* party, you would be mistaken.[3] His view of the political party system with its backroom wheeling and dealing in the interests of gaining and remaining in power, by any means, was less than flattering. The party clique-ism in every sense of that term, not to mention its perceived right to turn *Dáil Eireann* and its shadow 'the Higher House' into an elite club for the benefit of its extended families and cronies, was a situation that he found wanting.[4] Hence the subtitle of this account: Independent and Unrepentant, which, incidentally was not the original title chosen by my father for this story, who had an even darker view of politics and those who profess to live by it. Suffice it to say, some of what you have just read encapsulates the spirit of that earlier title.[5] With the exception of some necessary editing, little else beyond the title has been changed.

There is much in this autobiography that has now been overtaken by events that might beg the question: what would he have thought, among other things, of the revelations stemming from inquiries into the lifestyles of certain public figures in these days of alleged transparency? Lifestyles which, although not meanly supported by monetary rewards for services rendered, could not possibly be sustained on their official incomes, a feat which brings to mind that biblical story of the proverbial 'loaves and fishes' – never was so much done with so little. Bearing in mind his past experience at attempted palming and his referral to politics as a form of hell, a view not without some basis, he might have been disappointed at the blatant exposure, but not unduly surprised.

Who was this figure with whom this story concerns itself? Those of a certain age would not need to be reacquainted with this man. For good or ill they might have encountered him in real life as he walked the streets of Dublin complete with soft hat and bow-tie, but beyond that what do we know of him? In part he probably affects the life of which you now lead as the moon affects the tide – as everything reacts upon everything else. He was elected to Dublin City Council in 1955 and overall, with breaks, held a seat for nineteen years. It was on taking of a *Dáil* seat, against great odds, as an Independent in 1957 that he became known nationally. As fate would have it, he found himself holding the balance of power, sustaining a *Fianna Fáil* minority government in the early 1960s led by Mr Seán Lemass. This position was to put him under considerable strain when the *Fianna Fáil* government sought to introduce an unpopular tax known then as the turnover tax, the precursor of the value added tax (VAT) that we know today. His reward for this was calumny and abuse, not only from the opposition but oddly enough to a great extent, the party that he had supported, who, when the time was right went after his vulnerable *Dáil* seat with as much gusto as the rest of them. Such is politics!

Does this tell us who Frank Sherwin was? No. It tells us who Frank Sherwin the politician was. He came from a family of eleven but of that eleven only he and his sister Mary were to live into anything resembling old age. He did not own a car; his general mode of transport was a bicycle. He lived in a small two bedroomed house in the centre of Dublin. To my knowledge he had but one suit, if suit you could call it. He did not aspire towards the grandiose trimmings of public life. I guess it was through his more parochial corporation work that we get to see the man. His main concern was the people, and not merely his constituents. He gave much of himself to all who came to his door with problems, or approached him on the street, which constituted his office. He loved this close dealing with people and they could approach him anywhere and at any time. They weren't fobbed off with a wee card indicating the times of his clinic (constituency meeting centre). They all got the truth about where they stood without a show of political playacting, or trying to secure a vote while knowing, or not knowing as the case usually was, that there wasn't a hope. There were no woolly promises. He knew where they stood and told them there and then. That was the man he was, and it will be a long day before we will see his likes again, as was said at his passing. Some at first were taken aback by his bluntness before taking their business elsewhere to a 'hail fellow well met' typical charmer, who would promise whatever they wanted, and whatever colour they wanted it in. They would get the pleasantries and the usual letters in the post that amounted to what my father had told them within three minutes of their meeting.

However, in the greater majority of those cases, my father was able to send those callers away walking on air, for once he took on a case, he knew its outcome in advance, such was his experience of the system that prevailed. Mind you, I was occasionally to hear some amusing exchanges emanating from the vicinity of our hallway on the arrival of a return-caller to our doorway, which might go something like this: 'Any news for me, Frank?' the caller might say, a little intrepidly, keeping his fingers crossed. Now there were, it must be understood, times when my father genuinely would not remember what it was that he was to do for a caller, which of course led to the following: 'What was this I was to do for you? I see so many people. Remind me again.' I would note a darkening of tone on the part of the suddenly despondent caller, as he went through the motions of setting out his case once again while sending out strong mental images of which I was quite adept at picking up. He doesn't even remember me! Just like the rest of them! Just another politician! However this invariably turned out to be a hasty reaction. For on putting their case to him again he would come out with, 'Ah, sure I've done that! You'll be getting favourable news in a couple of days.'

'Just another politician' would not describe Frank Sherwin. On his passing, it was said that he was 'a giant among men' while former Dublin City Manager Frank Feely described him as 'the conscience of the City Council'. In 1982, Dublin City Council saw fit to posthumously name a new bridge spanning the River Liffey at Heuston Railway Station in his memory.

NOTES

1   There are echoes here of 1977 when the country reverted to its childhood and once again believed in that annual visitor from Lapland. There was but one catch - it wasn't Christmas!

2   *Dáil Éireann* equals the Irish Parliament.

3   Sherwin was a founder member of *Fianna Fáil*, that is, until certain inimical elements began to invade it, an unsavoury trait not peculiar to that party alone. Frank Sherwin insisted that he was not voting for the *Fianna Fáil* party, Mr Seán Lemass or the turnover tax – he was voting for a government.

4   The houses of the *Oireachtas* but notably the *Dáil* is creaking at the seams for the want of relief from these so-called dynasties that seem to take it for granted that there's a family seat for them in the *Dáil.*

5   Frank Sherwin's original title for his autobiography was *Politics is Hell.*

PART I
FRANK SHERWIN'S
POLITICAL HELL

The name Sherwin is uncommon in Ireland. According to my sister Mary who is interested in genealogy, the Sherwins came from England in the sixteenth century to escape religious persecution.[1] They were of Norman stock. A certain Father Ralph Sherwin was beheaded during the religious persecution when forty Catholic priests were executed and he was to become one of the religious martyrs who were canonized saints by the Pope in 1970. The remainder of the family came to Ireland and settled in the Naul, an area about sixteen miles north of county Dublin. Several graveyards in the area have tombstones with the name dating back several hundred years. My mother's maiden name was Mary Jane Ford, another uncommon name, although the name is world-known because of Henry Ford of motor car fame. Her father was Joseph Ford from Rush, north County Dublin. He was a well-known character. He always wore gentlemanly attire of an elitist sort and I was told that he always chaired public meetings when Parnell came to speak at Rush. He owned a number of buildings at the end of Parnell Street near Capel Street which were known as 'Ford's Buildings'.

When I became a TD and especially since my vote kept *Fianna Fáil* in power for a number of years, the name Sherwin became known nationally and anyone with a similar name was said to be my son or related to me. A case in point is that of a young man who was elected TD for Dublin South-West in 1970.[2] Almost everyone said that he was my son but he is not related to me in any way that I know. For a week after he was elected, I was congratulated all day and everyone was surprised when I told them he was no relation. Another man with the same surname, an RTÉ announcer, is supposed to be my son but that is not so. In fact, I have never met the man although my sister said that he is a second cousin. Whenever I answer the phone and give the name Sherwin, those on the line usually ask if I was related to Frank Sherwin so at least I have made the name known.

I was tortured five times during the Civil War (1922–23) and was incarcerated in seven different jails for twenty months. I came out of prison disabled and a nervous wreck and could not do any physical work. Despite this, I promoted 10,000 dances over thirty-five years, became a member of *Fianna Éireann* GHQ in 1925 and a member of *Fianna Fáil* Executive 1939–44. I was also a member of *Dáil Éireann* for seven years from 1957–65 and a member of Dublin Corporation serving as Alderman for seven years from 1955–67. My vote made Mr Lemass *Taoiseach* in 1961 and kept him in power for three and a half years, for which the former President of the Republic Mr Seán T. O'Kelly said I saved the country.[3] In a leading article, *The Irish Times* said that I was 'the linchpin that kept the government in power'.[4]

Later, in 1964, I sued *The Irish Times* for libel in the High and Supreme Courts and won my case, *The Irish Times* agreeing to pay all expenses and insert a statement in all daily papers declaring that they never questioned my honour as a politician.[5]

Frank Sherwin

NOTES

1   Mary Sherwin, sister of Frank Sherwin.
2   Seán Sherwin, a member of the Fianna Fáil Party, was successful in the Dublin South West 1970 by-election.
3   '*Taoiseach*' is the Irish for 'Prime Minister'.
4   See *The Irish Times*, Wednesday 10 July 1963, p. 7.
5   The phrase 'all daily papers' refers to the following articles: 'Sherwin libel action is settled', *The Evening Press*, Thursday 27 October 1966, p. 1; 'Sherwin action settled', *The Evening Herald*, Thursday 27 October 1966, p. 1; 'Sherwin Libel Action', *The Irish Times*, Friday 28 October 1966, p. 1; 'Settlement in Sherwin libel case', *The Irish Press*, Friday 28 October, p. 3; 'Sherwin libel case is struck out', *The Irish Independent*, Friday 28 October, p. 12.

1

SMALL BEGINNINGS

I was born in poor circumstances in a city tenement, 35 Upper Dorset Street, in 1905. These tenements were formerly occupied by a single family during the period of the Irish Parliament which was abolished in 1800. They were the Dublin homes of aristocrats who represented Britain, not Ireland. In later years the tenements were to be bought up by slum landlords and let out to poor people. It was not uncommon to have a poor family of six to twelve living in one room. If you had two rooms, you were doing well. The toilet was usually out in the yard, two of them to serve about sixty people, and one cold water pipe. Some people managed to keep them clean but most of the time they were filthy. The hall door that led to the street was open day and night which resulted in the hallways being abused. Later we moved to Broadstone Avenue, and then to Linenhall Street. I am now residing in a corporation dwelling, Church Terrace off Church Street. All places of residence were a short distance from one another.

My father, Christopher Sherwin, was employed as a carter by Cartons, a well-known poultry firm at Halston Street. He worked from 8 a.m. to 6 p.m. but because wages were small, he worked an extra early shift, 5 a.m. to 7 a.m. so actually worked from 5 a.m. until 7 p.m. He was a very religious man, always praying and attended morning Mass and evening devotions. He never drank, smoked or was heard to utter a swear word. He was very quiet and never raised his hand against any member of the family except once, when he found out that I was skipping school. His only hobby was an odd shilling on a horse or a Gaelic football match. My mother, Mary Jane Sherwin (née Ford), was very talkative and always singing. She was in poor health and died at 42 years of age. I remember when I was about 9 years old, one of the children died. The day after the funeral my mother told me that an angel appeared to my father during the previous night. Now, I have always found it difficult to believe in apparitions but if such things happen, then my father would have been the type of person to whom such a thing would happen.

When we went to live at Broadstone Avenue, I met a boy, Willie

O'Reilly, who remained my companion for the next fifty-five years. I remember one incident when I was about 7 years of age, a boy by the name of McCluskey got a penny from a relation because his father had died. At that time (1911) I had never seen a penny, as my father had only eighteen shillings a week to keep a family of nine. Anyhow, McCluskey bought this packet of squibs, one of which he fired into the air which accidentally went into an open window setting fire to the curtains. Both McCluskey and I ran into our homes. The excitement brought other people out to see what was going on. My brother Joe came to the door as did a woman from across the street and as soon as she saw him she immediately said that it was Joe Sherwin who had set the place on fire. The woman had had a row with my mother some weeks earlier and was looking for a way to get even. Joe was about 9 years of age at that time. He was charged in the District Court and was fined £1 or a month in a reformatory. Poor Joe had not even been on the street. McCluskey told us that he admitted to his mother that it was an accident and that he had thrown the squib but he was told to keep his mouth shut. As we could not afford to pay the £1 fine, Joe had to serve the month.

At about this time, I was attending Phibsborough National and became one of the 'school gang'. Not that I was always there, I skipped school now and then. We all had nicknames, I was known as 'Nauler' because I was always talking about the Naul where my father was born and where I went for summer holidays. Others were known as 'Far Kelly' and 'Modeller Murphy' because his people owned a dairy called the Model Dairy. He always had money when the rest of us had none. He used to bring in black and white pudding regularly which we would eat while doing our exercises. At the end of school term, when I was 14 years of age, I was told by the headmaster to remain behind when school finished. I knew that I was going to be caned as I had skipped school on the previous two days so I dived down the stairs and made for home and that was the end of my schooling. At that time most children finished school at 14 years of age. There were no jobs except as messenger boys, unless you were lucky enough to have a father who had a trade, as these jobs were a 'closed shop'.

When I was 10 years old, the 1916 Rebellion broke out, commencing on Easter Monday. We were then residing at 11 Linenhall Street. My father went to the Fairyhouse races that morning. He only attended race meetings once a year and then only because it was a Bank Holiday. The shooting commenced about noon and went on all day. We were expecting father home about 6 o'clock and were alarmed when he did not arrive. We were told that all transport had stopped. My father got home at about 12 o'clock that night, having had to walk fourteen miles along the rail tracks. The Republican Army erected barricades in North

King Street around the corner from where I lived. There was an army barracks fifteen yards from our home – Linenhall Barracks. There were only a few soldiers in the barracks as it was used largely for storage. The IRA decided to blow up the barracks' wall and they warned residents of the danger. At the time of the explosion, my father and all of the family were on our knees saying the Rosary. Only slight damage was done to the wall. Later the IRA set fire to the barracks and it burned for a week. During the five days that the Rebellion lasted, I was down town every day looking for food, as all business was at a standstill and no food could be obtained. My mother and I brought back food including salmon and sardines which we had never tasted before. On Friday night the British Army attacked the IRA in North King Street in strength. Heavy firing went on all night so we were really 'between two fires'. On the right, fifteen yards away, the barracks was blazing, throwing out intense heat, while thirty yards to the left a battle was raging throughout the night. Looting took place on a large scale during the five days. Some people took valuable furniture but we only took food as it was thrown out onto the street by looters.

On Saturday morning, before the surrender of the rebels in North King Street, members of the Staffordshire Regiment murdered thirteen innocent people who had been taking cover in cellars a short distance from where we lived. On that morning, all of our homes were raided. I was in bed, so were my parents. My father was told to get dressed. He and others were marched to Richmond Military Barracks for questioning but he was released later that day. The leaders of the Rebellion were executed which brought on a wave of sympathy. Songs and recitations appeared in many shop windows honouring those who took part in 'The Rising'. I remember one called *The Story of Easter Week*. I forget who the author was and I have never seen nor heard of it since. It went something like this as I learned it bit by bit from a shop window:

The Story of Easter Week
(Poet, unknown)

(1)
'Twas Easter Monday in Dublin,
The streets bore a festive air,
The people were holiday making,
For a while, free from work and care.
But what means the armed men marching,
Look from every side they pour,
But the people take little notice,
For they've seen them oft before.

(2)

But hark; that distant thunder,
O'er, the pattering bullets hail,
And the cry goes up 'what's the matter?'
And many a cheek turns pale.
Then the news goes quickly flashing,
A Rebellion again in sight, and
O'er the grey Post Office
The flag of SINN FÉIN flows high.

(3)

The City Hall, too, is taken,
That overlooks old Cork Hill,
The Four Courts, the College of Surgeons,
Jacob's and Boland's Mill.
And the news goes quickly flashing,
To the lands far across the foam,
That Ireland is fighting for freedom:
Not in Belgium, but here at home.

(4)

Now from out of some streets
Of the city, comes people of ugly mood.
The shops are looted and pillaged,
And children cry for food.
From the scene, the Police have vanished,
Now powerless for good or ill.
And some of their scattered members,
In death lie cold and still.

(5)

Away in Ashbourne Village,
Brave Thomas Ashe holds sway.
His men over England's forces,
Have completely gained the day.
But while waiting a message from Dublin,
Anxious thoughts on each face you read,
As they pray to the 'God of Battles',
That their Rising may succeed.

(6)

Three days pass slowly over,
And Dublin is still being held,

By a handful of Irish Insurgents
With courage unparalleled.
But with the closing in of
That day of darkness,
The British troops advance,
With engines of death and destruction,
Like the battle fields in France.

(7)
Away on the coast of Kerry,
Roger Casement has landed there.
The Germans have sent on a vessel,
With rifles and arms it bears.
But Casement has been captured,
No help now, the cause to save.
So the German ship and cargo,
Are sunk beneath the waves.

(8)
Now the Clergy sought the leaders,
And implored them with faces grave,
To lay down their arms to England,
Civilian lives to save.
See O'Connell Street is burning,
And buildings ruddle and reel,
And the Irish Republican Army,
Is hemmed in with shot and steel.

(9)
They decide now to surrender,
In written words they sent,
Signed by Pearse and McDonagh,
Seán McDermott and Éamon Ceannt.
Away now, in a gloomy prison,
Where walls frown grim and high,
Ah: England's day of vengeance,
Now dawns in that 'blood red sky'.

(10)
They died, but oh they conquered,
These men whom their land would save,
A firing party at day-break,
A hasty quicklime grave.

Think not of them with sorrow,
Nor mourn
For the cause they died,
For their deaths saved
Ireland's honour,
What matter else besides?

I was inspired, as were many, by the songs and stories of Easter week. About July 1918, Willie O'Reilly and I joined the *Fianna*, a militant boy scout organization which was founded in 1909. Members of the *Fianna* fought in Easter week and several were killed or executed. I became a member of D Company 2nd Battalion. Later this company became B Company 1st Battalion. I never missed a parade until 'the Truce' with the British, on 11 July 1921.[1]

I have mentioned my grandfather, Joe Ford. He was an extraordinary character. He was always singing, dancing or talking. No one could get a word in edgeways! When he had finished talking, he would tell you that he never told lies but that he told 'queer stories'. When he was young, he was always in trouble with the police. The local landlord prohibited the taking of seaweed for manure so he organized the locals to resist. He always took a few drinks but it did not take drink to put him in form. Everywhere he went he sang and he compelled everyone in the company to sing with him, keeping time with his hefty walking stick which he banged on the table or tapped on the floor. He wore a fur hat and wrist watch, a frock-coat, hard collars and cuffs and always had a flower in his coat. He sported a moustache and goatee beard. When I was a child, I asked him why he dressed like that and he answered: 'When you see me once, you always know me again!' During the Great War of 1914–18, he composed many songs and recitations. I remember one – *Tramp, Tramp, Tramp, we have the Germans on the run.* He sent it to King George V and received an acknowledgement.[2] He caused a rumpus everywhere. When he was 80 and ill, his daughters thought that he was finished and sent him to the old men's home in Kilmainham, but when he recovered he was once again his old self. He had all of the old men on the warpath. The nuns begged his daughters to take him out but they refused, so they evicted him. When he died at 88 years of age, he was buried in the old graveyard in Rush next to the landlord he was always at war with. Old people at his funeral said: 'Well, he won't talk anymore.' He was known to the family as the 'Oul Fella' but to others as 'Blah Ford'. He had ten children, eight of whom lived to be over 80. In fact, three of his daughters living in Boston, USA in 1971 were aged 83, 86 and 88 years of age.

In about August 1919, I was employed as a harness maker's

apprentice which was becoming an obsolete trade as it was difficult to obtain employment. My brother Joe was employed by the same firm, namely O'Donoghue's of Wood Quay. My first week's wage was five shillings or twenty-five new pence. I received sixpence from my mother for pocket money. I spent this small sum on Saturdays: four pence on the cinema and two pence on sweets. A year later I had ten shillings weekly and received one shilling and sixpence pocket money. Again I spent four pence on the cinema and two pence on sweets which left me with a shilling which I put into the post office as I was saving up for a bicycle. With fifteen shillings, I was able to buy my first bicycle, a second-hand one. When I left O'Donoghue's I was earning only fifteen shillings weekly after serving two and a half years.

Having left O'Donoghue's, I joined Scanlan's before entering the National Army (the Free State Army) in April 1922, which meant an improvement in pay – twenty-five shillings weekly. It was difficult to get into the army in 1922 but my cousin John Connolly, who was a staff captain on the Adjutant General's Staff, fixed it up for O'Reilly and myself. All members of the First Battalion IRA signal class were captured at a meeting in Parnell Square shortly before 'the Truce.' A new class was formed and O'Reilly and I were chosen to represent the *Fianna* Company. Between the *Fianna* and the signal class, I was to give four nights a week to the movement over the next ten years.

NOTE

1   Frank Sherwin applied in May 1942 for the Service (1917–1921) Medal in respect of his membership of B Company, 1st Battalion of *Fianna Éireann*, Dublin. The Medal was awarded and was issued to him on 14 December 1942. He was awarded the Truce Commemoration Medal in 1973.

2   George V, the second son of Edward VII and Alexandra, was born on 3 June 1865 and died on 20 January 1936. He reigned from 6 May 1910 until his death. Sherwin saw this reply when he visited Ford's daughter in Boston in 1971.

2

THE WAR OF INDEPENDENCE AND CIVIL WAR[1]

The War of Independence broke out on 21 January 1919, when famous freedom fighter Dan Breen and others attacked two armed police men who were guarding gelignite.[2] Both police officers were shot dead. This caused a sensation and it was to be the first blood spilt in the War of Independence. On the same day, the *Dáil* or Parliament of the Republicans met in the Dublin Mansion House, the residence of the Lord Mayor. Breen's attack on the police was carried out without the approval of the *Dáil*, an illegal parliament in the eyes of the British. Dan Breen was an uneducated man as were many but he was intelligent and had the right spirit. If it had rested with the *Dáil*, they might never have declared war on the British but Michael Collins, Director of the IRA Intelligence, was delighted and stated that this form of attack should be kept up and it became the general rule so the *Dáil* had no choice but to accept responsibility.[3]

Collins was a Cork man and ruthless with a clear goal. His aim was to destroy the British spy system and he largely succeeded. The Irish had not the means to fight a conventional war. We had to depend on guerrilla warfare, in other words, 'hit and run'. The majority of the IRA continued to work at their civilian jobs and slept at home. Only a small minority were full-time soldiers and they were on the run, that is, they did not sleep at home. However, they could be surprised if informed on and this is where the British had the advantage. Collins succeeded in gaining the support of several British agents and with their support he seriously damaged the British spy system. His special squad shot spies out of hand. In this way, large numbers of IRA men escaped arrest.[4] It was to be said that there were never more than 1,500 men in the field against the British. That could be true, but if you counted all of the men and women who were active from the beginning of the War of Independence until 'the Truce' with the British, on 11 July 1922, and include all of those who were in jail, the number involved could be around 15,000.[5] There were, however, another 30,000 active reserves, many of these men were murdered or arrested. It was not as some writers think, that some men were anxious to fight and others not, it was a question of some men being privileged by getting the opportunity and other men anxious to fight but being denied the chance. Guerrilla warfare is fought with small numbers because they could hit the enemy and get away. Whenever large numbers were engaged, as in the burning of the Dublin Custom House, half of the men engaged in the operation were killed, wounded or captured. The reserves were always there to take the place of casualties. As long as there was a large reserve, the war could go on indefinitely. If the British thought that there was no large reserve then they would not have agreed to a truce in 1921.[6]

The most outstanding figure in the War of Independence was Éamon De Valera.[7] He was President of the illegal Republican Government. His father was Spanish but his mother was Irish. He was born in America and this fact saved his life when he was sentenced to death for his part in the 1916 Rebellion. He came to Ireland when he was a child so he was as Irish as the rest of us. He had fixed principles, was honest and wanted nothing but complete independence. When the War of Independence ended, a treaty was signed with the British, but certain articles were repugnant to many Irish republicans, especially 'The Oath to the British King'. In my opinion, there would have been no civil war had it not been for this condition. De Valera rejected 'the Treaty' and influenced most republicans by his stand. Collins controlled the Irish Republican Brotherhood (IRB), a secret organization which penetrated every national body including the IRA. He also influenced most of the 'gunmen', for he was their boss as Director of Army Intelligence. About 70 per cent of the IRA opposed 'the Treaty' but the majority of the *Dáil*, and later the majority of the people, supported it. The partition of Ireland was already established and a government of former British planters was functioning. The planters were a million strong, protected by the British Army. We could not end partition by force so partition was not the real issue when discussing 'the Treaty'; it was 'The Oath to the British King'. Men who had been taught to hate the British king were now being asked to swear allegiance to him.[8]

The majority of the IRA leaders held a convention and decided against taking orders issued by the new provisional government or any other authority including Mr De Valera, thus inviting a civil war. These 'anti-Treaty' men were sincere and it would have paid them to accept 'the Treaty' as most of them would have acquired jobs or employment in other services. They were civilian soldiers and had fought the British in the War of Independence. Many were brigade area commanders. Many commanded 'flying columns'. Some were members of General Headquarters staff but they had no political experience nor in-depth political sense, no clear goal. They were heading for a bloody civil war and they could not stop themselves. They refused to accept advice from Mr De Valera who sensed what was going to happen. Some had become 'Little Caesars'. They controlled their brigade areas and would take no advice or orders. There was no supreme military leader who could command them all. Napoleon said that one bad general was better than two good ones.[9] He meant of course that were there only one man in command, he would take great care, for he would know that should there be failures, he would be held responsible. Where there were many generals, each claiming to be the leader, then one would leave responsibilities to another.

The whole Republican movement was in confusion, whereas Collins was in supreme command of the government forces. He was building up a new national army. The Republicans occupied the Four Courts (Law Courts) and other buildings. Had the IRA meant business, they should have prevented Collins from establishing the army. They should have arrested the provisional government and shot them. I am not saying that they would have been right in doing so. They had a military advantage for several months after 'the Treaty' was signed and they still had this advantage up to the time the Four Courts were attacked. They lost this advantage, however, when Dublin fell to the Free State forces. Dublin was the capital city and full of unemployed men. The government had unlimited arms and money and thus could build up a large army as soon as they had that city in their hands. Having lost the city, the Republicans were beaten and should have called off the fight.

After the fall of the Four Courts, Liam Lynch was accepted as Chief-of-Staff.[10] He was an able guerrilla leader from the south but he knew little about conventional warfare. He prolonged the Civil War unnecessarily. He only recognized the Republican Civil Authorities towards the end of the fighting, when all hope was long gone, but even then he insisted on his right to decide 'peace or war'. Just before he was killed in action, he voted against a ceasefire. The decision to fight on was carried by just one vote. At the following meeting of GHQ or what was left of it, the Republicans unanimously agreed to a ceasefire. By the end of August the whole country was in the hands of the government and the Republicans were forced to depend on guerrilla warfare, a type of fighting that they could not win, because most of the people supported the government and former comrades who were fighting for the government lived in every area. Thousands of ex-British soldiers joined the new national army, including many who had fought against the IRA during the War of Independence.

Michael Collins, the Commander-in-Chief of the National Army, while on an inspection of barracks in the Cork area, was ambushed and killed on 22 August 1922. According to evidence, only the rear guard of an IRA column attacked his convoy which consisted of about thirty men, including an armoured car. Had Collins taken a little more care, he would not have been shot. He stood up in the middle of the road when he thought the fight was over and was hit by chance. One of the officers with Collins when he was shot was Commandant Joe Dolan, a 'gunman' who later boasted to an English Sunday newspaper about all of the men he had shot during the War of Independence but he never mentioned the men, his former comrades, whom he murdered during the Civil War. I was his victim the morning that I was arrested, when he tortured me four times in the same day. Several books have been written about the Civil War. They deal largely with events leading up to the attack on the Four Courts and the fighting up to the period when Collins was killed but they gloss over the remainder of this tragic event. When Collins was killed the 'terror' began. Prior to Collins' death, the war was a pseudo-war. No one was murdered or tortured and many IRA were arrested and released but after Collins was killed, the 'murder gangs' took over, protected by members of the government. A law was passed making execution the penalty for possessing a gun and seventy-seven men were executed. Hundreds were murdered in cold blood while thousands were tortured. Regularly, men were found riddled with bullets all around the outskirts of the city. All over the country, similar murders took place and went on not only for the duration of the war but for months after it ended. Several months after the war had come to a close, Noel Lemass, brother of Seán Lemass, later *Taoiseach*, was found riddled with bullets on the Feather Bed Mountain, some ten miles from Dublin.[11]

I was a soldier in the Curragh Military Camp, some thirty miles from Dublin when the attack was made on the Four Courts. As mentioned earlier, I had joined up because I wanted an army career and hadn't reckoned on the Civil War taking place. However, when it did, I decided to leave but I could not get out of the camp until about a week after the government took the city. My brother Joe was then a prisoner in Mountjoy Prison. He had been captured during the week's fighting following the attack on the courts. I got back to Dublin with a forged pass but all of the IRA forces were scattered. The next day I took a train to Thurles, Tipperary, with the intention of contacting the IRA in Cashel some miles away but I could not get past the army patrols. I remained in Thurles that night and returned to Dublin the next day. I had £8 saved from my army payment. This trip had cost me £4.

Some weeks later I read in the newspapers that Frank Aiken had escaped from Dundalk Prison with many others and with the help of the IRA captured the town of Dundalk.[12] I rode my bicycle to Newgrange, Co. Meath, a distance of twenty miles, leaving my bike with my aunt, Mrs Collins. I then walked to Drogheda, a distance of nine miles. I was arrested on the Dundalk Road, just outside Drogheda and held prisoner for four hours. They let me out only on learning that I had an aunt at Newgrange but they were suspicious. I was told to get out of Drogheda immediately. I walked back to Newgrange, got my bike and cycled back to Dublin, arriving back at 3 o'clock in the morning. In other words: I cycled forty miles, walked eighteen miles and spent four hours a prisoner – all in one day!

I finally made contact with some of my former *Fianna* comrades when Alfred Colley and Seán Cole, two *Fianna* officers, were murdered in a lane at Whitehall near Dublin. On the same day, another IRA man was found riddled with bullets at Raheny. They were all murdered by the Free State Murder Gang. They were the first to be murdered. These three men were shot while Collins' body lay in state at the City Hall, Dublin; the date was 26 August 1922. Cole and Colley were engaged in trying to reorganize the *Fianna* when they were shot. At the funeral, I met my former O/C, Tony Black, and he told me that he would send for me later.

About the middle of September, four *Fianna* units were formed. I was appointed in command of the full-time squad (the unemployed men). We were all told to raid a post office for money. The IRA had no money and men did not get paid. They fought for their principles but many were 'on the run' and were billeted in the homes of supporters. Money had to be commandeered to pay for the upkeep of the men. Government money was taken and in many cases, goods were taken from shops. The IRA knew that these shopkeepers would be compensated. One squad was captured outside a post office. Another turned up but changed their minds. The third squad never met and only my squad succeeded in getting £20.

Arising out of these failures, the *Fianna* was disbanded again and my squad was the only active *Fianna* unit in the city. The O/C, Tony Black, appointed me his deputy and I was brought to *Fianna* General Headquarters for the first time.[13] It was the home of Acting Adjutant General Alfred White, at Peter's Place. He appeared rather effeminate to me. However, I was soon to learn that he had great courage and accepted responsibility. I was the only member of the active Dublin *Fianna* who knew of his address.[14] On the day following the post office raid, I was followed about by an Intelligence Officer named Byrne. He was an old member of my former company. I reported this matter to White and he instructed me to take my men from Doody's Dairy and join up with 'The Plunkett Flying Column' operating at Ballinscorney in the Dublin mountains, an uninhabited and wild area. There was an odd dwelling here and there. You could see the city from this spot and could see an enemy approaching for miles. We were billeted in a house owned by a man named Daly.[15] The column was resting as they had suffered some casualties in an attack on a barracks some weeks previously. In this area you seldom walked the roads as there was always a chance of surprise as many men gave information following torture after arrest, this being the order of the day. You kept to wild mountainside and crossed bogs and rivers to get around and it was most tiring. The men were hungry as there were about a dozen to be fed. Occasionally they killed a sheep because the column was not active. I decided to go back to the city and bring back some food. This turned into many a sensation for me.

We raided grocery stores and commandeered a load of food, having already commandeered a taxi, and made for the Dublin mountains. We had to pass Portobello Military Barracks, the headquarters of the army, to reach our destination. As we passed the barracks, Eason, our driver, put on speed, which caused the car to skid, hitting a lamppost. This damaged the car and left us shocked but luckily uninjured. We realized that we were in real danger as there were only four of us and we had only two revolvers. No motor vehicle came in sight, only a horse and dray which was useless if we were chased, but we had to decide quickly so we loaded the horse cart and made for Rathfarnham some miles away, the end of the city proper. Our hearts were in our mouths expecting every minute to see soldiers after us but we were in luck. When we got to Rathfarnham and turned towards the village of Tallaght, we stopped a closed van, loaded it and made for the mountains. Tallaght was about half way between the city centre and Ballinscorney where I had left the remainder of my men. There could be road blocks at Tallaght but once again we were lucky. About three miles from our destination, we rested at the home of one of our supporters named Kelly. This was at a mountain village called Castlekelly. We proceeded towards Ballinscorney when the closed van broke down. Eason spent an hour trying to get the car going but failed. In the distance, we saw a man on a horse making towards us at great speed. It was our friend Kelly. He told us that a large force of soldiers were looking for us in Castlekelly. We were thinking of dumping the food and walking the rest of the way when an ass and cart appeared trekking down the mountain. We loaded our stuff on the cart and proceeded but it was necessary to push the ass and cart up some of the mountain. We left the motor vehicle across the narrow road to block our pursuers. Finally reaching our destination, we dumped the stuff under some hay, some distance from Daly's and waited, but no soldiers appeared.

That night, at about 11.30 p.m., one of our scouts informed us that many lights could be seen coming up the mountain some miles away. It was dark as it was the middle of October. It was obvious that the lights were from convoy cars so we crossed the mountain behind us and made for the village of Lacken. It was so dark we could not see where we were going. One of our men, whose name was Dolan, was a kind of Indian scout and knew that area well. He led us across the mountain through bogs and across rivers and streams. Each man held on in file. We walked about twelve miles and stopped at the school master's home that night, arriving there at about 3 a.m. Next day we returned to Ballinscorney and learned that the whole area had been raided on the previous night but the goods had not been found. However, some supporters had been arrested. It turned into a day to remember and all for a load of food. We only remained in the column for about twelve days as we were not active. The only activity while we were there was the capture of a mail van some miles away. We came back to the city on about 1 November 1922 and again were billeted at Doody's Dairy. We carried out some activity every day. I received a note from the IRA Adjutant General to get some typewriters. We got three. Tony Black, who had appointed me his deputy, disappeared. I never met him again but I was told that he had been arrested shortly before Christmas. Where he was between the times that he appointed me his deputy (about the middle of October) and the time that he was arrested, I do not know.

On the night of 7 November 1922, we damaged the signal cabin and cut the telephone wires at the Liffey Junction railway station on the perimeter of the city. On that night, I climbed the telephone pole and cut the wires. By mistake, I cut into an electric cable. I was almost thrown off the pole. My right arm was seized up and when I got down, my hand was bleeding. We had arranged to attack two despatch-riders at Whitehall on that morning but cancelled the job because of the heavy firing in the area and the activity of patrols. I was arrested at about 11.30 a.m. on 8 November 1922 and brought to Wellington Barracks.[16]

On the morning of 8 November 1922 the IRA attacked Wellington Barracks and many soldiers were killed or wounded. The *Fianna* took no part in this. Following the attack, patrols searched in all directions and one of these patrols raided our headquarters. I suspect that some of the local people were suspicious and advised the soldiers to raid the dairy. There were six men billeted at Doody's Dairy. I told the men to make themselves scarce but one man named Rochford, a stage actor by profession and a bit of a dandy, delayed getting out. While waiting for Rochford to leave, I stalled with another man by the name of

Moore when the soldiers entered the room. We had no guns in the room we occupied; our 'dump' was in the adjoining chamber. When the arms were found, there was pandemonium. Soldiers rushed here and there. They captured five revolvers, about six hand-grenades, a quantity of ammunition and much equipment. This included three typewriters and about £2,000 worth of stamps taken some days earlier from captured mailbags.

Old Mr Doody, who wasn't a member of the IRA, was arrested with us. His wife let us use the premises. She was arrested next day and interned. To our surprise, our two men who had left earlier had been arrested at the street door. They must have come along just as the raid took place and were pointed out by some of the local people who had crowded around the dairy. Captain O'Doherty, who was in command of the soldiers, kept shouting: 'We have captured thousands of pounds' but this was not so. He was referring to stamps for which we had little use. We were marched between two files of soldiers to Wellington Barracks about a mile away. Some of the people in the streets shouted and jeered at us. Perhaps they knew some of the soldiers who had been shot that morning but, anyhow, most of the people were against us during the Civil War. Thus began my twenty months in hell or perhaps I should say fifty years because I still suffer from the effects of those twenty months.

I found myself in seven different jails. I was charged before two civil courts. I was arraigned for Military Court Martial. I was tortured five times. I went on hunger strike and was in real danger of being murdered or executed. I came out of prison physically crippled and a nervous wreck. When we were arrested, we were taken to the Intelligence Office, referred to later by the prisoners as 'the knocking shop'. There was much excitement inside and outside the barracks because of the attack that morning and on the way to the Intelligence Office I saw a dead horse. I was brought in first. The rest were lined up outside the door. There were four officers around a table. I did not know any of them at the time. They surrounded me and asked for my name and address. They then searched me, which was followed by many kicks and blows, about thirty in all. I was put outside of the door, dazed and bleeding from nose and mouth. Another prisoner by the name of Clarke was brought in. There were cries and moans followed by silence for several minutes. The door was opened and there was a shout: 'Bring Sherwin back.' There were, of course, soldiers guarding us outside the door. When I entered for the second time, they demanded information about White, my O/C, that is, his home address and mentioned a job that they suspected us of planning. This was the main piece of information that my torturers wanted to know.

Had I confessed, White and others would have been murdered. I was also accused of being O/C of the Active Service Unit and they then asked the other prisoner who was still in the room to confirm what they said and he did. I refused to answer so I was punched and all of my clothes were dragged off me until I was naked. They put me across a table and twisted my arms. They lashed me across the back. As far as I could see, they had sticks, belts and a bayonet scabbard. They all lashed me, stopping now and then to see would I talk but I did not. I was lashed for about twenty minutes receiving hundreds of blows, and was in agony but still semi-conscious. They then threw a jug of water in my face and called in the soldiers to put my clothes on and take me to the guardroom. The prisoner who gave me away was in the office through all of this.[17] I did not say that he gave me away to save him embarrassment but the other prisoners knew. Had he taken his beating like the rest of us, I would have got away with one beating but he could not take it.

One man in particular was the leader in these assaults, he was Commandant Joe Dolan.[18] Another was Commandant Frank Bolster. I was never certain as to the identity of the other two. These men were often mentioned in Republican papers as murderers and torturers. Two hours later, I was taken out of the guardroom by Dolan and two soldiers and brought again to the Intelligence Room. Only Dolan and Bolster were present. Dolan said that I would not get out alive unless I talked. They both punched me. I was prodded with a wire and received several blows on the head with a revolver. Dolan did most of the attacking. I was in such a daze that more blows made little difference. I was in a state of shock and pain and bleeding all over. The soldiers were again called in and they had to carry me across to the guardroom. I received some first aid from the prisoners as the guardroom was full. I lay on the ground unable to move.

About an hour later the soldiers took me out again and brought me to the Intelligence Room. Again only Dolan and Bolster were present. Dolan had his hat on and a rifle in his hand as if he were going out on a raid. He started jabbing me with the rifle. He got me into a corner and kept jabbing me all over. He was in a state of frenzy and shouting like a lunatic. He set his rifle down and ran in my direction to choke me. He tried to shove the muzzle of the rifle down my throat. Then he took a razor from the drawer of the table and went to cut my throat. Bolster held his hand and said: 'Leave him alone, he won't talk.' He then left the room shouting: 'I am taking you out tonight as a hostage but you will not be coming back alive.' Bolster did not beat me on this occasion. I was again carried out to the guardroom and lay on the floor until later that night when I was removed to a wing of the barracks. I did not sleep that night as I lay on a mattress on the floor. I was in too much pain. Next day the prisoners inspected my body. There were hundreds of cuts and marks on my back. My face was swollen, my nose was broken, several teeth were missing or loose and I had cuts and lumps on my head with bruises all over my body. I could not stand or move. I remained in bed for about nine days. I received no medical attention other than some first aid treatment from a soldier.

There was a reign of terror in the barracks for the next few days and doctors were not allowed to give medical attention. Two of the prisoners who inspected my body were Seán Lemass (later *Taoiseach*) and Mr Tom Walsh, an O'Connell Street outfitter, who gave me his overcoat and told me to keep it as I had only my blanket.[19] That day Dolan came into the wing and took two prisoners out. One came back later with his back cut to pieces, his name was George White. He later had to receive treatment in a mental hospital. Another man by the name of Tom Hendrick was brought back in a coma. He did not regain consciousness. The prisoners demanded doctors from the soldiers but no doctors came. He was later removed on a stretcher to hospital. I was told afterwards that he had been removed to a mental home.[20]

Let me say here and now that I never suffered any ill-treatment from the ordinary soldier, and as far as I am aware, nor did anyone else. The people responsible were the officers, especially the Intelligence Officers, and they had full protection from the top.

Many of those who took the side of the IRA in the Civil War did so reluctantly. When the Four Courts were attacked, everything was in the melting pot. Most of those who had taken part in the War of Independence were dragged into the fighting, including Mr De Valera. It might have been better had he kept out of it, as he might have been able to influence the IRA to cease their activities much earlier than they did. I suppose he would have been arrested anyhow. Most of the IRA members were young men who knew nothing about politics. They were sincere and believed that those who supported 'the Treaty' had betrayed the country and I was one of them. We certainly did not fight for gain. Since I left the National Army in July 1922, I had only received £1 from my O/C and half of this small sum I put behind a picture in my home. It was still there when I was released in 1924. The other half, amounting to ten shillings, was in my jacket when I was arrested and it was taken from me.

Looking back now, I know that it was wrong to fight the government by force as they had a mandate to rule, but something like this happens in most countries when they first get freedom. Had the IRA some dominant, clear-sighted military leader in command, it would not have happened. While I may excuse the tough action against the IRA by the government, I can never excuse the wholesale murders of helpless prisoners and the torturing of thousands, especially when they were former comrades, who had given years of labour to the national cause. I will not accept that the government did not know. They did know and the murder gangs were protected by members of the government. It is known that Kevin O'Higgins, the tough Minister for Justice, challenged other ministers about these murders.[21] He stood over official executions but he was against unofficial killings. Most of the murder gangs and the ministers who protected them were members of the secret society – the Irish Republican Brotherhood. When O'Higgins was shot in 1927, many thought that members of this murder gang had killed him because he put down a mutiny in the army when the Civil War was over, but I believe that he was shot by the IRA as he accepted full responsibility for these official executions, totalling seventy-seven. When he was shot, Republicans cheered everywhere. It slaked their thirst for revenge. When Collins was assassinated, everyone was sorry and Republicans in jail prayed for his soul.

On about 28 November 1922 I was removed to Oriel House, the headquarters of the political police. They threatened me but did not ill-treat me. After some days, I was brought to the District Court and charged with the raid for typewriters. I was remanded and spent a few days at the Bridewell Prison. Later I was removed to Portobello Military Barracks and was charged by Court Martial for taking part in a raid while in possession of firearms. At that time, possession of a gun meant death by firing squad. My cousin John Connolly who got me into the National Army in 1922, who was then a staff captain stationed at Portobello Barracks, told my sister that he had seen a report that I was to be executed.[22] I was then two months past my seventeenth birthday. I could not officially be executed until I was 18 years of age but this detail would not stand in the way of the murder gangs. On the day I was brought to Portobello, I was taken to the Intelligence Room. Dalton, the Director of Intelligence, again demanded information.[23] I refused to answer so he punched and kicked me around the office. I was bleeding again and felt very weak from the previous beatings. Four soldiers took me out to the guardroom. One of the soldiers knew me and delivered a message to my home.[24] Dalton shouted at me when I was being taken from the office: 'You will be dead within a week.' I knew that my age saved me as they could not officially execute me at 17 years of age but they could torture or murder me. There were four cells in the guardroom with a prisoner in each. They were myself, Patrick Rigley, later O/C of the Twenty-Sixth IRA Battalion during the Emergency 1939–44; Fred Cogley, a journalist, and Major Robinson, an ex-British army officer and a cousin of Erskine Childers, an Englishman who had helped the Republican cause.[25]

The day after I arrived in Portobello, an officer arrived at my cell and read from a charge sheet. I was accused of being in possession of a gun when carrying out a raid for typewriters and other charges. I was told that I would be tried in a few days. At the same time I was asked if I was prepared to sign a form agreeing not to take up arms against the government again. I refused to sign this form. Had I done so, I would have been released, as two of my men who were also charged signed this form and were later released, along with hundreds of others.

My trial was postponed, which I believe was due to my being under 18 years of age as the officer called again to enquire as to how old I was. I was removed to the political wing of Mountjoy Prison, a few days before Christmas. There were about 200 prisoners in the wing. I met several prisoners there who were to become prominent politicians at a later date, e.g. Dr Jim Ryan, who later became Minister for Finance,[26] and Gerry Boland, who later became Minister for Justice and was father of an even later minister for local government.[27] The prisoners were able to meet one another as they had broken off the locks of their cells. They had freedom within the wing. While there, I got a dose of scabies and did not get rid of this skin disease for the next two years.

Towards the end of May 1923, all prisoners were removed to Tintown Camp at the Curragh. That was, all prisoners except me. As each man's name was called to leave the wing, I alone was left behind in the big wing. I thought that it could have something to do with my trial. I called the guards and asked to see the governor. When I entered the office, he shouted at me and told me that I should have gone to another camp some weeks before and ordered me down to the underground dungeon. This was a dark place, flooded and full of rats. I did not sleep that night and got no food. The next day a soldier came with some tea. I asked to see the officer who came down later. I explained to him that there could be a mistake as my brother was a prisoner in another wing and had been removed to Newbridge Camp some weeks earlier. I was taken up and put into another wing where I met my O/C, Alfred White, the *Fianna* Acting Adjutant General. I also met Seán Harling, who was O/C of the Dublin Brigade *Fianna* at the time that Cole and Colley were murdered.[28] White told me not to trust Harling who was in charge of a line of communications between the prisoners and the IRA on the outside. He suspected that Harling was disclosing the nature of the communications to the Free State authorities. Harling had been arrested and released and then rearrested. Some weeks later all prisoners were removed to Tintown Camp No. 3 and all young prisoners were ordered into Hut No. 16. In about August all of the prisoners were ordered to go on hunger strike to demand their release, as the Civil War had been over since 24 May when the IRA, or what was left of it, were told to dump their arms. Before the Civil War ended, the Deputy Chief of Staff of the IRA, Liam Deasy, was captured and sentenced to death.[29] He appealed to the IRA on the outside to lay down their arms. This act no doubt saved his life. To his credit, he had tried to stop the war before he was captured but had some of the unfortunate 'rank and file' who had been executed made this appeal, they would have been accused of cowardice.

Of all the insane acts carried out by the IRA leadership, the order 'to shoot government deputies on sight', issued in November 1922 was the worst. The government had over 12,000 prisoners on their hands and we had lost the fight at least five months earlier. Arising from this order, two deputies were shot on the Dublin quays. One, Seán Hales, was killed.[30] He was a brother of Tom Hales who was fighting on the Republican side and was in charge of the area where Collins was shot.[31] The government ordered four of the Four Courts leaders to be executed without trial as an official reprisal. No more deputies were shot. Why did they not realize that something like this would happen before acting on the decision? Why did they not do this when they had the military advantage? It certainly highlights the hopelessness of the leadership outside. The order to go on hunger strike was another foolish act. It was a new tactic 'to fight on an empty stomach'. After the first few days, the boys became weak. It was difficult at the beginning but you got used to it. We drank water with a little salt. We would not last more than a few days without water. After the fifth or sixth day we took to our beds. After that, few people spoke and the hut became like a morgue. After twelve days, the boys in Hut No. 16 were ordered off the strike but the older prisoners continued. When some prisoners died, the rest were ordered to take food.

In about November the government began to release the prisoners. Every morning, an officer arrived at the huts and told prisoners to pack up for release. At the beginning of December 1923, my name was called and I packed up thinking that I was going home, but I was put into a tender and brought back to Mountjoy Prison. I was put into one of the wings that had been vacated six months earlier. I thought that I was all alone in a big wing but next morning I found that there were three other prisoners in the cells. They were political prisoners who had been arrested over some land trouble. Before Christmas, I was brought to the District Court and again charged with the raid for typewriters. I was remanded to the Central Court, Green Street. A solicitor named Reid called to see me. He was sent by the IRA to act in my defence. I told him of all the ill-treatment I had received and gave him the names of the witnesses. He took my statement down in shorthand.[32]

I was charged at the Central Court in January 1924 and sentenced to twelve months in the criminal part of Mountjoy. When one of the witnesses told the court that I had been tortured in prison, the judge ordered him off the stand. When I arrived in Mountjoy, I was put into a cell with two others. One was an imbecile and was in for sodomy. I did not know what this meant but when I was told, I banged at the cell door and demanded that I be removed to another cell and I was removed. Here, I was surrounded by many criminals. I could have escaped all of this had I signed a form stating that I would not take up arms again but I had strong principles and I never believed in giving in to anyone.

A large warder named Crosby was in charge of the prisoners and it was his practice to put them through exercises before breakfast each morning. On the first morning, I could not do the exercises as I was very weak. At this time, I suffered badly from nerves, pains in the head and back and gastritis as a result of the hunger strike. Warder Crosby shouted at me and said that he 'would see me' when I went back to the cell. When Crosby came into the cell, he went to strike me but I warned him that I was not a criminal and that he would be sorry if he hit me. I told him that I was a political prisoner. He then left the cell. That evening he came again to the cell and was very nice. He said that he would excuse me from exercises and that he would put me in the boot repair shop, where I could take it easy. It seems that he had made enquiries about me and found out about the IRA connections. Later he confided to me that some of the IRA told him all about me.

In about June 1924, I wrote to Kevin O'Higgins protesting about being treated as a criminal and to my surprise, he ordered my release, so I finally came out of jail. I think I was the last IRA man to be released having spent twenty months in seven different prisons.

Allow me to elaborate a little further on the conditions in jails at this time. The conditions in jails or places of detention during the Civil War depended on whether it was temporary or regular abode. There was some sort of organization in the latter case but in the former, conditions were bad. Prisoners were interrogated and beaten, some brutally. Bedclothes were dirty and the prisoners were restricted to very confined areas. Generally speaking, conditions depended on the period of the Civil War and the type of officers in control. For instance, when Collins was killed, the brutality peaked: therefore what was happening on the outside greatly influenced how we were treated on the inside. The Intelligence Officers were a law unto themselves. They were usually drunk and trigger-happy. Wellington Barracks, later called Griffith Barracks, was the worst but there were other bad areas as well.[33]

Some weeks before I was arrested, the vice-vicar of St Paul's, Mount Argus, County Dublin, Father Smith, complained to President Cosgrave that a prisoner, Fergus Murphy, had been almost beaten to death with rifle butts at Wellington Barracks.[34] Cosgrave denied the charge but Father Smith stressed that when one of his priests tried to gain admission to the barracks, he was told that the prisoner was not there but prisoners on the compound shouted that he was there and was dying. On the morning that I was arrested, officers fired into a crowd of prisoners on the compound and wounded five and on the same morning a man named Spain was wounded and captured. He was put against a wall and shot dead. Commandant Joe Dolan was the worst terrorist in the barracks. He was a sadist. He is quoted in historian Carlton Younger's book *Ireland's Civil War* saying: 'We had to learn to kill in cold blood and we got used to it.' He was referring to men he had killed during the War of Independence but it did not trouble his conscience during the Civil War either.[35] Both Joe Dolan and Charles Dalton, two of the men who tortured me, were later treated in mental hospitals.

The prisoners in Wellington Barracks were sullen and defiant but some were simply scared. When I was removed to Oriel House at about the end of November, I mixed with about twenty other prisoners. Some were non-political and were there on criminal charges. They were light-hearted, cracked jokes, played cards and talked about drink and women. We slept on the floor, as there were few beds. After a few days, I was removed to the Bridewell, a place of detention adjoining the courts. I was charged with the typewriter raid. I was there about two days. I was alone in the cell and slept on a wooden plank.

I was removed to Portobello Military Barracks on about 2 December for Military Court Martial and detained in the guardroom. There were four cells and five prisoners including myself. Three of the prisoners were of the officer class. They talked about the war outside and the mistakes that had been made. One of the prisoners, Simon Kane, a wild character from Co. Clare, was detained in my cell. He was always talking about the police whom he had killed during the War of Independence with his 'Peter the Painter' (revolver). I was removed to Mountjoy Prison a few days before Christmas. They had deferred my trial, perhaps because I was only 17 years of age. At that time, several young men of 18 years of age were officially executed and three *Fianna* boys were murdered at Clondalkin. One of the officers who had tortured me was known to be responsible. Mountjoy Prison had several wings. Criminals were confined to some and the political prisoners to others. The military governor was Paidín O'Keefe, a prominent member of the Gaelic League. He was short, erratic and comical to look at. None of the prisoners, even his own men, took him seriously. He was often drunk and used strong language. The prisoners were confined to the wing. They played cards but spent most of their time making bags, mats and other articles. At night they held concerts which included Irish dancing and cooked some of their own food. When the lights were turned off, they lit candles made from grease and a piece of rag. Most of the prisoners had scabies. There were about 500 political prisoners in Mountjoy at that time.

During May, the prisoners were removed to Tintown Camp (Curragh Camp, County Kildare). Some were sent to Newbridge some miles from the Curragh. The camps were okay, with certain freedoms within the barbed wire fence around the camp. We had our own cooks and camp officers. We had the usual concerts, dancing and sports. The prisoners, who included many from the country, spent much of their time making articles as souvenirs. You could hear the 'tap tap' all day as they made rings from silver coins. I carved a Celtic cross out of a piece of wood. At this time, the Civil War was over. About the end of November, I was removed and taken back to the same wing at Mountjoy Prison. The wing was filthy, full of rubbish and just as it had been when the prisoners left it six months before. There were no locks on the cells so we had the run of the wing, which could hold 150 prisoners. The other prisoners played cards and talked about drink and women. About this time, I met a prisoner by the name of Flannery from Galway, who had been on remand for some months. I arranged to meet with him at Mass every Sunday if I were sentenced, as remand prisoners could receive a visit weekly. I arranged with my sister Mary to visit Flannery regularly. In that way, I heard all of the news and could send out messages.[36]

The food was bad. Porridge and a cup of cocoa was served in the morning. For dinner, we received three potatoes (one usually bad), cabbage and a small piece of meat which tasted like rubber. Then there was more cocoa and a very small loaf with margarine at 5 o'clock in the evening. No more food was offered until the next morning at 8 o'clock.

Some writers say that there were atrocities on both sides in the Civil War but this was not so. There may have been isolated cases but it was no organized policy of terror. No person captured by the Republicans during the Civil War was murdered or ill-treated. We knew that we had no chance of winning the war; therefore, there was nothing to be gained by revenge. In fact, we would have been big losers if we had tried, as the government had 12,000 prisoners. We, on the other hand, could not keep prisoners.

As already stated, the terror began when Collins was shot. It's significant that Commandant Joe Dolan was with Collins when he was killed. Commandant Charles Dalton, who beat me up at Portobello Barracks, was a brother of Major General Dalton who was in charge of the convoy. Again I consider it a strange coincidence that the last barracks inspected by Collins in Cork before he was shot was commanded by Captain Bob Conlon, my former *Fianna* Company O/C (D. Second Battalion 1919). One of the first men murdered following the death of Collins was Alf Colley, my former *Fianna* Company O/C (B. First Battalion) in 1920.

NOTES

1   The original chapter title was: 'The War of Independence and the Civil War'.

2   Dan Breen (1894–1969) was an Irish freedom fighter and a *Fianna Fáil* politician. Breen joined the Irish Volunteers in 1914. On 21 January 1919, the day the first *Dáil* met in Dublin, Breen took part in an ambush at Soloheadbeg. The ambush, led by Seán Treacy, attacked a group of Royal Irish Constabulary men who were escorting explosives to a quarry. Two policemen were killed and the entire episode is considered the first action taken in the War of Independence.

3   Michael Collins was born on 10 October 1890 near Sam's Cross, West Cork. He was Commander-in-Chief to the Irish Free State Army. On 22 August 1922, he set out from Cork in a convoy. On the return trip, they passed through Bandon where his convoy was ambushed at a place known as *Béal na mBláth* (the mouth of flowers) where Collins was killed.

4   Many of Collins' 'gunmen', later on during the Civil War, murdered their own former War of Independence comrades. They became known as the 'Free State Murder Gang' and Sherwin was to become a victim of two of them.

5   An editorial decision was made regarding spelling. Changed 'gaol' to 'jail'.

6   During the Civil War there were no reserves. All men were engaged and when the Civil War ended there was practically no-one outside to carry on.

7   Éamon De Valera was born on 14 October 1882. He joined the Irish Volunteers in 1913. As a Commandant, he took part in the 1916 Easter Rising. He was sentenced to death, the sentence being commuted to penal servitude for life. He was released on General Amnesty in 1917. De Valera was elected Sinn Féin MP for East Clare in 1917 and re-elected as parliamentary representative for Clare at subsequent general elections until his election as President in 1959. He founded the *Fianna Fáil* Party in 1926 and from 1932–37 he was President of the Executive Council of the Free State and Minister for External Affairs. He was President of the Council of the League of Nations at its 68th and Special Sessions, September and October 1932 and President of the Assembly of the League of Nations in 1938. Following enactment by the people of the Constitution, Éamon De Valera became *Taoiseach* and Minister for External Affairs from December 1937 to February 1948. He was *Taoiseach* again from June 1951 to June 1954 and March 1957 to June 1959. On 25 June 1959, he was inaugurated as third President of the Republic of Ireland. He died on 29 August 1975.

8   In 1932, the Republicans were elected to power and they got rid of the

objectionable articles in 'the Treaty', thus proving that there was no need for a civil war.

9   Napoleon Bonaparte, (spelt *Buonaparte*) France's greatest military genius, was born on 15 August 1769 in Ajaccio, Corsica. He began his military career as a second lieutenant in the French artillery and rose the ranks to become First Consul of France. He crowned himself Emperor and by 1807 ruled territory that stretched from Portugal to Italy and north to the river Elbe. Napoleon's attempts to conquer the rest of Europe failed. He was defeated in Moscow in 1812 and in 1815 to the Duke of Wellington at Waterloo. He was sent into exile on the island of St Helena where he died in 1821.

10   General Liam Lynch was born in 1893. He joined the Gaelic League and the Ancient Order of Hibernians and in November 1914 joined the Irish Volunteers. In the autumn of 1915, he took up full-time duties with the IRA. By January 1921, Lynch was Commandant of the Cork No. 2 Brigade. He was then appointed Divisional Commander of the 1st Southern Division with Brigades from Cork, Kerry, Limerick and Waterford. When the Army Convention finally met on 8 April 1922, the Army was placed under the control of a sixteen-man Executive with Liam as Chief-of-Staff. The result was that when the Civil War broke out Liam Lynch was in control of the whole Republican armed forces. While initially the IRA outnumbered the Free State Army, this changed rapidly through recruiting to the army and soon Lynch's defensive line from Waterford to Limerick was under severe pressure. On 10 April 1923, Liam Lynch was shot and later died from his injuries.

11   See *Parliamentary Debates Dáil Éireann*, entitled 'Dublin Man's Disappearance', Vol. 4, dated 27 July 1923, col. 1537 involving Ailfrid O'Broin, Kevin O'Higgins Minister for Home Affairs (replying for the President) and a Mr Johnson. O'Broin refers to '... the disappearance of Mr Noel Lemass on 3 July 1923 in broad daylight in a much frequented thoroughfare of the city'. There is a reference to his disappearance in Macardle's *The Irish Republic*. It states that on 3 July 1923, 'Noel Lemass is arrested by Free State forces. His body is discovered in the Dublin mountains on 12 October 1923.' See Dorothy Macardle, *The Irish Republic*, New York, Wolfhound, 1999, p. 862.

12   Frank Aiken, senior Irish politician, was born on 13 February 1898 and died on 18 May 1983. Aiken joined the Irish Volunteers in 1914 and commanded the Fourth Northern Division of the Irish Republican Army in the War of Independence. He was first elected to *Dáil Éireann* in 1923.

13   The Vice-O/C and several others had been arrested, no doubt due to some of the arrested men giving information.

14   When Sherwin was arrested, this was the main piece of information that his torturers wanted to know. Had he confessed, White and others would have been murdered.

15   Michael Daly was later arrested and Sherwin met him in Mountjoy Prison. He gave evidence to the Pensions Board about Sherwin's state of health, compared to what he knew of him prior to his arrest.

16   Wellington Barracks was later called Griffith Barracks after Arthur Griffith, one of the founding fathers of the Irish Free State. Arthur Griffith was born in Dublin on 31 March 1871. He joined the Gaelic League and in 1898 edited *The United Irishman*. In a series of articles, Griffith outlined a new policy advocating abandonment of parliamentary action at Westminster and passive resistance to British rule in Ireland. These articles, which cited the example of the Hungarians under Deák after 1848, were published in 1904 in a pamphlet entitled *The Resurrection of Hungary*. At a convention in 1905, Griffith expounded

this policy under the name Sinn Féin, chosen to emphasize the idea of national self-reliance. Griffith supported the Irish Volunteers, set up in 1913, and took part in the landing of arms at Howth in July 1914. He also took part in the Easter Rising of 1916 and was imprisoned. After the execution of the leaders, public opinion turned in favour of Sinn Féin and its name became synonymous with Irish freedom. Griffith stood down as president of Sinn Féin in favour of De Valera and in the general election of 1918, they gained an overwhelming victory. The elected members assembled as *Dáil Éireann* and proclaimed themselves the parliament of Ireland and declared a republic. De Valera was elected President of the Republic and Griffith its Vice-President. While De Valera was in the United States from June 1919 to the end of 1920 to enlist American support, Griffith acted as Head of the Republic. Sinn Féin courts were set up and British rule ceased to operate. However, this civil resistance to British rule was accompanied by guerrilla warfare under the leadership of Michael Collins and Richard Mulcahy. Griffith was arrested in November 1920 and imprisoned in Mountjoy Jail until July 1921. Pressure of public opinion in America and Britain led to a Truce in July 1921 and Griffith was chosen to lead the plenipotentiaries to the negotiations that resulted in the Anglo-Irish Treaty of 6 December 1921. He defended the Treaty as he thought it gave Ireland the opportunity to advance to full freedom. The Treaty was ratified by sixty-four to fifty-seven votes and De Valera, who had opposed it, resigned. Griffith was elected in his place. In the general election of June 1922, the Treaty party won fifty-eight seats, the Anti-Treaty side thirty-six, with the remaining thirty-four shared by Farmers, Labour and Independents. Civil War began with the shelling of the Four Courts (held by anti-Treaty forces) on 28 June 1922. Griffith died suddenly on 12 August 1922 and is buried in Glasnevin Cemetery, Dublin.

17   The prisoner, James Clarke, later sent evidence to the Pensions Board and was in court to give evidence on Sherwin's behalf when he took a libel action against *The Irish Times* newspaper.

18   According to Richard Abbott and Mick O'Farrell, RIC Sergeant Daniel Roche, who had been brought to Dublin from Tipperary to identify Seán Treacy, was shot and killed by the squad at the corner of Capel Street and Ormond Quay on 17 October 1920. The members of the squad were Joe Dolan, Tom Keogh and Jim Slattery. Paddy Daly and Bill Stapleton were also present. O'Farrell contradicts the location by claiming it was Parliament Street. See Richard Abbott, *Police Casualties in Ireland 1919–1922* (Cork: Mercier Press, 2000), p. 134 and Mick O'Farrell, *A Walk through Rebel Dublin 1916* (Cork: Mercier Press, 1999), p. 25.

19   Seán Lemass was born in Capel Street, Dublin in 1899. He served as a young Volunteer in the 1916 Rising, escaped deportation and returned to the Volunteers as a full-time officer. Following his arrest in 1920, he was interned in Ballykinlar for a year. He opposed the Treaty, fought in the Four Courts during the Civil War and was subsequently imprisoned in the Curragh Camp and Mountjoy Jail. On his release, he returned to the political side of the Republican movement and was elected TD for Dublin South in 1924 but abstained from taking his seat. Influential in founding the *Fianna Fáil* Party in 1926, he was appointed Minister for Industry and Commerce when the party entered government in 1932. He was Minister for Supplies during the Emergency from 1941–45. In 1945, De Valera nominated him as *Tánaiste* and he succeeded De Valera as *Taoiseach* in 1959. In January 1965, Lemass visited Belfast in an attempt to break down the cold war between north and south. In that same year, he re-established free trade with England, seeing this as a prelude to a joint entry into

the Common Market (now the European Union). One of the greatest innovations of the Lemass years as *Taoiseach* was the introduction in 1966 of free second-level education, which revolutionized Irish education. Second-level education ceased to be the privilege of the better-off but was opened up to all in accord with the Proclamation of the Republic by the leaders of the Easter Rising. During Lemass' time in government, Irish troops joined the United Nations Peacekeeping Force for the first time. He is remembered for building up Ireland's industry and infrastructure and founded many state bodies to achieve this, such as *Bord na Móna, Aer Lingus* and Irish Shipping. See Liam Skinner's draft unpublished biography entitled *Seán Lemass* (c. 1960), which is located in the University College Dublin Archives.

20   When Sherwin took the libel action against *The Irish Times* in 1964, he gave the names of Dolan, Bolster and another torturer, a Commandant Charles Dalton, who was to beat him up later at Portobello Barracks.

21   Kevin O'Higgins was born in Laois in 1892. He joined the Irish Volunteers in 1915 and was imprisoned in 1918. While in prison, he was elected MP for Queen's County at the 1918 Westminster Election. In 1919, he sat as a Sinn Féin TD in *Dáil Éireann* and was appointed Assistant Minister for Local Government under Wiliam T. Cosgrave. O'Higgins was strongly in favour of the Anglo-Irish Treaty which was signed in London on December 1921 and paved the way for the Irish Free State in 1922. After the deaths of Arthur Griffith and Michael Collins in August 1922, William T. Cosgrave led the government, first as Chairman of the Provisional Government and from December as President of the Executive Council. O'Higgins became Minister for Home Affairs (renamed Minister for Justice in 1924) and Vice-President, positions he held until his death. In 1923, they formed *Cumann na nGaedheal*, precursor to *Fine Gael*. In 1923, O'Higgins established the *Garda Síochána* as an unarmed police force and diffused the crisis of the Army Mutiny in 1925. O'Higgins was shot on his way to Mass at his home in Booterstown, Dublin on 10 July 1927 by members of the IRA.

22   This refers to an exchange between John Connolly and Mary Sherwin.

23   See Charles Dalton, *Charles with the Dublin Brigades 1917–21* (London: Peter Davies, 1929).

24   This soldier, James Farrell, later gave evidence to the Pensions Board about Sherwin's condition when taken from the Intelligence Office.

25   Robert Erskine Childers, author and Irish nationalist, was born on 25 June 1870 and was shot dead by the Irish Free State firing squad on 24 November 1922. It was in Childers' yacht that the guns were brought into this country for use in the 1916 Rebellion. Childers was hated by the Free State government, supposedly because he was not on their side. He was captured a few weeks before in possession of a small revolver. He had been a prisoner in this guardroom and was executed at Beggars' Bush Barracks. His son was later Minister for Health in the *Fianna Fáil* government and President of Eire.

26   Dr James Ryan was born on 6 December 1891 near Taghmon, County Wexford. Ryan was the medical officer in the GPO during the Easter Rising and was imprisoned in Wales until 1917. He was elected a Sinn Féin abstentionist MP for Wexford South at the 1918 Westminster Election. He was also a member of the Second *Dáil* where he opposed the Treaty. He was elected an abstentionist Republican TD in the 1923 General Election. Following the 1926 Sinn Féin *Ard Fheis*, he joined Éamon De Valera in the *La Scala* theatre as a founder member of *Fianna Fáil*, after the motion on giving recognition to *Dáil Éireann* failed to win a majority. He was re-elected TD for Wexford in every subsequent election until he

retired from the *Dáil* before the 1965 general election. Ryan was a minister in all of De Valera's governments: Minister for Agriculture (1932–47), Minister for Health (1947–48) and Minister for Finance (1957–65). He died on 25 September 1970.

27   Gerald Boland was born in Manchester, England on 25 May 1885. Boland joined the Irish Volunteers, the IRB and fought in the Easter Rising at Jacob's Biscuit Factory. He fought with the Old IRA during the War of Independence and took the Republican side in the Civil War. Boland won election to the Fourth *Dáil* as a Republican TD for Roscommon and was re-elected at each subsequent election for this constituency until he lost his seat in 1961. He became a founder member of *Fianna Fáil* in 1926. He entered the *Dáil* with the other party members after the passing of the Electoral Amendment Act encouraged the party to abandon the policy of abstentionism. He served as Parliamentary Secretary 1932–33 and was appointed to the Cabinet in 1933 as Minister for Posts and Telegraphs and for the next fifteen years served in all of De Valera's governments. He is best remembered as Minister for Justice (1939–48). During the Emergency, Boland introduced strong measures against the IRA such as internment and military courts that resulted in a number of executions. In 1948, *Fianna Fáil* ended up in opposition to the first coalition government. Having lost votes to the *Clann na Poblacta* party, their entry into coalition with *Fine Gael* assisted *Fianna Fáil*. Boland returned to Justice when *Fianna Fáil* returned to power (1951–54). He was not reappointed after the 1957 general election. He lost his *Dáil* seat at the 1961 general election and won election to the *Seanad* that year. He retired from politics in 1969. He died in Dublin on 5 January 1973.

28   Seán Harling, born in 1900, was 16 at the time of the Rising. He was a friend of both De Valera and Collins and was used to carry messages between the various members of the first government, while they still had to meet in secret. See *Parliamentary Debates, Dáil Éireann*, entitled 'Woodpark Shooting: Proposed Tribunal of Inquiry', Vol. 22, dated 15 February 1928, cols 29–33. The debate took place between Seán Lemass and the then Minister for Justice, Mr Fitzgerald-Kenney. Fitzgerald-Kenney: 'I move that it is expedient that a Tribunal be established for inquiry into a definite matter of urgent public importance, that is to say, the facts and circumstances surrounding the shooting of Timothy Coughlin, at Woodpark Lodge, Dartry Road, on the 28th January 1928.' He continued: 'It is probably in the recollection of members of the House that on the date in question this young man, Timothy Coughlin, met his death. From the evidence of the principal witness examined at the inquest, an Intelligence Officer named Seán Harling, it appears that Coughlin and another man followed up and endeavoured to shoot Harling. A coroner's jury inquired into the matter, and they brought in the following verdict: "We find that the said Timothy Coughlin died on the 28th inst. from shock, haemorrhage and laceration of the brain caused by a bullet. We are of opinion that the circumstances of the cause of death be a matter of further investigation."' Lemass had the following to say: '... the witnesses at any rate who were in State employment, endeavoured to establish that the late Timothy Coughlin was on Dartry Road on that night for the purpose of shooting Mr Seán Harling. Mr Seán Harling... is an Intelligence Officer... We are particularly interested in the date on which Mr Seán Harling first became a member of the Intelligence Force of the State. It is not so very long since the individual sought for and obtained a position of employment in the *Fianna Fáil* organisation. Was he then in the employment of the Intelligence Department of the State? Was he drawing

money out of the taxpayers' pockets for the purpose of espionage?'

29   Liam Deasy was one of the military leaders in the War of Independence. Deasy was just 20 years of age at the time of the 1916 Easter Rising. He enrolled in the Volunteers in Bandon in 1917 and by 1921 was in command of the West Cork Brigade. See Liam Deasy, *Towards Ireland Free: The West Cork Brigade in the War of Independence 1917–1921* (Cork: Mercier, 1973).

30   Seán Hales, 'the Buckshot', was a native of West Cork and a friend of Michael Collins. During the War of Independence he commanded a Brigade in the West Cork area of the old IRA which included his brother, Tom Hales. Seán Hales was elected to the *Second Dáil Éireann* as a Sinn Féin TD for County Cork at the 1921 general election. He was originally hostile to the Anglo-Irish Treaty but soon viewed it as a stepping stone to Irish unity through military means. During the Civil War, he fought with the Irish Free State Army. The Hales' familial experience is indicative of the fratricide that occurred throughout the country at this time. His brother Tom opposed the Treaty and led the ambush at *Béal na mBláth* where Michael Collins was shot dead. Hales was the most senior Free State Officer in the West Cork area. In early December 1922, Hales was in Dublin with Pádraig Ó Máille, who was then the Deputy Speaker of the *Dáil.* Hales was shot dead, and Ó Máille wounded, by a group of anti-Treaty IRA. Apparently Ó Máille had been the target and Seán Hales was shot by mistake. In reprisal for Seán Hales' death, Rory O'Conner, Liam Mellows, Joseph McKelvey and Dick Barrett, who were imprisoned at this time, were executed by firing squad despite having nothing to do with his murder.

31   Tom Hales, brother of Seán Hales, was captured by the British Army in Cork during the War of Independence and was badly beaten and tortured in an effort to make him disclose the whereabouts of prominent IRA figures including Michael Collins. He never broke, though his co-accused suffered brain damage and died in hospital insane. The British commanding officer, a Major Percival, subsequently commanded the British forces in Singapore during the Second World War and surrendered to the Japanese.

32   Sherwin later acquired this written statement and sent it to the Pensions Board.

33   Dorothy Macardle, historian, republican, novelist and journalist was born into the Dundalk brewing family in 1889. She was an important republican publicist during the Anglo-Irish War and the Civil War and sat on the first executive of *Fianna Fáil*, a political party that had been formally inaugurated on 16 May 1926. Macardle also protested about the Conditions of Employment Bill (1935) which limited women's working rights. She was also interested in refugees and in 1951 was President of the Irish Association for Civil Liberties. She was author of *Tragedies of Kerry 1922–1923* but her best-known work is *The Irish Republic* (1937).

34   William Thomas Cosgrave was born on 6 June 1880 and died on 16 November 1965. Cosgrave served as Minister for Local Government from 1919–22, Minister for Finance 1922–23, President of *Dáil Éireann* and the Executive Council of the Irish Free State from 1922–32, Chairman of the Provisional Government in 1922, President of the Executive Council from 1922–32, leader of *Cumann na nGaedheal* from 1923–1932 and leader of *Fine Gael* from 1933–44.

35   See Carlton Younger, *Ireland's Civil War* (London: Muller, 1968).

36   When sentenced to twelve months in the criminal section of Mountjoy, Sherwin mixed with criminals who talked all of the time about the 'jobs' that they had done outside, the mistakes that they had made and of how cautious they would be next time. They were always picturing the great feasts they would have when released and they talked about women, of course.

3

POLITICS: NO PLACE FOR THE LONE MAN![1]

On my release from jail in 1924, I reported back to the *Fianna* and was appointed a battalion commandant. In 1925, I was appointed a member of General Headquarters staff. Both the IRA and the *Fianna* reorganized after the Civil War and were closely associated with the Sinn Féin Party that had forty-four elected deputies. The physical force movement remained strong until after *Fianna Fáil* were elected to government in 1932 because there was a fear that the Free State government would refuse to hand over power if they lost the confidence of the people. Things being as they were, members of the Free State government and the senior army officers urged President Cosgrave not to hand over power and to set up a dictatorship but to Mr Cosgrave's credit, he refused to listen to such suggestions.

When I became a member of *Fianna Fáil* GHQ, I met Countess Markiewicz for the first time.[2] I was not impressed. I found her indistinct, tiresome and publicity seeking. She presided over tea party-styled executive meetings during which there was nothing but prattle. I did not approve of the all too blatant subservience of the members towards such coercion. About this time the Sinn Féin executive asked for a meeting with the *Fianna Éireann* executive to discuss future *Fianna* policy. This was the first time that I was to meet Mr De Valera, as he was then chairman of Sinn Féin. I was also to meet Frank Aiken, future Minister for Foreign Affairs. Mr De Valera suggested that we should cease to be a militant organization, as times had changed. He offered to subsidize the purchase of scout handbooks and other material and we accepted his proposals.

Arising out of this change of policy, 'Madam', as the Countess was known, appointed Seán Harling Chief Scout for Dublin. Sometime prior to that, I had organized an Intelligence Unit in the Dublin *Fianna* and it came to my attention that Harling was a spy. One of the men who gave this information was Thomas Reynolds who later became a prominent member of *Fianna Fáil*. The *Fianna* Intelligence Unit was satisfied that Harling was a police agent. I discussed this matter with the Acting Adjutant General Alfred White, who had had his own suspicions of Harling when in Mountjoy Prison in 1922. I conveyed my suspicions to 'Madam', but she refused to listen. Harling was her part-time chauffeur, her *aide-de-camp* and her pet. In fact, according to evidence admitted later by him at a court of inquiry, he was made a present of a car by her. For my trouble, Madam warned me that she would have me expelled from the *Fianna* if I repeated my remarks about Harling. Under the circumstances, I refused to take orders from Harling, as did most of the officers of the Dublin *Fianna*. Madam came to my home at Linenhall Street and told me that she was appointing me Deputy-Chief Scout under Harling and asked me to co-operate with him but I refused. She then made an amazing statement that Harling was doing intelligence work for her, which she supplied to the top leaders. This proved that he was more dangerous than I had thought because he was giving her useless information and getting important information in return as well as getting to know people who were engaged in IRA intelligence work. I told 'Madam' that she was a fool. At that, she said that she would have me expelled from the *Fianna*. I immediately resigned and so did most of the other *Fianna* officers.

Following my resignation, I organized a youth club comprised largely of ex-*Fianna* members. We ran dances and soon had a substantial fund. We called the club 'The Cole and Colley', after the two *Fianna* officers who had been murdered in 1922. After this first venture into the dancing business the members of the club suggested that I should run dances myself as I was not employed and that they would all support me. I took to this suggestion and made thirty shillings on my first promoted dance; this was in 1926. This was the first money that I earned since leaving the army in July 1922 and as already mentioned, the only other money that I received was £1 from my O/C before my arrest and £5 from the 'White Cross', a prisoners' aid society, on my release from jail. I remember at this time having no seat in my pants and asking a wealthy relation for the loan of a £1 to buy a new pair. I did not get it. I was asked just how I was going to pay it back. At that time, single men did not get public assistance.[3] After making thirty shillings on my first dance, I knew that this could be my lifeline. It could be my main form of support as it did not involve much physical effort and I was to depend on running dances for the next thirty-five years, to which I shall return.

After I resigned from the *Fianna* and organized 'The Cole and Colley Club', I attended Mr De Valera's meeting at the La Scala Theatre in May 1926, when he formed *Fianna Fáil*.[4] He had resigned from Sinn Féin because they refused to agree to his proposal to enter the *Dáil*. His view was that to remain outside the *Dáil* was to remain in the wilderness, and while certain people were satisfied to make idle protests and remain martyrs, the ordinary people thought differently. They wanted peace and progress and you could only pursue that by possessing power. I reported back to my club and I recommended that we should join the new party as a '*cumann*'. My proposal was unanimously agreed to.

We applied to the organizing committee which met in O'Connell Street. We received a reply recognizing our club as a '*cumann*' and we were invited to send a representative to the next meeting of the organizing committee. I attended the meeting so I was the first chairman of an organized *Fianna Fáil Cumann* in Ireland as the party was only then getting established. We were not invited to the next meeting but the secretary received a communication to the effect that they would continue to recognize the *cumann* but not if Frank Sherwin was a member. The *cumann* secretary replied on the instructions of the members that if Frank Sherwin was not good enough for *Fianna Fáil*, neither were they. Another communication was received from the secretary of the organizing committee which stated that they would not object to Frank Sherwin being a member but not as a representative on the organizing committee. The *cumann* decided that this was adding insult to injury and instructed the secretary not to communicate with *Fianna Fáil* any further.

Some weeks later a member of the organizing committee who lived near me told me that Madam Markiewicz had been appointed Chairman of the organizing committee and when she learned that I was a member she objected and told the members that it was either me or her. Several members objected to her attitude, but she impelled them and had her way. Thus *Fianna Fáil* lost a strong youth club with substantial funds and all because I had warned her that she was being used by a police spy. This was my first lesson in politics. It proved that democracy was merely a front and that rules are made to hold down the followers but not the leaders.

Madam Markiewicz was to die in 1927. Shortly after she died, the IRA was satisfied that Harling was a spy and decided to shoot him. Two men fired on him at Dartry, a short distance from his home, on 28 January 1928. He returned fire and killed one of the attackers, Timothy Coughlin, on whose body was found a *Fianna Fáil* membership card. *Fianna Fáil* demanded an inquiry because he was shot in the back of the head but they were more concerned with propaganda because he was a member of the *Fianna Fáil* party and they were anxious to know how long Harling had been a police agent. He had been employed at *Fianna Fáil* headquarters as a courier having got the job through Madam Markiewicz's influence and was thus in a position to know what was going on at *Fianna Fáil* executive meetings. An inquiry was held and their findings were that Coughlin fired at Harling and that he was killed by Harling in the return fire, which was a correct interpretation of events. Harling was asked how long he had been an intelligence officer but he refused to say and claimed privilege, which was allowed. His superiors also refused to say anything, except that Superintendent Ennis said that he had known Harling for nine months. Harling's brother-in-law gave evidence. He admitted that he had been sentenced to twelve months' imprisonment for bank robberies but was released in 1924. He was in Mountjoy Criminal Prison in 1922–24. Harling escaped to the United States but later returned.

On Christmas Eve 1929, I was struck down with a stroke which left me paralyzed. I could not walk nor could I use my arms. I was helpless. That night I remained in my bed in agony. On the following day, Christmas Day, I was taken to Jervis Street Hospital by my old friend John Dillon. They x-rayed me, then put yards of plaster around my back that enabled me to walk by inches but every movement was painful. I found that I could neither turn the knob of a door nor strike a match. My right arm was useless. I could use my left arm a little.

The x-ray showed no broken bones as nerve injuries cannot be seen by x-ray. I was told to get violet-ray and massage treatment. I went to St Vincent's Hospital for this treatment but I only got temporary relief which left me disappointed. Dillon had some knowledge of massage so he treated me every night at about 6 p.m. for the next ten years, with the exception of the fifteen months that I spent in the United States. I wrapped a long sash around my back and under my groin. This gave me some support. I tried several doctors but they did not know what was wrong with me so I decided to go to America. My brother Joe was in Boston so I decided to call there first.[5] My primary reason in going to America was to get cured as I was disappointed in the medical profession in Ireland. I also hoped to make big money in the dance business. I had saved about £400. (Ir. Punt) = £2,000 Ir. Punt (1972) = €25,220 (Feb. '06); $31,680 (Feb. '06); £17,240 sterling (Feb. '06). Most people go to America with nothing but their fare. I went with a small fortune. I was examined at two hospitals in Boston, but they could do nothing. I made for New York residing at Woodside, half an hour's journey by subway from New York proper. I attended Bellevue Municipal Hospital as soon as I arrived there. The doctors there said what the doctors said elsewhere, that there were no bones broken, and advised heat and massage. I attended three days a week for the next twelve months, but again no cure, only relief. It took about five hours daily to get this treatment because the hospital was an hour's journey. There was always a big queue and the treatment took an hour. My money was going quickly as it was expensive to live in the United States unless you were earning a living. I decided to look for a job that would not entail physical work. I got a job from 6 p.m. to 12 midnight in a swanky indoor golf course. All I had to do was to shove a roller on a sand-walk about ten minutes every half hour. The roller was a little heavy so I told the chief attendant who was a North of Ireland man and fond of drink. He told me to empty the water from the roller into a pond where there were goldfish and, to my embarrassment, the goldfish died but he said nothing about it. About this time, I was recommended surgical belts around my back which held back my shoulders and gave me some support. I also had a broad belt around the small of my back with straps under my groin that tightened on the front of my belt. Between these belts and daily massage, I managed to do a little work, but the chief attendant was eventually sacked because of his drinking and the new chief attendant ordered me to fill the roller so I had no choice but to give up the work.

I had made enquiries about dance promoting but I found that things were very different in America from the way they were at home. Anyhow, I had made up my mind to return to Dublin, as I had grown much weaker than when I was at home as a result of not being able to walk more than a few hundred yards without severe pain in the lower part of my spine. Everywhere I went entailed walking more than I could, whereas at home I could catch buses everywhere or I could ride a bike, which required very little physical effort. I decided not to go home until the end of the summer of 1931 as I could then start the dance business immediately. At that time, most dance halls in Dublin closed during the summer.

In the meantime, I joined 'The Burns' Detective Force', a private agency who wore uniforms and carried guns. I was sent on duty guarding New Jersey pier, a short distance from New York. The hours were long, twelve hours a day, but later it became easier – six hours daily. I sat most of the time as I could not walk for long, nor could I stand for any length of time. I was to have another more embarrassing moment the day after I joined. I was told by another guard to put on the lights in a large shed. It was dark and he said that the switch was in the corner. I pressed down a switch which turned out to be none other than the fire alarm, so within minutes, dozens of fire brigades arrived at the pier. I only remained on this job about three days as it entailed a lot of standing. I then decided to apply to an employment agency for the handicapped, but I heard nothing so I gave up and waited to go home. I had only a little more than my return fare. I had lost my £400, plus about £800 which I could have earned had I not gone to America. In other words, I lost the equivalent of £6,000 (at 1972 value) and all because of my physical disability.

My US venture was my greatest disappointment. Before I left Dublin I organized special dances and parties to celebrate my departure. I gave out my photograph as a souvenir. All Dublin, at least all who knew me, wished me well but I found myself in a strange land where you met nobody that you knew unless you had addresses. They were certain to live fifteen or twenty miles away and if you called on them, they were probably out. At home in Dublin I was making good money and was engaged in a form of business that was most enjoyable. It was a sort of dream world where boys and girls could dance to lovely music and hear good singing every night. I had medical aid and massage that at least gave me some relief and companions I could trust. In the United States, it was like being in jail all over again. I felt like going home the month after I arrived but pride would not let me and I was hoping against hope that I would get treatment that would cure my physical ailments. Apart from the hospitals that I have mentioned, I went to others, including 'quacks'. I even considered joining the US army. I thought that power and determination, of which I had plenty, would defeat what was wrong with me. Tears often came to my eyes on finding that I could not overcome these problems that afflicted me and I was to realize this predicament far away in a foreign lonely land.

I never gave in. It is not in my nature. It was this faith that carried me through all difficulties before and since. I made my way to the US recruiting office. I was told that I would have to take out my first citizenship papers before I could join. I applied for my papers in the courts and again made my way to the recruiting office. The Medical Officer tested my eyes and heart. He then told me to bend and touch my toes. This exercise was part of my daily programme otherwise I would not have been able to do it. I passed, and was told to come back in a week to sign the final papers. During the week, I slept on what I was doing and came to the conclusion that I was only fooling myself. I would not last a day and knew it. I believed that I could do almost anything, except the physical. Experience had taught me that if I engaged in physical work I would pay for it with severe pain in the spine and head, no sleep for days and palpitations in the affected parts including the heart. Instead, I joined the YMCA on 23rd Street. They offered steam baths, massage, a gym and an indoor swimming pool. I got all the treatment, but again only relief, no cure. One morning I dived into the 6ft 6in part of the pool. I thought that I would come up in the 4ft part but when my feet came to the bottom I found that the water was well over me and it began to choke me. It was a frightening experience. I dived or walked to get near the rail but it was nowhere near. I got the sensation that I was drowning. It has been said that when a person is drowning, all their past life comes back to them in a flash. Something like that happened to me but determination saved me. I made a ferocious dive while still under the water and came to a wall. I grabbed the rail and was safe. I learned the lesson that had been taught many times: 'Never swim unless there are other people around!' At the time that I dived in, there was nobody in the pool area and I could not swim a stroke.

I might have lost my mind were it not for the convivial moments at the address where I resided. The owner was a man named Trehy, a publican from Kilkenny. His mother and unmarried brothers lived a few doors away. There were also two musicians from Dublin who had played for me before they came to America, which was why I had made for this address, having received particulars from one of their relations. The Trehy brothers had a 'still' in their basement. They brewed poteen for their own use, and that of their friends. This was the period of prohibition, gangsters, 'speakeasies', and so on.

When I arrived home, I looked around for a hall in which to run dances and I booked three nights and a Sunday afternoon at 44 Lower Gardiner Street, the Dublin Trades Council Hall. The secretary was P.T. Daly, a former Labour councillor and Big Jim Larkin's right hand man.[6] He was Larkin's choice as secretary of the Irish Transport Union, when he (Larkin) left for America in 1914. However, James Connolly got the appointment.[7] The hall held about 180 dancers but 450 turned up the first night I opened. They were leaving as others came in but nobody asked for their money back. I made £20, the cost of my fare back from America. This was a great reception, but obviously I did not make that sort of money on future dances nor did I expect to. However, I made about £12 weekly, quite impressive at that time, 1932.

At this juncture I shall take the reader, if I may, on a short sojourn through my dancing business and my experiences of it, both good and bad. This will include my meeting with my future wife, Rosie, after which we shall return to take up this story and my re-entry into the jungle that is the wheeling and dealing of politics, 1932-style. This is not to imply that this 'style' did not apply across the board, that is, to all parties and in my view, to all times. I continued to expand my dance business. In time I was to run twenty-seven dance halls, not all at the same time of course, and it is upon this topic and some of the hypocrisy surrounding it that I should like to express a few comments. In the early days, people who ran dances were looked upon as 'agents of the Devil', but later on, the parish priests were to become the biggest promoters because they found that there was money in it. Actually, where it was a person's livelihood, they took good care to see that their dances were properly conducted because any disorders or complaints reduced numbers and could cause the place to close. It was a major job to keep dances going from year to year.

I met my future wife Rosie early in 1934. She was a very good-looking girl and a good dancer and inevitably, I had plenty of competition. Until then I had never kept company with girls. In fact, I was shy of them. Although I had been running dances for some seven years before meeting Rosie, I never danced and the first time that I got on to the floor was the day that I met her. She came into my hall at Lower Gardiner Street on a Sunday afternoon. I invited her and her companion to a dance that I was running that night at Dún Laoghaire. Just before the last dance, I took her up and managed to get around. Rosie and I were to be married in 1937. We were to go on to have nine children, six boys and three girls. A person who ran dances for a livelihood usually ran the risk of attack from thugs or gangs trying to force their way into the dance. I was injured on four occasions by this type but when you consider that I ran about 10,000 dances over thirty-five years, I was quite lucky. No thug or gang ever got into my dances but if they did and I could not get them out myself, I got the police.

I had one rare experience. In 1938, about six fellows calling themselves 'The Hoyer Gang' came into my hall at Lower Gardiner Street. My sister and sister-in-law were the only ones present. It was about 7.30 p.m. and none of my regular customers had yet arrived. I was sitting at a small table near the entrance door. A room behind me led to the bandstand. The gang got around me and demanded that all of their gang was to get into the dance every night for nothing and that I was to pay them protection money. I told them that I would do no such thing. I then received a number of blows. I retreated to the bandstand where there were a number of chairs for the band. I swung a chair and knocked one of them out. I then jumped onto the dance floor and ran towards the exit. Two of the gang blocked my way. I shoved one so violently that he in turn shoved one of his pals down the steps on to his face. With that, they seemed to have had enough as one shouted to the other: 'This fella is mad! Let's get out of here!' I was not to see them again.

My most serious injury befell me one night on stopping a thug from forcing his way into my hall. He butted me in the face and knocked me down. He then kicked me in the head and chest. People pulled him away. That night, elsewhere, the same thug inflicted on a man injuries that required seventeen stitches. He was arrested and got two years' imprisonment. I spent that night in Jervis Street Hospital. In spite of the above, I met thousands of decent people in the dance game and thousands met their marriage partners in my halls.

I had been studying 'The Theory and Technique of Dancing' for some time past with the object of teaching dancing with the help of several good dancers. One of these in particular was Jimmy O'Brien, who gave exhibitions, but the day I got on to the floor with Rosie was the first time that I had actually danced with a girl.

Shortly afterwards, I began teaching dancing, having mastered the theory and technique. I practised the lady's and gentleman's steps alone until I became an expert. I explained the steps and O'Brien would dance them. We would then take up those who lacked the nerve. I found that I could dance the lady's steps without much physical effort so I took up the gentleman and in time I could dance very well both as a lady and a gentleman. In fact, I did a course in London under Victor Sylvester who was a one-time world champion dancer.[8] I also took an examination in London for a dance diploma but again came up against my injuries. I passed on theory and technique but narrowly failed on actual dancing. When I was expected to be up on the balls of my feet, my right heel was on the ground because I had little power in the right leg. I later wrote to the dancing board and they said in reply that if I had had a doctor's certificate at the time of my examination that they would have allowed a pass.

I found that the knowledge of theory and technique of dancing gave me better poise and balance. A good dancer held the weight of his body slightly over the balls of his feet that enabled him to dance without effort and move around as light as a feather. In my case, my injuries were all over my back so that when I danced as a lady, I stretched back from my hips. It brought relief to my back and exercised the muscles of my back that were functioning. Actually, dancing was a form of physiotherapy for me. I usually danced the slow dances and avoided the quick ones. It is well known that dancing, like swimming, has cured or relieved people who suffer from physical ailments. In my case, I could not be cured. I was suffering from damaged or severed spinal nerves and arthritis had set in. I am certain that had I not taken active steps myself, I would have been permanently bedridden or wheelchair bound. All of the time that I went about looking normal physically, I couldn't do any work as my right hand was practically useless.

It was commonly assumed that young people had immoral relations because they danced together and it was further assumed that immoral women patronized dance halls. There was no truth in these assumptions. The halls were licensed and usually closed at 11 p.m. Those who came to my dances were usually working class people. It was the only enjoyment that many of them had as wages were small in the old days and admission prices were eight pence to one shilling. It was a cheap night's enjoyment. Were you to go to a pub, you would spend ten times as much. Dance halls enabled thousands of young people to meet a variety of the opposite sex and so most of them had true love affairs. When people choose their partners from a small selection, they have not much choice and such marriages are often dull. Immoral women don't attend ordinary dances. If they did, they would earn nothing, as there are no facilities for that kind of business in licensed dance halls. The modern night club or striptease joints may attract such people but not ordinary dance halls.

I make no apologies for running dances and am most grateful for the support that I received over the years from thousands of decent young people, and I am glad that I was instrumental in thousands of couples meeting their true loves in my halls. I am further glad that I was to go on to meet many of my old dance clients at tenants' and old-folk' outings and to learn that they were still having a dance and keeping themselves young at heart.

I have referred at some length to the dance business because it was my only form of employment. Now after that detour through my dance promoting we will return to the main story and take it up from 1932. Shortly after returning from the United States in 1932, I met Barney, brother of Liam Mellows, one of the Four Courts leaders, who was shot in an official reprisal in November 1922.[9] He was an applicant for a disability pension and was on his way out of Bricin's Military Hospital. I was on my way in for medical examination. We went into a pub opposite Kingsbridge now called Seán Heuston.[10] We talked about old times and he told me that just before Madam Markiewicz died, she admitted that she had done me a great injustice but she never had the decency to clear my name with *Fianna Fáil* and others.

I rejoined *Fianna Fáil* in 1932 to help with the general election of that year. I joined the 'Father John Murphy *Cumann*' and later became chairman.[11] I was, however, to find myself opposed by a clique on the Constituency Council who wanted all nominations as public representatives for themselves. I was looked upon as an outsider. The clique had the support of the National Executive clique. All political parties have cliques at all levels. Every constituency council is controlled by one or two individuals, often business people who spend money on drink. They have a number of 'paper clubs' in their pocket and they pay the affiliation fee. New members are not wanted unless they are supporters of those who run the set-up.

In recent years there have been many rows at constituency level. The public seldom know of these rows because there is an unwritten law that the public must not know about fixing, bribing or other accusations in case they get wise to the kind of business politics is. All the parties take advantage of these rows in other parties but they are all agreed on one thing: that it is bad for business. They feel that they should stand together for fear that the voters might take it into their heads to say: 'A plague on all your parties.' For this reason, the row is quickly swept under the carpet. Young people join extremist parties or groups because they feel they are not wanted in the larger parties unless they are supporters of the cliques, this among other reasons.

In 1939, I was elected to the National Executive of *Fianna Fáil*. I had worked hard in the party, and I ran dances for several *cumann*, so I got their support. When the war broke out in 1939, I was chairman of the Old *Fianna*, so I asked Seán Saunders, who was the former adjutant of the Dublin Brigade *Fianna* (1921) to join me in calling a meeting of all old *Fianna* and we offered ourselves to the government as a defence force.[12] We were accepted, so Saunders and I marched 200 old *Fianna* into Collins' Military Barracks. The old IRA was accepted at the same time. I told the doctors what was wrong with me. They told me that it was a reserve battalion and I would only have to do a few hours' training, that I could try it and if I could not carry on that I could always resign. They also said that many of the men were old and not in particularly good health, and that I might not be any worse than some of the others. I was selected as a member of an NCO's class and received high marks in the examination and was appointed 'Sergeant Instructor' in charge of recruits attached to Headquarters Company.[13] Alfred White, the former Adjutant General of the *Fianna*, was Battalion Adjutant. He knew of my physical handicap so he excused me from all route marches, so all of my work was in the barracks and I was more or less my own boss.

I had one advantage over the other members of the 26th Battalion – I was a marksman. When I was young, I always fired at fancy fairs and won many prizes. The principles governing shooting from pellet guns and the real thing is the same. You hold the rifle firm with the left hand and the butt pressed into the shoulder. You keep the foresight on a level and in the centre of the back sight. You press the trigger with the forefinger of the right hand and of course, keep your eye on the bull's eye or target. You must make certain that there is not the slightest movement of the rifle as you press the trigger. You must be determined, and at the moment of pressing the trigger, 'tense'. Of course, when firing a real gun you may have to fire at a distant target, therefore you must allow for distance. You must train yourself to judge distance. On a rifle, there is a gauge, which allows you to raise the rear sight according to the distance required. I got the best score at the miniature rifle range and when the battalion went to Kilbride for testing with service rifles, I again got the best score and a hundred members put a shilling in a hat so I won £5. When I was training recruits, I only used my hands for about twenty minutes out of two hours' training. That was about my limit. Of course, I had my surgical belts on and had to tighten them when giving instruction. I had a good grip with my left hand but little or no grip with my right.

While heavily involved with these activities I continued to attend hospitals and doctors and received electric treatment at the Richmond Hospital. I attended the Meath Hospital and was treated by Surgeon 'Daddy' Houghton at the Orthopaedic Clinic, Merrion Square, and I had treatment from a blind masseur which cost me £1 for each massage. I attended the Bray Clinic, run by Mr Lindoph who catered for all hospital rejects. People came to him from all parts of the country. Some resided at his home, which included many priests, and I once met the late Denis Guiney, the owner of the biggest store in Dublin, Clery's of O'Connell Street, while I was there.[14] I went to many unqualified people, including a bonesetter, but made certain they were of good reputation. In fact, I went to everyone and anyone to try to cure this complaint, which I knew had cost me a fortune and a life of agony.

In 1942, I was nominated by *Fianna Fáil* to contest the local elections. I did not succeed but I got 532 votes. I was new at the game and I focused on addressing meetings when I should have spent more time canvassing. In 1943, the war situation had eased so the political parties arranged for a general election. I was nominated by the *cumann* and I knew that I would have a good chance of being elected. It was the practice then and it is still the practice for outgoing deputies to be selected, which meant in this case that only one outsider had a chance.

Whenever there is a general election and especially a by-election, there is always a lot of wire-pulling, wangling and fixing to get the nomination. In recent years much publicity has been given to these tactics, but as I said previously, most of it went on behind the scenes. People with money use it liberally to bribe delegates and every effort is made to get the executive clique on to their side. In this case, the executive clique was against me because I was not a founder member. In politics, it does not matter whether you are good or bad. Those who want the same honours as you will vilify and plot against you. An American writer (Kane), who was a cousin of President Kennedy, advised the president not to trust anyone in politics because there are no friends in politics, only fellow conspirators.[15] Had I not been kept out of *Fianna Fáil* in 1926, I would have been a founder member with as much influence as any other member. The convention was held at Gardiner Row on 11 May 1943, presided over by Gerry Boland, the father of Kevin Boland.[16] Gerry Boland was a tough and impulsive individual. He was the Honorary Secretary and head of the National

Executive; at least they took his word for everything. He was honest but under the paid secretary's influence.

Every *cumann* was entitled to send two delegates. Two delegates turned up claiming that they represented a *cumann* that had been defunct for many years, but according to the constitution of the party, no new *cumann* could be formed without first getting the sanction of the Constituency Committee. Delegates pointed this out to the chairman but he ruled that they were 'in order' and could vote. He was hostile to me at the time.[17]

Accepting new *cumann* or clubs on the eve of an election is an old trick but it is only possible if you have the paid General Secretary or the chairman of the convention on your side. The General Secretary can accept an affiliation fee or he can refuse and in this case he was the 'chief' conspirator against me. Candidates are not present at conventions but later on I was informed that I had been selected by two votes. There was a tie on the first ballot but on a second vote, somebody had changed his mind. The mystery was solved some days later when the secretary of the 'John Mitchel *Cumann*' confessed to me that the opposition had offered him a job if he double-crossed his *cumann* who had instructed him to vote for me.[18] He was married, had several children and was unemployed. He said that Seamus Davin, who was the General Secretary of the party, was to get him the job.[19] He said that it had been on his conscience and that he was glad that he had changed his mind on the second ballot. He then told me that another important member of the 'Casement *Cumann*', who had decided to vote for me agreed to double-cross his *cumann*.[20] The paid General Secretary bribed his son by promising him employment. He, however, failed to get himself selected as a delegate, but up until the last minute before the convention, he tried to get one of those who had been selected to attend the convention to back out and let him deputise. However, they insisted on going themselves, although they had no suspicions of him. You can judge from the above what kind of business politics is and it's equally bad in all political parties. Winston Churchill said that democracy was the worst possible system but no better has so far been devised.[21]

When the National Executive met to ratify those selected, the executive clique lobbied the top leaders not to ratify me but to appoint the man that I had beaten and they decided to do just that, although they also decided not to ratify Éamonn Cooney, the outgoing deputy, because he was too fond of his drink.[22] They decided to add insult to injury by selecting the chief conspirator, Seamus Davin, and another crony, John O'Connor, a solicitor, who I don't think was a member of the party at the time.[23] These two men had no popular support and most of the members did not work in the election. As a result of the confusion caused by the conspirators and the blindness of the National Executive, the party lost a seat in Dublin North-West. An *Ard Fheis* was due to be held and all *cumann* were invited to send in the names of those they wanted as their constituency member on the National Executive. Those who got the most votes were the ones selected. Davin, the paid General Secretary, would know who was lucky as he opened all correspondence. I knew that I was selected because I knew how the *cumann*s voted, for these votes are open and known at *cumann* meetings. Davin held back the result of our constituency, perhaps with the approval of other executive members. As a result, I was not present at the first meeting of the National Executive following the *Ard Fheis*. The clique in my absence suggested that our constituency should be reorganized because a seat had been lost. This was agreed. A member of the executive clique was appointed to carry out the reorganization. He proceeded to invite six *cumann*, those who were opposed to a few individuals and me. He ignored the eight *cumann* who supported me. He constituted the 'rump' as the Constituency Committee, thus eliminating eight active *cumann* without giving them a hearing. He invited Bob Christie, the secretary of the Constituency Committee, probably because he had the minutes book and other material, but Christie had supported me so he was deprived of the secretaryship. Christie knew that he wasn't wanted so he resigned from *Fianna Fáil*. This new reorganizer's name was Seán Bonner, an amateur and a lackey of Davin's. I met him later outside the Metropole cinema and I told him that it had been a great swindle. He replied in a venomous tone: 'Well we got rid of you anyway!' and this was obviously the only purpose of the exercise. We appealed to the National Executive but we received no reply.[24]

In 1943 the *Fianna Fáil* Executive refused to ratify my selection as a candidate for the *Dáil*; one of the excuses put forward was that I ran dance halls. The joke was that many IRA veterans after the Civil War had no choice but to run dance halls. The other option open to them was to emigrate, as thousands did. Tom McGrath, a 1916 veteran, ran dances in the Rotunda Winter Gardens until the day he died and Mick Fitzgerald, another 1916 man, ran the National and later became a dance teacher along with many others.[25] In fact, on the day after I came out of jail in 1924, I was invited to a dance hall at Loftus Lane, Dublin, by the *Fianna* Brigade Staff, which was run for funds. These dances were 'jazz', except for the odd Irish dance, but Irish dancing did not pay.

When I first joined *Fianna Fáil*, I ran many dances for *Fianna Fáil* clubs to raise funds, and to think that they accepted the excuse that I ran dances as a reason for not accepting my nomination? They never opposed publicans. In fact, they welcomed them because they had money and I suppose gave out free drink. It can be proved that drink is the cause of most unhappiness in homes and it was drink that conditioned people into acting immorally because drink encourages men to look for loose women and encourages decent women to become immoral. In fact, it is the cause of most crime and turns some people into brutes.

There was no *Ard Fheis* convention until 1945 because of the second World War, so I was a member of the National Executive for four years. I got to know most of the party leaders but only a few members of the Executive. Whenever Mr De Valera attended, his every word and gesture was law. Everyone called him 'Chief'. Everyone revered him, just as people revere the Pope. He did not mix with the ordinary people and there was a lot of mystique about him. He once said that whenever he wanted to know what the Irish people were thinking, he looked into his own heart. He depended a lot, however, on what his aids told him and if they were against you, you were 'out in the cold'.

Every constituency in the twenty-six counties was entitled to elect a member of the Executive but only the Dublin members usually attended. Apart from these delegates, fifteen members were elected by the *Ard Fheis*. Only a few ministers or top leaders were members. There was a paid General Secretary and all business was handled by him before it came before the Executive, which could do you a bad turn or a good one depending on the prevailing mood. Usually these secretaries have a small clique of executive members around them and they can do a lot of fixing, a situation that exists in all political parties.

I would soon learn that people who have political ambitions will sell their souls and much else and that they would stop at nothing to gain political honours. I also learned that political parties practised the same corruption to get the votes of the people. Many profound writers say that politics is not immoral but amoral. You can make what you like out of that. I know it means that people who lie and cheat in the name of politics do so because they would not succeed or survive if they did not, although many may be honest people. The trouble is that corrupt people have a field day in this profession and every party is invaded by such people. That profound political authority, Edmund Burke, said: 'The surest way that crooks can triumph in politics is for honest people to keep out of it.'[26] Huxley, referring to Father Joseph, who was a rogue as a politician but a religious mystic in his private or religious life, said: 'Pious men have entered politics to elevate it to their own high moral level only again and again to be dragged down to the low level of those they tried to elevate.'[27] Edmund Burke also said that the voters were just as corrupt as those they elected and that no reform would ever change their nature.

After the let-down in 1943 I parted with *Fianna Fáil* for the second time. I decided that if I hoped to get anywhere in politics the political party route was not the way. I considered strongly the option of becoming an Independent. This move, however, would take money and I was already in debt. I have said it before and I will say it again: politics is no place for the lone man, except if he has money to throw away. Looking back over my life in politics I can think of many other than myself that had to struggle against debt in order to survive as an Independent. Alfie Byrne, who was an Independent all of his life and got out of it more money than most, nevertheless died broke.[28] He said to me several times: 'They could never beat me but they could bankrupt me', but what can you do when you love the game and when the 'fixers' will not give you a chance in a party? Anyhow, parties stink to some people, including myself. It's very hard to be honest with voters, especially when 90 per cent of all people only want pleasant news. The party men agree with everybody without meaning a word of what they say. I know that there are well-meaning party men, but they have found that it is dangerous to differ with those who want something. You are compelled to avoid telling the truth, even though you do not lie, and this gets sensitive souls down – once again proving my point, that politics is no place for such people.

I cannot imagine Christ being a politician; He'd make enemies everywhere. He would lose His deposit in every election. An election period is a nightmare to an Independent and especially to his family, as they depend largely on them and a few friends to help. Some people offer their services during an election but they cannot be depended upon. During the general election of 1969, I gave 1,000 circulars to a person who offered to canvass for me. Two days before the election, I was informed that no circulars had been distributed. I called at his home and found the circulars in the same spot where I had left them two weeks previously. Another fellow called and offered to give out circulars and I gave him about 1,000. Next day he called me on the phone saying that he was in a pub nearby. When I arrived, he said that he needed £3. I gave him £1 and told him that I would see him later. I never heard of him again and much worse, he never gave out the bills. Another fellow who got circulars was seen that same night giving out leaflets for another party and in another case a fellow just put the circulars down a toilet, according to a witness. My wife was my best canvasser. She took the worse areas: all of the high tenements. She canvassed three weeks day and night in every election, twice when she was over six months pregnant. My three daughters and members of my wife's family did the same, and to think that I had to fight all of the big parties with this handful?

On polling day, my wife and family remained all day outside polling stations, canvassing voters going into vote. They depended on me giving them a bottle of milk and sandwiches, as they never left the booths from 9 a.m. until 9 p.m. I could only afford to have canvassers at about a quarter of the polling stations. All day I kept going around keeping them supplied with leaflets or refreshments. During the general election of 1969, I actually called at every dwelling in the constituency to put leaflets into letter boxes. This took a month to do as there were over 30,000 residences to visit. As a rule, not only I, but most of my family were in a state of collapse when polling day was over. You keep going while the fight is on. You live on your nerves but actually fall asleep every day for a fortnight afterwards. Politics never paid. I don't think that it ever pays an Independent. In fact, it bankrupts most of them. During the general election of 1965, when I lost my seat, another Independent went forward in my area. He was fairly well off. He received 500 votes less than I did and his election agent, who was a friend of mine, told me that he had bills for £2,500. During the general election of 1969 a councillor who went forward as an Independent in another constituency got about 600 votes and it cost him £3,500. Compare my total election costs when I was elected in 1957 (£150). So you see, I performed miracles with practically nothing, just faith and determination or, as Churchill put it, 'with blood, sweat and tears'.

In 1957, an unemployed man named Jack Murphy was elected. At that time there was an unemployed organization in Dublin so he had the full support of that body plus a sympathetic support from others who subscribed funds. He was elected on the crest of a wave. He did not know much about politics and only spoke about the unemployed from time to time, but no attention was paid to him. When I was elected in a by-election six months later, he told me that he was fed-up as he was getting nowhere in the *Dáil.* A few months later he told me that he was going to resign, an unheard of thing for a poor man to do. He said that the unemployed and every 'toucher' in Dublin were all looking for money and that he had no peace at home with people calling looking for a handout. The next day he resigned and later went to Canada. He came home some years later. People think that when you are a TD that you are a millionaire. Party men are well-off as a rule because they have good jobs or a business and most if not all of their election expenses are paid from party funds. An Independent has not only to live but there are expenses in connection with his job as a public representative, but the biggest burden of all is the fact that he has to pay practically all the costs of elections, as Independents rarely get subscriptions. When elected, most Independents are heavily in debt.

When I lost my seat in the *Dáil*, I was dependent on a small weekly IRA pension of £3.50, but people continued to touch me for money and still do. It's no wonder that Murphy got out and it's no wonder that everyone wants to get in on a party ticket. Party men can refuse to give and say or do anything, knowing that with party support they will get back. For the loner (the Independent), however, it is an endless uphill struggle.

NOTES

1   The original chapter title was 'The Dance Business – I meet Rosie and enter Politics'.

2   Constance Gore-Booth was born in London in 1868 into a wealthy family that had a large estate in county Sligo. Her father, Sir Henry Gore-Booth, was an explorer. In 1898, Constance met Count Casimir Dunin Markiewicz while in Paris and they married in 1901, making Constance Countess Markiewicz. In 1908, the Countess became actively involved in nationalist politics. She joined Sinn Féin and *Inghinidhe na hÉireann* – a women's movement. In that same year, the Countess stood for parliament. She contested the Manchester constituency where her most famous opponent was Winston Churchill, but was unsuccessful. In 1909, she founded *Na Fianna Éireann*, which was a form of Boy Scouts but with a military input, including the use of firearms. In 1911, the Countess was jailed for the first time for her part in the demonstrations that took place against the visit of George V. In the lockout of 1913, she ran a soup kitchen to aid those who could not afford food. During the Easter Rising of 1916, having joined James Connolly's Irish Citizen Army, she was second in command at St Stephen's Green. She was arrested, held in solitary confinement in Kilmainham Jail, brought before the court martial and sentenced to death. However, General Maxwell, the officer commanding the court martial procedure, commuted her sentence to life imprisonment. The Countess was released from prison in 1917 along with others involved in the uprising, as the government in London granted a general amnesty for those involved in the Easter Rising. It was around this time that Markiewicz, born into the Church of England, converted to Catholicism. In 1918, she was jailed again for her part in anti-conscription activities. While in prison, she was elected an MP standing as a Sinn Féin candidate at the 1918 Westminster election – the first woman ever elected to the British Parliament. The Countess refused to take up her seat as it would have involved swearing an oath of allegiance to the king and recognizing British jurisdiction in Ireland. Instead, she took her seat in *Dáil Éireann* where she was made Minister for Labour, the first woman anywhere in the world to attain such a position at national government level. During the War of Independence, she was either on the run from British authorities or in prison. As the then leader of *Cumann na mBan*, she fiercely opposed the Anglo-Irish Treaty of December 1921 and supported Republican forces. The Countess was re-elected to the *Dáil* but her republican views led her to being sent to jail again. In prison, she and ninety-two other female prisoners went on hunger strike. Within a month, the Countess was released. In 1926, the Countess joined *Fianna Fáil* led by Éamon De Valera. She died in 1927.

3   Since Sherwin's release from jail, he was very weak and regularly attended
       hospitals and doctors. His former O/C, Alfred White, who was a corporation
       official, got him a job about five months after his release on a building site at
       Glasnevin. The wages were fifty shillings weekly, good at that time. After working
       for ten minutes, Sherwin fainted and was brought home in the overseer's car.
       The next day he tried again but again fainted. He could not work and any
       attempt to do so caused severe pain in the spinal region and head.

4   La Scala Theatre and Opera House was located just off O'Connell Street Dublin
       and opened to the public on 10 August 1920. Despite its name, it functioned as
       a cinema. Paramount Pictures took over the building and renamed it The
       Capitol. A live show was run every week to accompany the current film. The
       Capitol continued as a cinema until 1972. It was demolished along with the
       adjacent Metropole Cinema and a branch of the department store chain British
       Home Stores was built on the site. This in turn closed and was replaced by a
       branch of the Irish Penneys chain.

5   Joseph Sherwin, brother of Frank Sherwin.

6   James Larkin was born in Liverpool in 1876. Larkin supported policies that
       promoted social equality, justice and cultural and social achievement.
       Throughout his life, he was committed to revolutionary socialism, the
       destruction of capitalism and conveyed a hatred of exploitation and strong
       identity with the underprivileged. In 1906, Larkin became full-time organizer of
       the National Union of Dock Labourers (NUDL) and in 1908 he was sent to
       Dublin to mobilize port workers there. In 1911, he established a weekly
       newspaper the *Irish Worker and People's Advocate* which reached a circulation of
       20,000 and was arguably the most effective propaganda sheet at the time. He
       established the Irish Transport and General Workers Union (ITGWU) and
       acquired Liberty Hall as its headquarters in 1912. Larkin's confrontation with
       the Dublin United Tramway Company (DUTC) precipitated the 1913 Dublin
       Lockout. Defeat devastated his union. In October 1914, Larkin left for the
       United States to raise funds to rebuild it. While there, he opposed American
       entry into the First World War, acclaimed the Russian revolution and was
       imprisoned for almost three years during the 'red scare' of 1919 before being
       deported in 1923. He was elected to the *Dáil* on two occasions and died in 1947.

7   James Connolly, an influential trade union leader and great Irish revolutionary
       socialist who played a leading part in the Easter Uprising of 1916, was born on
       5 June 1868 at the Cowgate, Edinburgh. He came to Dublin in May 1896 as paid
       organizer of the Dublin Socialist Society and organized the Irish Socialist
       Republican Party, and by 1898 he had established the first Irish Socialist paper
       – *The Workers' Republic*. Connolly went to the United States and, on his return to
       Ireland, he became the Belfast organizer for James Larkin's Irish Transport and
       General Workers Union. In 1913, he co-founded the Labour Party and the Irish
       Citizens Army (ICA) at Liberty Hall, the headquarters of the ITGWU. The ICA
       was established to defend the rights of the working people. In 1914, he helped
       organize opposition to the Employers Federation in the Great Lockout of
       workers that August. He became Acting Secretary to the ITGWU in 1915. In
       1916, Connolly took part in the Easter Rising at General Post Office Dublin. He
       was arrested and, on 12 May 1916, he was executed by firing squad.

8   In 1922, Victor Sylvester and Phylis Clark of England won the World
       Championship for Ballroom Dancing and ballroom dancing split into
       professional and amateur levels. Sylvester's early career as world champion
       exhibition dancer also included teaching ballroom dancing with his sister Gwen.

His world championship programme had consisted of the English waltz of not more than a right turn, left turn and change of direction but in 1926–7, the waltz movement was changed to step, side and shut. As early as 1930, Sylvester wrote that 'position, balance, hold and time should be explained first and steps last even though the pupils ask for steps first'. Victor Sylvester's Ballroom Orchestra was one of the leading dance bands of the 1940s era. In the late 1920s and early 1930s, there was a lack of good dance recordings that featured a contrast, and tempo was something Sylvester needed for his dance studio – The Victor Sylvester Studio. Sylvester assembled a few musicians and made his own recording featuring songs with a pronounced beat. Among his releases were *Ballroom Dancing with Victor Sylvester and his Ballroom Orchestra* and *Dancing on my Heart* and he authored *Modern Ballroom Dancing*. His jazz-oriented orchestra included stars such as Tommy McQuater and George Chisolm. Sylvester also had a jive band and his first description of jive was published in Europe by 1944. The boogie, rock and roll and the American swing also influenced this dance. At 17 years of age, world champion ballroom dancer Monica Needham turned professional and took up a teaching post in the Victor Sylvester Studios in London. She gained invaluable experience teaching beginners' classes where they had 200 students, medal work and children's Saturday morning classes where they had approximately 250 pupils. Monica and husband Michael were presented with the Carl Allen Award for Outstanding Couple by Prince Charles in February 1970.

9   Liam Mellows was born in 1895 and educated in County Galway where he joined *na Fianna*, the Republican boys' movement founded by Countess Markiewicz. In 1915, he was arrested under the Defence of the Realm Act and interned for four months in Mountjoy Jail, Dublin. On his release, Mellows went 'on the run' but was arrested in Galway in early 1916, deported to England and interned in Reading Jail from where he escaped. He returned to Ireland to command the western division of the IRA during the 1916 Easter Rising. Mellows escaped to the United States where he was imprisoned without trial in the Tombs, New York, on a charge of partaking in an Irish–German plot to sabotage the allied forces during the First World War. He was released in 1918 and went on a lecture tour of America, collecting money for the IRA before returning to Ireland in 1919. Mellows became IRA Director of Supplies during the War of Independence. He opposed the 1921 Anglo-Irish Treaty, and on 25 June 1922 he and fellow Republicans Rory O'Conner, Joseph McKelvey and Dick Barrett, among others, took over the Dublin Four Courts. They were bombarded from a gunboat on the River Liffey which the Free State had borrowed from the British Army, and after two days they surrendered. They were imprisoned in Mountjoy Jail where Mellows and O'Conner contributed to a handwritten notebook of short stories, poems and articles dated 6 October 1922 and entitled *The Book of Cells*. Mellows' article was entitled 'The People's Republic'. On 8 December 1922, Mellows, O'Conner, McKelvey and Barrett were executed by the Free State firing squad, allegedly as a reprisal for the shooting of Seán Hales. See 'Parliamentary Debates', *Dáil Éireann* entitled 'Questions on the Adjournment', Vol. 5, 25 September 1923, preceding col. 81. The *Ceann Comhairle* states: 'I have to inform the *Dáil* that I have been notified by the Governors of the under-mentioned Military Prisons and Internment Camps that the following persons who have been returned to serve in the *Dáil* are detained pursuant to the provisions of the Public Safety (Emergency Powers) Acts, 1923: – Charles Murphy, Daniel Corkery, John Buckley, Barney Mellows, Austin Stack, Michael

Kilroy, Patrick McCarvill, Gerald Boland, Ernest O'Malley, Peadar O'Donnell – Place of detention, Mountjoy Military Prison, Dublin'.

10   Sherwin is referring to Heuston railway station named in honour of Seán Heuston who was one of the sixteen executed leaders of the 1916 Rising.

11   The Irish folk song *Boulavogue* tells the story of a Catholic priest Father John Murphy (1753–98). At first, as the United Irish, founded by Wolfe Tone, struggled to start the Rebellion of 1798, Father Murphy convinced his flock to surrender their arms and sign an oath of allegiance to the government. However, upon seeing the slaughter of his congregation, he led them into rebellion and paid the ultimate price. Father John Murphy was hung, his body burned in a barrel of tar and his head placed on a spike.

12   There was an interesting article entitled 'Tattoo at Baltinglass '98 Commemoration Ceremony', which appeared in *The Leinster Leader* dated Saturday 26 September 1948. The 'Tattoo' was a succession of scenes based on the life of Michael Dwyer during his insurgent campaign in Wicklow, 'The Massacre of Dunlavin', in 1798. This scene opened at the residence of a Colonel Saunders of Saunders Grove. Saunders was accused by a Yeoman captain of harbouring rebels. Saunders protested but nineteen of his men were marched to a summary court martial and brought before a firing squad in Dunlavin Green. The order was to execute in groups of five. Finding that one group had only four men, the spy Hawkins, who had already given information leading to the arrest, was forcibly compelled to take his place in the group of four to make up the five and was executed with them.

13   NCO stands for Non-Commissioned Officer.

14   Denis Guiney was a farmer's son from County Kerry who left school at 13 years of age. His first shop in Talbot Street, Dublin, burned down during the Civil War. He bought Clery's in 1941 for £317,430, a huge sum at the time. In business, he was ahead of his time with his practice of bulk buying, heavy promotion and quick turnover of goods. Denis Guiney died in 1967.

15   Joseph Nathan Kane was born on 23 January and died on 22 September 2002. He was the author of such reference books as *Famous First Facts*, *More First Facts*, *1,000 Facts Worth Knowing*, *Facts about the States* and *Facts about the Presidents*. Kane is certainly one of the most important figures in the field of factual information and his books can be found throughout libraries across the United States. Texts read by Sherwin on the subject of the Kennedy family include: *Kennedy and the Press* edited by Harold Chase and Allen Lerman (New York: Crowell, 1965), *The Kennedy Family*, by Joseph F. Dinneen (born 1897) and *Kennedy campaigning* by Murray Levin.

16   Kevin Boland (1917–2001), was elected to *Dáil Éireann* in 1957 as a *Fianna Fáil* TD. He served as Minister for Defence (1957–61), Minister for Social Welfare (1961–65) and Minister for Local Government (1965–70). He holds the distinction of being one of only five TDs to be appointed a minister on their first day in the *Dáil*.

17   At a much later date in 1969, Sherwin was to meet Gerry Boland in Westmoreland Street and they got talking. He said that he realized afterwards that he had made a great mistake in allowing the bogus delegates in to vote against Sherwin.

18   John Mitchel was born in 1815 in Dungiven, County Derry. Mitchel studied law by correspondence at Trinity College Dublin and after graduation he practised as a solicitor in Banbridge, County Down. In 1842, he contributed a series of articles to *The Nation* and in 1945 Charles Gavin Duffy invited Mitchell to edit the

paper. In the same year, Mitchel published *A life of Hugh O'Neill.* In 1847, Mitchel left *The Nation* to found *The United Irishman* in which he advocated the use of physical force to dissolve the Union between England and Ireland. Mitchel was charged with publishing treasonous articles and was sentenced to fourteen years' penal servitude in 1848. He was transported to Bermuda and Van Dieman's Land (now Tasmania) from where he escaped to the United States in 1853. In 1854, Mitchel published his *Jail Journal* or *Five Years in British Prisons.* In New York, Mitchel edited *The Citizen Magazine* which had a circulation of 50,000. He supported the Confederacy during the American Civil War and moved to Tennessee where he edited *The Southern Citizen.* In 1860, Mitchel travelled to France to solicit funds for the Fenian Movement. In Paris, he published a satire entitled *An Apology for the British Government in Ireland* (1860). On his return to New York, Mitchel was imprisoned at Fortress Munroe for supporting the Confederacy in articles he had published in the *New York Daily News.* Mitchel's release was effected by the Irish Republican Brotherhood and he spent the duration of the American Civil War in Virginia. In 1874, Mitchel returned to Ireland and in 1975, he was elected a Member of Parliament for Tipperary on an abstentionist ticket. John Mitchel died in Newry on 20 March 1875.

19   A lecturer at GMIT Galway of the name Seamus Davin died on 8 January 2003.

20   Roger Casement, patriot and participant in the Easter Rising, was born on 1 September 1864 and died on 3 August 1916. He was hanged and buried in England but his remains were re-interred in Glasnevin Cemetery in 1965.

21   Sir Winston Leonard Spencer Churchill (1874–1965), statesman, author and Prime Minister of Britain from 1940–45 and 1951–55.

22   Sherwin is possibly referring to Éamonn Cooney, TD, member of the *Fianna Fáil* Party and a member of the 10th *Dáil Éireann* (1938–43).

23   Perhaps this John O'Connor was associated with the O'Connor family of John O'Connor Solicitors, a family-run law firm based in Clare Street, Dublin. One of their family members was Judge John William O'Connor.

24   Twenty years later Sherwin would put his head on the block to save *Fianna Fáil* from destruction by preventing a general election on the turnover tax issue.

25   There was another Mick Fitzgerald who was the IRA commander and 1916 veteran who died in Cork Prison while on hunger strike. This Michael Fitzgerald was head of his battalion, 'the Fermoy Company', of which Lar Condon was Vice-O/C.

26   Edmund Burke was born in Dublin on 12 January 1729. He acted as private secretary to the Chief Secretary for Ireland until 1765 when he became a Member of Parliament. He died on 9 July 1797.

27   Father Joseph du Tremblay was born on 4 November 1577 in Paris and died on 18 December 1638 in Rueil, France. He was a French Capuchin monk, mystic, religious reformer and confidant and agent of Cardinal Richelieu. He was generally known as the *Éminence Grise* or grey eminence. Aldous Huxley, born on 26 July 1894, produced forty-seven books in his long career as a writer despite remaining blind all his life. He died on 22 November 1963.

28   Alfie Byrne (1882–1956), was one of Dublin's most beloved Lord Mayors. He was a TD and served as Lord Mayor from 1930-1939 and 1954–55.

4

FROM THE DOLE TO THE *DÁIL*[1]

I gave too much of my time to the Twenty-Sixth Battalion and the *Fianna* during the war years. I also drank a lot more than usual, as after the Twenty-Sixth Battalion activities there were a lot of drinking sessions. I seldom drank on my own as I always had a lot of company. My business deteriorated during the war because many people were in the Free State Army or in England earning the big money, but I neglected my business and began to draw on my savings. In 1944, I could not pay my way so I had to give up 44 Lower Gardiner Street. I also had a small dance school in O'Connell Street but I had sold my amplifier and other equipment. I was forced to close this school and I found myself drawing public assistance for twelve months. I had about £800 saved before the war yet I had nothing in 1944 and was on the dole in 1945. Had I minded my business, I could have held on to my savings and I could have made a fortune out of dances and other business when the war was over. There were great opportunities for those with money.

The owner of my dance school on the top floor of 55 Lower O'Connell Street took action in the courts for possession because I owed him a year's rent.[2] The school was closed but I planned to reopen it. I told the court that I was prepared to pay my rent and as much again off arrears but the owner insisted that he wanted possession and that he did not want dances on his premises. The judge asked him if there were dances on there when he bought the premises. He admitted that there had been so he was told that when he bought the premises, he bought a dance studio with it. The judge made an order agreeing to my offer. I got a loan of a record player and an old radio which had a good output. By this means, I was able to reopen my dance school with records instead of a band. The war was over so business improved but I could only earn a limited return which was not enough to keep my family and pay the rent on the studio. I began attending auction rooms on the quays. I bought portable goods, which I resold, and with the proceeds from that venture, I bought two more. In this way I made a few extra pounds each week. Therefore, between the dance school and the auction rooms I started to save a little. For a while I opened a second-hand shop and one of the children helped. I continued with these activities until 1960, after which I gave them up with the intention of devoting all of my time to politics and people in need. That was the biggest mistake of my life. Every other politician improves their business. They do not trust voters and with the benefit of hindsight, I can see that they are right. For instance, when I lost my *Dáil* seat in 1965 I had no business, no pension and was incapable of working as I could not use my right arm. Yet, nobody helped me in spite of all of the slanderous statements made by cowardly politicians in the *Dáil*, where slander is privileged. When I took *The Irish Times* to court, not one person came forward to say that I had ever done anything dishonourable. In fact, *The Irish Times*' witnesses on oath said that I never did anything dishonourable to advance my political career and I won my case.

Having left *Fianna Fáil* for the second time after the 1943 letdown I stood as an Independent for the first time in June 1945. I was then on the dole. A friend of mine by the name of Belton, who had a small printing works, gave me a few hundred small posters free of charge.[3] My brother-in-law, Jack Kinsella, and I got up at 5 a.m. and posted them up in the area. If we posted them up at night, they would be pulled down or covered over by my opponents. I received thirty shillings from some friends. That was the only money we had throughout the campaign, but as this small sum was useless, we spent it on a few beers at a local pub which opened at 7 a.m. after our morning's work. I addressed a number of small meetings, often about six adults and a couple of dozen children. I spoke from a kitchen chair. In spite of these terrible difficulties, I received 522 number one votes and I had 968 votes when eliminated.

After this first venture as an Independent, I was to try out the party system once more by joining a newly formed political party in 1946 called *Clann na Poblachta*.[4] I thought that it was a party with a difference, a party comprised of super Republicans. I joined a club in the North City and as usual, because I was a dance promoter, I was asked to run dances to raise funds. I made £40 for my club. I also helped other clubs. I became a member of the Club Committee. When I had been a member for about three months, I was told by a friend, Paddy McBrin, who was a member of the Constituency Committee, that members of the Constituency Committee had been discussing me, and that they had agreed to bar me from any important position and block me from becoming a candidate for future elections. When I heard this, I realized that it was *Fianna Fáil* all over again. At this point I decided never again. I had had a bellyful of party politics. It seems that once people enter politics, they change. They become jungle animals and the so-called rulers of political parties are only there to keep 'the rank and file' under control.

I fought the next local elections as an Independent in September 1950, by which time I was earning some money and I spent £40 on the campaign. I received 743 number one votes and had 906 when eliminated. I could have won this election. Another local man – Michael Mullan, General Secretary to the Irish Transport and General Workers Union, split my vote but I expected to get about 500 of his preference votes if he were eliminated.[5] Another candidate named Mullen stood for *Fine Gael* and on two occasions Michael Mullan got a lot of votes when the *Fine Gael* candidates were eliminated.[6] They were obviously intended for the *Fine Gael* Mullen. On this account, Michael Mullan went ahead of me although I was in front of him at the outset.

I was finally elected an Independent councillor to Dublin City Council in 1955, when I was to meet up with a few unusual characters and opportunists. Before I attended my first meeting of the Dublin City Council I had a deputation to my home asking me to nominate a Jim Carroll as Lord Mayor.

I had never met Carroll nor had I heard of him. I thought that he had a cheek to expect to be nominated for the high honour of Lord Mayor of Dublin before he had attended one council meeting, especially when this office was the main goal of all the outgoing members of the council. I refused to nominate him and told the deputation that he should prove himself first. Denis Larkin, the son of Big Jim Larkin, was elected Lord Mayor in 1955.[7] Larkin was also elected chairman of the Housing Committee in the following year and remained chairman until 1967. I became Vice-Chairman in 1957 and remained in that position until I lost my Corporation seat in June 1967. I considered Larkin to be a particularly coercive individual who adamantly decided on things himself. I was to have many rows with him. He always believed in big houses and objected to building one-room dwellings for old people. When the housing emergency began in 1963, following the collapse of several old tenements when old people were killed, he then ceased to object to old people's dwellings. Up until 1963, only about 1,400 old people's dwellings were built. Since then, over 6,000 have been built. Most of my rows with Larkin were over his refusal to build enough small dwellings. Nevertheless, he gave a lot of time to housing matters and was one of the few who was well-informed on the subject. The lack of houses has been a political issue for some years and all opposition parties and protest groups have blamed the government. There has never been any shortage of money for municipal housing and all planning has been in the hands of the

Housing Committee of which Denis Larkin was chairman. As I said, he dragooned his way through, especially on the Housing Planning Committee. This committee decided how many and what kind of dwellings would be built. Larkin was a prominent member of the Labour party and it was also the Labour party who introduced differential rents, including the inquiry into family means. The Labour party is foremost in condemning differential rents, especially the inquiry into income and also into the shortage of dwellings when their own supporters are responsible for both. However, that is politics: a two-faced game. They would not get away with it if voters were a little more aware, but this applies to all political parties.

When I was elected, Alfie Byrne was Lord Mayor. He was the most successful politician of all time. He was a British MP and later a TD for the best part of his life. He was Lord Mayor of Dublin for ten years largely because he constantly supported the *Fine Gael* party in the *Dáil,* even when they were in government and won their support in return. The *Fine Gael* party also got the support of his son who was also a TD. There was obviously an agreement on these lines. Alfie's area was in the Dock Constituency which was largely comprised of labourers or poor people who hated all governments. Nevertheless, they supported Alfie even when he regularly voted for legislation proposed by the *Fine Gael* government, including unpopular legislation. Alfie had a way with people. He mixed with the poor and the kids and he gave out thousands of pennies and shillings annually. In this way, he earned himself a good name but he was actually bribing them. He was always criticizing the government that he was voting for, especially when prices of food were increased. He was really deluding the people because prices increased as wages increased and because the government increased taxation because more social benefits and other improvements were necessary. Alfie, I was told, was asked by the *Fine Gael* party to join the government but he refused. If he had, he would not have been able to do all of the things that he was always shouting about without increasing taxation. It was much safer to talk about grievances and avoid responsibility. I felt he never really did anything constructive but he was a lot better than many of the other duds who did nothing or gave nothing away. He was okay to me.

When I voted for the small turnover tax in 1963, most of these people let me down, although what I did put pounds into the pockets of 300,000 people on social benefits and the workers gained six times more than the tax cost, but workers and poor people are ill-informed when it comes to economic matters. They see or hear of the odd shilling that some politician gives to somebody and consequently think highly of them, but they cannot see the pounds given to 300,000 poor people through some form of taxation that another politician votes for, and because he voted for it they condemn him. Such is the logic of many of the working class and because this is the way that most of them think, they are bamboozled from birth to death.

Then there was a character by the name of Miss Susan Bowler on the City Council. She was a solicitor but what made her unusual was the fact that she hardly ever talked. Perhaps she had no interest in council affairs. In the seven years that she was a member I can only remember her speaking about four times at City Council meetings and then only for a few minutes, which I thought unusual for a solicitor. She seldom attended committee meetings and when she did, she only remained a short while. She was elected to the council in 1960. I was elected Alderman, receiving 2,200 number one votes. Miss Bowler came next with 1,261 and P.J. Burke, TD, who was sent in to the area specially to capture the aldermanship, received 1,212. He was a *Fianna Fáil* candidate and Miss Bowler was an Independent. Miss Bowler had never been heard of before the election, nevertheless she came second. She toured the whole area giving out loads of sweets to the children near my home. In her election appeal she said: 'The Dublin Council is dominated by political parties and this has resulted in the shameful welter of corruption, graft and skull-drudgery, which bedevils the civic administration of the city. If you elect me, I promise that I will strive fearlessly to fight against this shameful state of affairs.' When elected, she never opened her mouth and later she joined the Labour party, one of the alleged corrupt parties in the council.

Another unusual individual was Peader Cowan, a solicitor who got two years in Mountjoy because he misappropriated money belonging to a client. He had been a TD some years earlier. He was largely responsible for bringing down the inter-party government comprising all parties other than *Fianna Fáil* in 1951. He was ambitious and always tried to monopolize all discussions at meetings. His views seldom made sense to me and after he came out of jail he was again elected to Dublin Corporation in 1960. He and I were always at variance and according to many councillors, I was the only person who was a match for him. Again, he was a likeable fellow.

In 1956 I decided to nominate Jim Carroll as Lord Mayor. Although I was not impressed by his contribution as a councillor, he was an Independent and it was the practice for all Independents to nominate one of their own. He was not successful in the bid. About this time, Jimmy O'Brien, who helped me in the dance business and who knew Carroll, warned me that Carroll was not to be trusted. He added that I would regret helping him as he would double-cross me whenever it suited him. When I told O'Brien that he was mistaken, he answered 'wait and see', and of course, he was right. We nominated Carroll because he threatened to split the Independent group but on one condition, that if he were eliminated, he would then vote for Denis Larkin, the Labour candidate. When he was eliminated, we all voted for Larkin except Carroll. He voted for a *Fianna Fáil* candidate, without giving us the slightest hint of his intentions. We swore never to trust him again. However, because he threatened yet again to split the group, we nominated him and he was elected Lord Mayor the following year.

Carroll was elected Lord Mayor by me and nobody else. I got The *Fine Gael* leader, Jack Belton, to agree to support Carroll if they thought that they would not win themselves. I was with Jimmy O'Keefe, later Lord Mayor, again by my vote.[8] After asking Jack Belton to support Carroll, Belton asked, 'Who was Carroll?', and 'Why should he be Lord Mayor?' I put it to Jack, 'What difference is it who he is if it means keeping out a political opponent?' He agreed with my suggestion so everything was arranged as I had planned it. Carroll promised me that should he win I would be his deputy.

I fought my first general election in 1957. It takes a lot of money to fight *Dáil* elections. I spent £80, while others spent £500 and £1,000. I got the third highest vote, 2,300 number one votes, but I did not get enough preference votes. This was a three-seat constituency.

Carroll was a TD having been elected in the general election of 1957. As I have said I had not been successful in the general election but I wanted all the publicity I could get in case there should be a by-election or even another general election. The Lord Mayor got many invitations to functions every other day. He could not attend them all, so he would send a deputy and this was where the let-down came in. I was asked once to deputize, a month before the next mayoralty election was due. Although Carroll had agreed that the rest of the Independents would be supported in turn, he insisted on putting himself forward for a second term. In fact, he insisted on going forward every year for the next eight mayoralty elections. He objected to giving any other Independent a chance. As I have said, he asked me to deputize for him about a month before the next election was due, obviously to get my support, but by that time I had had enough of Carroll, and so had the rest of the Independent group. When the next election took place, he got three votes, one of those being his own. Councillor Lehane voted for him and the only other vote that he got was from Councillor Rory Cowan, who had been brought over from England, where he had been working during the previous months.[9]

Carroll disappointed everyone as Lord Mayor. I felt apathy and general ennui during his time in the Council Chair during which he was always to be found smoking big cigars and the like. His father, a former member, was a most virile character. He often bragged that he was so poor when the children were small that they had to eat off orange boxes. I was told that he had been barred from the Mansion House where the Lord Mayor resides. Denis Larkin was to say to me many times afterwards that the worst thing that I ever did was to make Carroll Lord Mayor.

The Lord Mayor's full title is 'The Right Honourable the Lord Mayor of Dublin'. There are three Lord Mayors in Ireland residing at Cork, Belfast and Dublin. Only the Dublin Lord Mayor can use the prefix 'The Right Honourable'. This additional title was granted by Charles II in thanks for Dublin's support of his father Charles I in the English Civil War between king and parliament.[10] We are a republic. We are doing away with 'wigs in courts'. We have ceased to address High Court judges as 'My Lord'; nevertheless we continue to call the temporary chief citizen of Dublin 'The Right Honourable the Lord Mayor of Dublin'. When I was first elected to the Corporation, I proposed a motion which was passed, that the title be simply 'Mayor'. If plain 'Mayor' is good enough for America and France, it should be good enough for us. It requires legislation in the *Dáil* to make this change, let's hope that the necessary legislation is passed soon. I consider it a joke to make 'some party dud' Lord Mayor one day then he's nobody the next. Half of those who have been Lord Mayors since the foundation of the Irish Free State were duds and gave no service, or so it is thought.

Every party selects one of their own as a candidate for the mayoralty. The person selected is often one who has never attended any committees where all the municipal work is done. They may be nobodies who have never made any worthwhile contribution to council affairs. They may be mummies who never open their mouths and they may be someone who had bribed his colleagues with money. When a party selects a candidate, that person may look for the support of other parties or individuals and may offer money or other inducements. Shortly after I was elected to the City Council, I was making my way to the funeral of an old member of the council, P.S. Doyle, when I overheard two councillors in conversation.[11] They were discussing how a member of the council became Lord Mayor. From the conversation, it was obvious that one candidate offered a councillor £300 for his vote. The opposition offered £200, so the former won as one vote decided the issue. I am aware myself of candidates for the mayoralty giving councillors money and plenty of drink for their support.

We are all familiar with the ballyhoo at US conventions to select candidates for presidential elections. The election of Dublin's Lord

Mayor is much the same in miniature. You have all of the hullabaloo, all the caucus meetings to select candidates within parties and groups and later between parties and groups. You have the 'deals', party strategists studying the weak points in councillors to see who could be influenced by money or drink, or who would be influenced by promises of other appointments or the following year's mayoralty election. Phones ring day and night for the week preceding the election. On the night of the election, the gallery of the City Hall is full, the only occasion in the year. All the media is there, especially television. Every councillor is present; the recent dead are represented, as meetings of councils are called to elect someone to fill the vacancy. Councillors come or are brought from hospitals and their sick beds. They even come from overseas, from as far away as the United States because many Lord Mayors are selected by a majority of one vote.

On the night of the election, all the candidates are praised from the ground up by supporters. It's largely a huge palaver, or rigmarole to use a better term. There is usually a lot of double-crossing or inculpating by some councillors who only hours before had made undying promises to certain candidates. When the Lord Mayor is elected, all retire to the Mansion House for free drinks. The House is full, people are there who have no right to be there but inveigle themselves in somehow. Many notables are present, including Cabinet ministers or party leaders depending on the politics of the new Lord Mayor. His or her victory is considered a major political victory because much political mileage can be made out of it. All of the councillors present sing the praises of the new Lord Mayor, including councillors who hours earlier had not a kind word for him or her. The outgoing Lord Mayor becomes 'nobody'. He is not even mentioned, as if he had never existed or as the saying goes 'The Lord Mayor is dead! Long live the Lord Mayor!' Several times I have asked Jack McCann, the playwright, to write a play on the election of the Lord Mayor.[12] It would be a great farce and a smash hit!

My greatest achievement was the winning of a by-election in October 1957, some months after the general election in which I had been unsuccessful. I beat all the parties, *Fianna Fáil, Fine Gael,* Labour and Sinn Féin. No man ever before, with my difficulties, had won a by-election. It was almost impossible to win such an election as the parties swamp out the lone man in publicity, in canvassing and in transport and money. I had a bicycle, not a single car. I did, however, get the support of about twenty helpers other than my family under the direction of Paddy McBrin. The election cost me £150, having received about £50 in subscriptions. I also owe my victory to the fact that I was a councillor and met thousands of people in that capacity. I also wrote regularly to the press, especially *The Evening Mail*. The children gave me considerable help, they marched around the area with banners singing – 'Vote, Vote, Vote for Frankie Sherwin – Vote, Vote, Vote for him again.'[13] When I was introduced to the chairman of the *Dáil*, called '*Ceann Camhairle*', *Fine Gael* deputies cheered. Mr Lemass, the *Taoiseach*, interjected: 'You have nothing to cheer about.' I had done the impossible. I had made my way from the dole to the *Dáil*. My supporters were largely people whom I had got to know through the dance business and others who had been influenced by my letters to the papers. I was also a councillor and that gave me a platform for my views, but most of my supporters were traditionally opposed to the government, any government, and I lost their support later because I supported Mr Lemass as *Taoiseach*.

I was not a political opportunist, I had come up through the national movement and I always had the welfare of the country in mind. I worked hard as a public representative and it was against my nature to lie to people with a view to gaining an advantage. I had no choice but to vote for Lemass. It was the people's fault if no party could form a government and I hold that I came to their rescue in ensuring that a government was formed. Only cowards would avoid this responsibility.

NOTES

1   The original chapter title was: 'On the Dole – Elected Councillor and TD'.
2   It wasn't merely for the back-money owed in rent that the owner wanted my father off the premises; he had other more mercenary ideas in mind. The owner of the building was a man called Enock. He was, in fact, a new owner who, upon taking over, set out to rid the building of the presence of the old established tenants all with a view to giving the rooms, which were generally used as offices, a lick of paint and charging many times the old rent from new tenants. My father was the only one he could not shift and it was not for the want of trying. They both grew old together staring one another down. The studio was not released until after my father's death at which time I imagine the owner was too old to care.
3   Jack Belton, died on 9 May 1963.
4   *Clann na Poblachta* was a political party founded in 1946 by Republican activists Seán MacBride, Noel Hartnett, Jack McQuillan and Michael Kelly. Its leader was Seán MacBride and it quickly established a strong presence in the political arena of the day. It won 13.2 per cent of the 1948 general election and joined the first inter-party government with *Fine Gael, Clann na Talmhan* and the Labour Party. There was internal dissension, however, between MacBride and one of his ministers, Dr Noël Browne, Minister for Health, over the Mother and Child Scheme. Browne's scheme brought him into conflict with the Catholic hierarchy and MacBride would not support him. After Browne's resignation and the resulting fallout, the party never recovered its position, although it continued to contest elections until 1965.

5   Michael Mullan, Labour Councillor, TD and Secretary of the Irish Transport and General Workers Union, was referred to in an article in *The Irish Independent* of 5 October 2003 by journalist Nollaig O'Gadhra. It was entitled 'Proinsias MacAonghusa'. It referred to MacAonghusa's defence of the PR voting system which he wrote in 1959. On retiring from politics, De Valera tried to abolish PR in a referendum, while at the same time contesting the presidential election. The system was retained by a slim 33,000 majority. Most of the 'Nos' were in Dublin and Cork, mainly as a result of Proinsias' pamphlet, instigated, according to O'Gadhra, by ITGWU General Secretary Michael Mullan, who distributed it through union activists in working class areas.

6   Fred Mullen, *Fine Gael*, had hoped to become Lord Mayor of Dublin 1968–69 but lost out to Frank Cluskey when the council was abolished.

7   Denis Larkin was born in Dublin in 1908. He was a Labour TD representing Dublin North-East, General Secretary of the Federated Workers Union of Ireland, served as Lord Mayor from 4 July 1955 to 1956 and was President of the Irish Congress of Trade Unions. He died on 2 July 1987.

8   James O'Keefe was Lord Mayor of Dublin 1962–63.

9   See *Parliamentary Debates, Dáil Éireann* entitled 'The Committee on Finance', vol 110, 19 May 1948. MacEntee refers to Deputy Con Lehane's 'highly edifying' leaflet and states: 'Every one of these statements of policy and of programme emphasised that if *Clann na Poblachta* were to secure a majority at the general election and were to form the Administration, great works of national development would be undertaken by them.' See also *Parliamentary Debates Dáil Éireann* entitled 'Committee on Finance, Vote 3, Department of the *Taoiseach* (resumed)', vol 112, 23 July 1948, col. 1522. The *Taoiseach*, John A. Costello, states: 'Deputy Con Lehane gave complete expression to my view this morning when he appealed to us in the *Dáil* and to public men generally not to foster or create a war phobia or a war psychosis, not to aggravate the natural fears of the people.' Lehane is also mentioned in *Parliamentary Debates Dáil Éireann* entitled 'Local Election Bill, 1947–48 from the Seanad', vol 110, dated 14 April 1948 and *Parliamentary Debates Dáil Éireann* entitled 'Local Election (County Administration) Bill, 1950, Committee Stage Resumed, vol 124, 21 February 1951. See *Parliamentary Debates Dáil Éireann* entitled 'Cancellation of *Telefís Éireann* Interview', vol 205, 7 November 1963, col. 1171. The Minister for Posts and Telegraphs, Mr Hilliard, states: 'The decision not to broadcast the edition of *An Fear agus a Scéal* in which Mr Con Lehane was interviewed was taken by *Radio Éireann* on its own initiative for reasons which were given in a statement issued by the Director-General. I do not think it would be proper for me to question the level or the time at which this particular decision was taken.'

10   Charles I was born on 19 November 1600 and died on 30 January 1649. He was King of England, Scotland and Ireland from 27 March 1625 until his death. Charles II was born on 29 May 1630 and died on 6 February 1685. He was King of England, Scotland and Ireland from 30 January 1649 (*de jure*) and 29 May 1660 (*de facto*) until his death.

11   Peadar Seán Doyle (Ó Dughghaill), TD and Lord Mayor of Dublin (1941–43).

12   Sherwin may be referring to John McCann, *Fianna Fáil* man, playwright and Lord Mayor of Dublin 1964–65. McCann resided at 6 Lennox Street and was father of Donal McCann, the stage and screen actor, who died on 18 July 1999.

13   Éamon Sherwin, born 17 July 1951, warmly recalls canvassing with his brothers Alan, Liam and Vincent with their father.

5

POLITICS: THE ART OF DECEPTION

Many people in public life use, or try to use, their position and the associated publicity to advance their business interests. The public think that public representatives will gain advantages for them and that is why many business people aspire to be representatives. These business people are prepared to spend a lot of money to get elected. Money alone will not get you elected, but where you are in competition with someone who is no better known than yourself, then money can decide the issue.

Some business people get contracts or influence the terms of contracts by being public representatives. I know of one case where a councillor kept lobbying corporation officials to put sewerage along a country road near Dublin. The pressure was kept up privately or in corners at planning meetings. The land was agricultural. If there were sewerage facilities, the value would increase fourfold. It would become industrial or housing land and the owners stood to make about £30,000 or more. Business people as a rule are bad representatives because they give little time to public affairs but at election times they take a few weeks off and bribe the voters with small sums of money or drink. Many voters are influenced by these bribes to the disadvantage of poorer but more conscientious candidates.

I mention these cases to show the sort of business politics is and the people I have mentioned are no worse than most politicians are. Democracy is an evil system, but there is no known alternative except dictatorship. With dictatorships, dictators can be both benevolent and progressive. The trouble is when they die or retire, tyrants may take their place and then it takes assassination or revolution to produce a change. The answer is not easy, but it is essential that there be a free press, a free radio and television system, and well-meaning, outspoken Independents in all democratic assemblies. Independents are worthy of support because they stand on their own two feet. There are good men in political parties but there is also an army of opportunists who have no faith in their own ability to become elected by their own efforts. They know that it is the parties that nominate them, and that they stand a good chance because party supporters will support anyone that the party puts up. A US politician, who was discussing the issue, once said if their party put up a walking stick, it would be elected, and this is largely true, which is why two-thirds of all party representatives are 'duds'.

Independents must earn every vote. They must slave for the people. They must be always on the lookout for people in trouble because unless they make many friends and keep themselves actively in the public eye they are in danger at every election. A party man knows that even if he hides from the people in trouble and does not attend meetings, he has the party machine and the party supporters behind him when an election takes place. Local councils are mainly concerned with local matters such as rates, rents and amenities. They have no political power but they are invaded by politicians because they can be used as political platforms or in the case of Dublin and other areas, they are after the 'plum job' of Lord Mayor. By right, only ratepayers, corporation tenants, Independents and community associations should be elected to councils. It is a joke to think that councillors who seldom if ever attend committee meetings should have the power to say how rate money should be spent. There are about seventy committee meetings held annually where all the work of Dublin Corporation is discussed and where decisions are made involving the following year's expenditure rates.

Those who attend these meetings get a good grasp of what it is all about and when the rates estimates meetings are held, just before the annual rate is struck, they contribute constructively. About two-thirds of the members of Dublin Corporation had a bad attendance record or they came in late or left early. At committee meetings all the administration and technical officers are present so you can elicit information. Apart from committee meetings there are council meetings when the press is present, so all the slackers and the know-nothings are present and they usually raise some irrelevant matter or gimmick just for a bit of cheap publicity. There are conferences held on the continent every few years. They are held in this country also. Whenever it appears on the agenda that members are to be selected to attend such conferences, political party members mobilize, including those who seldom or never attend, in order to capture the nominations for the trip. Ratepayers complain about the cost of sending councillors to these conferences. They are right to object to this waste if they are not going to get value in return. My own view is that these conferences are necessary because councillors have the final say in all expenditure and I think it is money well spent to have informed and experienced people in charge of that money, rather than 'duds' who know little or nothing. Critics exaggerate the cost of these trips. In one case sums of £6,000 and £10,000 were mentioned when in fact the cost was less than a quarter of the amount stated. Speaking for myself, I make no apologies for going to these conferences. I was Vice-Chairman of Dublin Corporation Committee that spends several million pounds annually on housing construction. I made a valuable contribution at all levels of corporation activity. I attended practically all committee meetings and other meetings of the corporation.

In 1964, there were seventy-seven committee meetings. I attended sixty-nine full meetings. In 1965, there were sixty-five meetings. I attended fifty-nine. In 1966, there were sixty-six meetings of which I attended sixty-three. I had the best attendance record every year. In fact, my attendance was equal to that of seventeen other councillors put together. Compare my attendance with that of Michael Mullan, one of my opponents, who did everything in his power to harm me during the 1965 general election, when I lost my seat in the *Dáil.* He was a Labour councillor and a TD. In 1964, he attended one corporation meeting according to official records. In 1965, he attended five meetings. In 1966, he attended one meeting. In other words, I attended 151 meetings in three years and he attended seven. He was elected an alderman at the local elections of 1967 and I lost my seat. As well as attending practically all official meetings from the day I was elected in 1955, I met people in trouble outside the housing and rent offices every morning at 11 a.m. when these offices were at the exchange buildings on Lord Edward Street. I heard all their complaints and made personal contact with corporation officers, which is the only way to achieve results. I helped thousands in this way because you can make a case. Many public representatives write letters and send on the official reply, which people in trouble do not understand. These letters are only used to bamboozle people into letting them think that something is being done. When the corporation offices were transferred to Jervis Street, I met the people in trouble every day at 2 p.m. A rent collector said to me, in the presence of other collectors, that I was the only councillor that ever really helped people in trouble. In fact, I met people in trouble all day, as I resided in the centre of my area. I always told them the truth but I found that it does not pay to tell the truth – people only want good news – which is the reason why pleasant perjurers are popular in politics.

Most of the people who came to me wanted dwellings. There is a priority system governed by housing law. The allocation of dwellings is the function of the City Manager and the Medical Officer. Councillors cannot get you a dwelling if you are not entitled to one and they cannot get you a dwelling until your turn comes up according to the priority system. I always questioned people who wanted dwellings about their circumstances. You get houses depending on the size of your family, the accommodation you had and the age of the children. Due to my knowledge of the working of the priority system, I knew where all applicants stood. People who wanted dwellings, however, did not care how many families there were who were worse off than themselves. They were only concerned with their own interests. The trouble was that because they would not take no for an answer, nor were they prepared to wait their turn, councillors had three choices: to tell the truth and take the chance of being abused, fabricate the truth or tell them that you would do your best, knowing that you could do nothing. I always told them the truth and got plenty of abuse or lost votes. At the same time, because of my knowledge and the fact that I usually checked up on their files, I helped many acquire housing because often there was evidence on their files that could advance their case which was not on the housing files, and it was the information on the files that decided their case. Not long ago, a parish priest, who was sympathetic because he knew of all the work I did, told me that I should not tell the truth if I thought that it would harm my chances of re-election but I just cannot prevaricate. It's not in my nature, and that is why I lost my seats in the *Dáil* and the corporation. Dan Breen, famous freedom fighter and ex-TD said: 'You must be a crook to get elected and re-elected', and so it would seem.

Before I finish with my corporation work and move on to my *Dáil* experience, let me say that many corporation committee meetings would have been cancelled had I not been on hand to constitute a quorum, as three was necessary to start a meeting and although there were eighteen members on each committee, it was sometimes difficult to get that small number. Often I was in some corporation department helping someone in trouble when I would get phone calls to come over so that the meeting could start.

Following the 1961 general election, when I was elected on the first count getting 5,356 number one votes, I found myself over a barrel. Until then I had been able to cast my vote however I pleased, and I was always criticizing the government. I was the hero of the hour but now no party could form a government. I could have acted the coward, as did several other Independents, or I could help form a government. About this time, there was a programme on television called *Hurlers on the Ditch*, in which representatives of the press formed the panel. They discussed the election several times and all agreed that the most important result would be a stable government without which the country would suffer. When I cast my vote for Mr Lemass, I was attacked and abused by many of my supporters, including members of the same television panel who had said that stable government was essential. The government lasted several years and it was during this time that economic growth in the country soared. It was the admitted beginning of prosperity, yet I was abused, not thanked, for my contribution.

Political parties are all the same. There are able and honest people in all parties. Some are able but not honest. There are a number who believe in the policy of the parties and there are a number of ambitious opportunists. These people are the fixers, the bribers and the people who control the caucus groups who arrange decisions, especially as to who should be nominated as candidates to fight elections. There is a constant war going on between the clique on the executive of the party and the clique at constituency level, as to who should nominate the candidates. Each party builds up a state of prejudice against other parties, especially among the people at large. Most followers follow and accept what their leaders say as gospel. What is said by parties most of the time are untruths. Let us consider the rise of Adolf Hitler.[1] What was his thinking? Hitler said the bigger the lie the better, and never reason with the working class, appeal to their emotions, in other words, to the selfish side of their nature and their ignorance. In fact, many politicians hold that a large number of the working class, or as many put it, the lower working class, are so naive you could sell them O'Connell Bridge.[2] According to all parties, the only honest people are themselves and all other parties are evil. This is not true – there is good and bad in all parties. Parties cannot tell the truth because their object is to get themselves into power, therefore they cannot give credit to others. Again Hitler said that we count on misery. Prosperity will defeat us and where there is no misery, it should be invented.[3] In *The Prince*, Machiavelli said that you should not be honest with those you want to influence.[4] Nevertheless, it is of great consequence to disguise your inclinations and play the hypocrite well, as people are so simple. Appear to have good qualities. It is honourable to seem mild and merciful, courteous and religious.[5] In *John Fitzgerald Kennedy: the Man and the Myth*, Lasky wrote that the political prizes go to artful dodgers, rather than the true believers.[6] Gore Vidal in 'The Holy Family', from *Collected Essays* said: 'For thousands of years the man-god was sacrificed to ensure with blood the harvest and there is always an element of ecstasy as well as awe in our collective guilt.'[7] Walter Lippman said that 80 per cent of voters have hereditary opinions and the battle of parties is to convince, bribe or bamboozle the other 20 per cent.[8] Lippman also said, and I quote Kennedy's *Profiles in Courage*, that exceptions are so rare that they are regarded as miracles of nature. Successful democratic politicians are insecure and intimidated men who advance only as they placate, appease, bribe, seduce, bamboozle or otherwise manage to manipulate the demanding threatening elements in their constituency.[9]

The decisive consideration is not which proposition is good but whether it is popular. It is not whether it will work well and prove itself but whether the active talking constituents like it immediately. In *A Doctor's Nigeria*, Dr Robert Collis said that the fact is that politics is not the pursuit of truth by every means. You must never agree with your political opponent or admit that anything he says can possibly be right. You must use every cunning device to trip him up, including misrepresenting him to your own advantage. You must utter half-truths with complete self-assurance, even though you know that they do not state the whole case; and having decided on a plan of action, you must discipline your supporters to follow it whether or not they agree.[10] Leo Durocher once said that nice guys finish last. Mean low-down bastards win.[11] Adler, in *Politics and the Common Man*, said that the tendency of party organizations is to serve the ends of power rather than justice to seek to out-bid their rivals for popular support by pandering to passion and ignorance, and generally to put party interests before those of the community is an evil inherent in the party system for which no remedy has yet been found.[12] Wolfe Tone wrote that what a man gains on the score of principles, he loses on that of common sense. In order to do any good within a party, a man must make great sacrifices, not only of his judgement but, what is much worse I fear, of his conscience also. If he cannot turn his mind to this, there is but one line of conduct for him to pursue, which is to quit the field.[13] Former American President Harry Truman, while speaking on the subject, said that if you can't stand the heat, get out of the kitchen.[14] Kane said that it takes three things to win at politics. The first is money, the second is money and the third is money.[15] Robert M. MacIver in *The Web of Government* said that in every community there are many people who are so engrossed in their private affairs or problems that they pay no heed to larger issues.[16] Others again have no understanding of political situations and their emotions are a response to the cheap appeals of those who play on them. The votes of morons count equally with the votes of the discerning. Lord Halifax said that the best kind of party is in some way a conspiracy against the nation.[17] I am quoting here from Hogan's *Proportional Representation*.[18] A member of the US Cabinet recorded in his diary, and I quote Kennedy's *Profiles in Courage*, that while he was reluctant to believe in the total depravity of the Senate, he placed but little dependence on the honesty and truthfulness of a large portion of the senators. A majority of them were small lights, mentally weak and wholly unfit to be senators. Some were vulgar demagogues. Some were men of wealth who had purchased their position. Some were men of narrow intellect, limited comprehension and low partisan prejudice; and I quote Rex Taylor's *Michael Collins*, who said that whenever he thought of politics, he thought of the false air which is part of most politicians.[19] However much we may blind the public and even ourselves into thinking that he is for party and country, it did not blind him into thinking the same way. To be a politician, one needs to keep tongue in cheek for all of the day and most of the night. One needs to have the ability to say one thing and mean another. One needs to be abnormally successful at the art of twisting the truth.[20] Christopher Hollis, former British MP, said that party politicians were insincere – they lied and deceived the people to get votes.[21] They looked upon the people as outsiders, and believed that no one had any conception of Heaven unless he had been a Member of Parliament and left it. Those who have never been in always think that they have missed something and those that are in know that they are in Hell. The only way is to have been in and then to have come out. This would appear to be true, and Hollis left Parliament more than for any other reason because he wanted to be free to talk about politics, which an MP can never do.

My own view of politics, based on experience, is that all politicians and particularly party politicians, falsify because their aim is to obtain power by fair means or foul. They have learned from experience that human nature is weak, selfish and largely ignorant. The truth does not pay, so even those who are honest and well-meaning are compelled to fabricate like the rest if they want to succeed in politics. Honest people may succeed if they are members of parties because they have an army of 'hatchet men' working for them, but it is difficult for honest people to rise in a party because of all the organized fixers they have to by-pass. Proportional representation enables candidates to win or lose often by a few votes, so bribery and outrageous promises are the order of the day. Pleasant lies, not truth, are the secret weapon.

The opposition have always had a field day on promises. The smaller parties are the most irresponsible because they know they are a long way from power and responsibility. Parties that come into power, often by outrageous promises, especially benefits without extra taxation, just ignore what they had previously promised and begin to increase taxation themselves. Parties looking for power always adopt Hitler's advice whether they know it or not. Misery will always get votes, so if there is no misery, they must invent it. Any progress that is made by a democratic government is a miracle. It is only because some ministers fight to bring success that progress is made, and that is accomplished despite not only the political opposition, but also in spite of the opposition of the ordinary people or lack of support of many who will benefit. There are individuals among the leadership of parties who do not equivocate but they may not tell the whole truth. On a radio show, Mr Lemass admitted this fact but all leaders condone the dissimulations of their colleagues, especially if the fabrications profit the party; at least they never deny them in public. When Oliver Flanagan TD slandered me in the *Dáil* in 1963, many of his colleagues said to me that he should be kicked out of the party, but the leaders said nothing and did nothing about it. Independents may prevaricate but not to the same extent as party men as they have no party to cover up for. They have no need to misrepresent other parties but for that again, some Independents just cannot lie.

NOTES

1   Sherwin was interested in Hitler's rise from that of a homeless penniless vagabond in 1909 to Chancellor of Intellectual Germany by 1935. Adolf Hitler (1889–1945) was born on 20 April 1889 in Braunau-am-Inn, Austria. At the outbreak of the First Word War, in 1914, he volunteered for service in the German army and was accepted into the Sixteenth Bavarian Reserve Infantry Regiment. After the war, Hitler joined the German Workers' Party and on 1 April 1920, under his influence its name was changed to the National German Workers Party or Nazi for short. At this time Hitler had formed a group of thugs to supress disorder at party meetings which subsequently became the *Sturmabteilung* or SA. During the summer of 1920, Hitler chose the swastika as the Nazi party emblem. By 1921, Adolf Hitler had virtually secured total control of the Nazi Party. By November 1923, Hitler plotted to overthrow the German Weimar Republic by force and on 8 November he led an attempt to take over the local Bavarian government in Munich in an action that became known as the 'Beer Hall Putsch'. He was tried for treason and sentenced to five years in Landsberg prison during which he dictated his thoughts and philosophies to Rudolf Hess, which later became the book *Mein Kampf.* Hitler was released from Landsberg prison in December 1924 after serving only six months of his sentence. By 1928, Hitler had created the infamous SS (*Schutzstaffel*), which was initially intended to be Hitler's bodyguard, under the leadership of Heinrich Himmler. The collapse of the Wall Street exchange in 1929 benefited Hitler and his Nazi campaigning. In February 1932 Hitler decided to stand against Hindenburg in the forthcoming presidential elections, and although he was unsuccessful, by the July elections the Nazi party had become the largest political party. On 30 January 1933, President Hindenburg decided to appoint Hitler Chancellor in a coalition government with Papen as Vice-Chancellor. The penultimate step towards Adolf Hiter gaining complete control over the destiny of Germany was taken on the night of 27 February 1933 when the Reichstag was destroyed by fire. This fire had been planned by the Nazis, Goebbels and Göering in particular. The Enabling Act placed before the Reichstag on 23 March 1933 was to allow the powers of legislation to be taken from the Reichstag and transferred to Hitler's Cabinet for a period of four years. By 14 July, Hitler had proclaimed a law stating that the Nazi Party was to be the only political party

allowed in Germany. On 30 June 1934, Himmler's SS and Goerring's special police arrested and executed leaders of the SA, including Ernst Roehm. President Hindenburg died on 2 August 1934 and Hitler became 'Führer and Reich Chancellor', and the title of President was then abolished. Between the years 1934–37, Hitler continued with his nazification of Germany and sought to release Germany from the armament restrictions of the Versailles Treaty. All youth associations were abolished and re-formed as the Hitler Youth organization and the Nuremburg Laws of September 1935 stated that Jews were no longer considered German citizens and therefore had no legal rights. In September 1936, Göering took over most of Dr Hjalmar Schacht's duties in preparing the war economy and instituted the Four-Year Plan which was intended to make Germany self-sufficient in four years. Hitler ordered the army to be trebled in size from the 100,000 man Versailles Treaty limit, to 300,000 men by October 1934. He also ordered the construction of warships, way above the maximum size decreed by the Versailles Treaty. The construction of submarines, also forbidden by the Treaty, had already begun secretly by building parts in foreign docklands ready for assembly. Göering was ordered to see to the training of air force pilots and the design of military aircraft. On 7 March 1936, German troops marched across the Rhine bridges in the demilitarized areas of Germany towards Aachen, Trier and Saarbrücken in breach of the Locarno Pact of 1925 stating that areas west of the Rhine were to be kept free of German military units. Thus Hitler had remilitarized the Rhineland and by October 1936, he had formed an alliance with Italian dictator Mussolini.

2   In America they say the Brooklyn Bridge.

3   Adolf Hitler, *Mein Kampf* (London: Friends of Europe, 1936).

4   Niccolo Machiavelli (also Nicolo, Niccholo and Nicholas, also Machiavegli, Machiavella and Machiavel), Italian essayist, dramatist, historian, sketch writer, biographer, dialogist, writer of novellas and poet. Machiavelli was born on 3 May 1469 and died of illness on 21 June 1527 in Florence, Italy.

5   Niccolo Machiavelli, *The Prince* was published in Geneva by Pietro Aubert in 1550. An early copy of an English translation is kept at the National Library of Ireland and dates back to 1720.

6   Victor Lasky was the author of *John Fitzgerald Kennedy: the Man and the Myth* (New York: Macmillan, 1963).

7   Gore Vidal (1925–) original name Eugene Luther Vidal, was a prolific American playwright and essayist. He was one of the great stylists of contemporary American prose and an active liberal in politics. In 1960, he ran unsuccessfully for the US Congress as a Democratic-Liberal candidate in New York. Between 1970 and 1972, he acted as Co-Chairman of the left-leaning People's Party. In 1982, Vidal launched a campaign in California for the US Senate. He came second out of a field of nine, polling half a million votes. He is the author of 'The Holy Family' from *Collected Essays* (1974) which is included in *United States 1952–1992*.

8   Walter Lippman, the son of second-generation German-Jewish parents, was born in New York City on 23 September 1889. While studying at Harvard University, he became a socialist, co-founded the Harvard Socialist Club and edited the *Harvard Monthly*. Lippman's *A Preface to Politics* (1913) was well received. He became a member of the US delegation to the Paris Peace Conference of 1919 and helped draw up the covenant of the League of Nations. His controversial books *Public Opinion* (1922) and *The Phantom Public* (1925) questioned the possibility of developing a true democracy in a modern complex

society. Between the 1930s and 1960s, Lippman wrote the nationally syndicated column *Today and Tomorrow* where he developed a pragmatic approach to politics. After the Second World War, Lippman upset leaders of both the Korean War, McCarthyism and the Vietnam War. Walter Lippman died on 14 December 1974.

9 John Fitzgerald Kennedy was born in Brookline Massachusetts on 29 May 1917. Upon his return from the navy after the Second World War, he became Democratic congressman for the Boston area and advanced to the Senate in 1953. In 1955, while recuperating from a back operation, Senator John F. Kennedy published *Profiles in Courage*, dealing with eight US Senators, namely John Quincy Adams, Thomas Hart Benton, Daniel Webster, Sam Houston, Edmund Ross, Lucius Quintus Cincinattus Lamar, George Norris and Robert Taft. The thesis of this book was that these men showed that conscience rather than political consideration has a way of running at critical moments in our history and that in retrospect the negative reaction directed at these men was unfair and undeserved. *Profiles in Courage* won Kennedy the Pulitzer Prize in history. See John F. Kennedy, *Profiles in Courage* (New York: HarperCollins, 1957). Kennedy served as thirty-fifth President of the United States from 1961–63. He was the youngest man elected President and the first Roman Catholic to hold that office. He was killed by an assassin's bullet in Dallas, Texas on 22 November 1963.

10 William Robert Fitzgerald Collis, *A Doctor's Nigeria* (London: Secker & Warburg, 1960).

11 Leo Ernest Durocher was born on 27 July 1905 in West Springfield Massachusetts and died on 7 October 1991 in Palm Springs California. He was a famous baseball coach and managed Brooklyn Dodgers (1939–46, 1948), New York Giants (1948–55), Chicago Cubs (1966–72) and Heuston Astros (1972–73).

12 Sherwin refers to Adler, author of *Politics and the Common Man*. Another text of the same title was written by H.T. Reynolds in 1974. Mortimer J. Adler, born 28 December 1902, died 28 June 2001, was author of *The Common Sense of Politics* (New York: Holt, Rinehart and Winston, 1971). No publication details for Adler, *Politics and the Common Man* were found. Sherwin may be referring to *Politics and the Common Man: An Introduction to Political Behaviour* by H T Reynolds (Homewood, Illinois: Dorsey, 1974).

13 Theobald Wolfe Tone, considered the first Irish Republican and commonly known as Wolfe Tone, was born in Dublin on 20 June 1763. He was a leading figure in the Irish Independence movement and is regarded as the father of Irish republicans. Wolfe Tone was called to the Irish Bar in 1789. He published a pro-independence pamphlet entitled *Hibernicus* in 1790 and in 1791 together with Thomas Russell and William Drennan founded the Society of United Irishmen in Belfast. In the same year, he published *An Argument on Behalf of the Catholics of Ireland* and in 1792 became Secretary of the Catholic Association with whom he worked until 1795 when he was exiled to America for his revolutionary activities. In 1796, he toured France and successfully petitioned the Directory to aid a rebellion in Ireland. In late December 1796, a fleet of 15,000 troops sailed with Tone for Ireland under the command of General Hoche. Bad weather scattered the fleet and they were forced to return to France. Tone petitioned the Dutch government and in July 1797, a Dutch expedition set sail but failed to land in Ireland. When the Rising occurred in May 1798, another French fleet of 1,000 troops under the command of General Humbert landed at Killala, County Mayo where they were met by the numerically superior English army

commanded by General Lake to whom they surrendered. Tone persuaded the French Directory to send another expedition to Ireland and in September 1798, a French fleet of 5,000 troops set sail commanded by General Hardy with Tone as *Chief de Brigade*. The fleet was apprehended by the British navy in Lough Swilly on 11 October 1798 and Tone was captured. He was imprisoned at Derry Gaol before being moved to Dublin where he was tried for treason and sentenced to death. When Tone's request for a military execution was refused, he tried to commit suicide in prison and died of his injuries on 18 November 1798.

14   Harry S Truman, thirty-third President of the United States (1945–53), was born on 8 May 1884 in Lamar Missouri and died on 20 December 1972 in Independence, Missouri.

15   Joseph Nathan Kane, an American writer and cousin of Kennedy, is quoted here.

16   Robert M MacIver, US sociologist and political scientist, was born on 17 April 1882 in Stornoway, Outer Hebrides Scotland and died on 15 June 1970 in New York. MacIver taught at the University of Aberdeen and later at Canadian and US universities, principally Columbia (1915-26). He believed in the compatibility of individualism and social organization and saw societies as evolving from highly communal states to states in which individual functions and group affiliations were extremely specialized. His works included *The Modern State* (1926), *Leviathan and The People* (1939) and *The Web of Government* (1947).

17   The Right Honourable Edward Frederick Lindley Wood, first Earl of Halifax, KG, OM, GCSI, GCIE, PC (16 April 1881 – 23 December 1959), known as The Lord Irwin from 1925 until 1934 and as The Viscount Halifax from 1934 until 1944, was a British Conservative politician. He is regarded as one of the architects of appeasement prior to World War II. During the period he held several ministerial posts in the Cabinet. He succeeded Lord Reading as Governor-General and Viceroy of India in April 1926, a post he held until 1931.

18   James Hogan, (1898–1963), revolutionary, historian, political scientist and activist, Director of Intelligence in the National Army during the Civil War and Professor of History at UCC (1920–63). Hogan's *Proportional Representation* is said to mark the beginning of political science in Ireland. See James Hogan, *Election and Representation, Part 1: The Experiment of Proportional Representation in Ireland* (Cork and Oxford, 1945). Other works read by Sherwin on the subject of proportional representation include works by Ferdinand Hermans, James Meridith and works by the Unionist Research Department and the United Irish League. See Bibliography.

19   See 'Agreement, Vision, Fear' in *Empire dies for Irish freedom* published by *Coiste na n-Iarchimí* on 7 January 2006. It refers to the uneasy mood of the Irish capital as outlined in Rex Taylor's biography of Michael Collins which evaluates the morale of the occupying forces on Dublin streets in 1921. Taylor's account of the life of Collins identifies the '....terror created by a force uncertain of the measure of its strength'.

20   Rex Taylor was born in 1921. See Bibliography.

21   Christopher Hollis, a right-wing Catholic and Tory MP. See Christopher Hollis, *The British Constitution in 1952*, Parliam. Aff. 1952, VI:165–172.

6

DÁIL ÉIREANN[1]

with introduction by Frank Sherwin Jr

Dáil Éireann is situated in Kildare Street, a short distance south of Dublin city centre. It has other names such as the *Oireachtas* or Leinster House. All of these names serve to denote the symbol of our democracy. It is on this democracy, and where it seems to be going, that I would like to dwell for a moment before we continue. In their foundation, such concepts are largely set up by those who still have about them that streak of idealism. However, gradually that awkward feature would appear to be rooted out, it being the inherent flaw of democracy. It is placed into the hands of mortal men who take it unto themselves and manipulate it to their own ends where it would seem to generate into an exhibition: of 'one-upmanship' and 'hoodwinking'. This was exemplified by one individual with a background in farming and a newcomer to the political scene who did not initially appear to know which party he was going to honour with his talents. He finally opted for the Progressive Democrats, who had him settled into the position of junior minister and it was from this position that he blatantly took credit for something in which he had no hand, with a view to enhancing his image in his own backyard. He then went on to disown the whole project when it appeared to be going 'pear-shaped'. A politician's eye is never off the next election! He does not stand alone in this playacting, as this autobiography will attest.

This neat trick is one of the great vote-grabbing ploys of the politician, when they will take a sudden great interest in your baby or even your dog, ready to kiss them on all four cheeks be it necessary, as they live out a cynical 'one born every minute' philosophy of treating the voter as a fool. That great idealistic notion soon degenerates into: 'How much is all of this worth to me?'

How did the democratic ideal degenerate to this level? Was it for this that those idealists of yesteryear battled and shed their blood after that long painful struggle to free ourselves from a domineering neighbour? We then hand that prize over to an even greater domineering neighbour, a neighbour who in time will tell us which brand of toothpaste we may use to brush our teeth. Don't get me wrong, the early notion of joining what is now the greater European Union looked very attractive. We all imagined we would be as equals in this union, at least I did. As time has borne out, some are more equal than others. It is something like the United Nations with its five permanent members. The man on the street, at least the man who drove on the street, or could afford to drive on the street given the high cost of motoring, naively imagined that he would at last be buying his motor car at European prices. 'Hope springs eternal in the human breast!'[2]

Let us return to some of the early rumblings of the European door opening, to admit to its fireside this little isle at the edge of the greater European continent, which is when we started to sit up and take notice. What was it that caused us – the Irish man and woman on the street, the ones that bothered with such things – to sit up and take notice? As I remember it, what grabbed our attention was money, a lot of money, £8 billion of the precious commodity. That was at a time when we were still counting in mere millions. 'Eight billion pounds', our leader Albert Reynolds informed us, more than once, in case we were not listening. There are still some out there who do not listen too much to politicians and their promises.[3] With naive hopes of getting our cars at European prices and those generous Europeans loading us down with money, the future looked rosy. Personally when I first heard mention of them giving us £8 billion, the first question to pop into my ever-curious mind was 'Why?' Why would they want to hand over their good money to a people known the world over for squandering its money on booze, which of course is not altogether true, although that is the impression and impressions tend to stick. They may know us a little better now, if they think of us at all, beyond what we are costing them. Incidentally, and keep it quiet, we still have a booze culture, it is just getting younger.

Anyhow, leaving that detail aside, what has been extracted from us by way of earning our easy loot? I remember the farmers being ecstatic for a while. They were among the first to receive and spend the cash. Then the elation seemed to fade somewhat when they realized that they were expected to be accountants as well. Their troubles did not end there, leaving aside the endless list of 'you must do' and 'you must not do' from the segregation of waste, to car tests.[4] Indeed, the latest of these dictates to register with us is the environment management charge. What is that I might hear some say? That is the sneaky little addition to the cost of everything from your new freezer to your electric light bulb. Now after that short preamble through the intricacies of living under the bureaucracy of 'Big Brother', I would like to look at our long-sought freedom and, not least, our democracy or what would seem to be left of it.

Recalling to mind our democratic vote on the Nice Treaty, which had to be dismantled to suit the agenda of certain politicians, one of which it would appear was appointed a minister on the strength of 'getting it through', prompts me to ask: what is this agenda?[5] Where do our politicians stand? Did they trade everything in for a greater stomping ground, without looking too closely at the 'terms and conditions apply' and, more importantly, where does our autonomy stand? Do we have such a luxury anymore? It would appear that Brussels tells our politicians to jump and they ask meekly 'how high?' Has our *Oireachtas* become a mere local government subject to Brussels? In view of all of this, I tend to ask, is there any point in having *Dáil Éireann* at all?

However, before we empty Leinster House, let us look at that august establishment at a time when that trace of idealism still struggled to flicker here and there in spite of the wind that sought to extinguish it. Let us consider the time before we really got down to rearranging the new-found democracy to suit our own ends, that is, before certain people saw in their position a means to making themselves rich.

When my father became a councillor in 1955, it was an unpaid position. He knew this and although he could have done with remuneration, he just got on with it. As I remember it, when he entered the *Dáil* in 1957 the allowance was in the region of £12 a week.[6] That figure was raised to some £20 per week in the following years but was then subjected to income tax. There were no extras in his case as he lived locally: no comfortable office, no secretary, no free post and no telephone, etc. These all existed in the future. To him it was a vocation. Had he enough to feed his family and bring his wife to an odd film he would have been prepared to do it for nothing. He was one of that old school and he was not alone.

In the recent past, one might have heard of the plight of former President of Ireland, Éamon De Valera, who confided to the doctor who was treating him for depression. His condition was attributed by the good doctor to De Valera's concerns over the state of his finances, that his pension of £1,200 (Ir. Punt) = £6,000 Ir. Punt (1972) = €75,660 (Feb. '06); $95,040 (Feb. '06); £51,720 sterling (Feb.'06) a year would not meet the expenses of his nursing home, not to mention the care of his ailing wife.[7] According to state papers released recently, after thirty years, the doctor took it upon himself to petition the then *Taoiseach*, Mr Jack Lynch, on behalf of the troubled former president. It was decided to increase the president's annual pension from the said £1,200 to £5,707. What the former president thought of this canvassing on his behalf is not recorded. The late president had militantly refused an increase in his pension some years earlier. Whatever you might personally think of Mr Éamon De Valera, you can be assured that he was not there to make himself rich. Incidentally, a president's wife, should she survive him, was expected to live on £500 a year.

Frank Sherwin Jr

Following the general election on 4 October 1961, the position of the parties was as follows: *Fianna Fáil*, seventy votes; *Fine Gael*, forty-seven votes; *Labour*, sixteen votes,[8] *Clann na Talmhan*, two votes; the National Progressive Democrats, two votes and *Clann na Poblachta*, one vote. The total opposition parties numbered sixty-seven.[9] The chairman of the *Dáil* does not vote unless there is a tie. There were six Independents but the opposition could never get the support of all the Independents. Even if they got their support, they could not count on them to be present at all times to vote, nor could they depend on them to support all legislation. Furthermore, no business could be done because there would have to be constant consultations between all groups and all Independents. A government of the opposition was out of the question. *Fianna Fáil* only required two votes to have an overall majority which would give stability. Three Independents decided to vote for nobody. I decided to support a government that would last a reasonable time in the interests of the country at large. I voted for Mr Lemass, I had no choice. I could have acted the coward. Before I cast my vote I made the following speech:[10]

As an Independent, I do not have to play the party game. I shall not make any speech on politics but I shall come down to the essentials. I am concerned only with the person who can form a government that has some chance of survival. I am not interested in voting for people – even though I may admire them – who can form a government that will only last only for weeks. I do not think the *Dáil* or the public want another election. In fact, members of all Parties have come to me and said they hoped Deputy Lemass would be elected [*Taoiseach*] because they did not want another election. Even members of the Opposition have said that to me.

I am concerned with figures, with the fact that there are seventy members of the *Fianna Fáil* party and all the others together comprise seventy-four. You, Sir [*Ceann Comhairle*] are one, and that leaves us with seventy-three. The seventy members of *Fianna Fáil* can all be 'whipped' into being here. That does not apply to the other side. There are six groups on the other side. Who can 'whip' the Independents into being here? Nobody. Who can 'whip' Dr Deputy Browne into being here? Not Deputy McQuillan.[11] I am concerned with forming a government. I would like to vote for Deputy Dillon and Deputy Corish, because both of these gentlemen have been very kind to me. In fact, if I ever encountered any hostility, it was from Deputy Lemass' party.

I am rising above all that. There is the country to be considered and not parties. There is the question of the country being able to carry to meet such problems as the Common Market and unemployment; there is the question of our boys in the Congo; there is the question of Partition. These are the matters we should consider, and not this little game. Everybody admits it is a little game. I would warmly support a national government, but such has not been proposed. Deputy Lemass has not said he is interested in such a proposal. It is up to Deputy Lemass whether he has a coalition.

I can help in forming a government that will last a reasonable time. Any other government would not last three weeks, let alone three months. As I said, we can play any little game we like. I shall say no more, except to emphasise that I am not voting for *Fianna Fáil* – I am voting for a government.

Mr Lemass was elected *Taoiseach* by seventy-two votes to sixty-eight. Three Independents did not vote; one, Deputy Finucane, voted with the opposition. Deputy W. Murphy, Labour, speaking later, said: 'The Deputy [Sherwin] is better than the men who kept out of it, who had not guts enough to go in.'[12] The 'Leader' section in *The Irish Times*, issued on 12 October 1961 said: 'It's a credit to the good sense of the *Dáil* because of relief which all parties feel at the fact a government with some reasonable state of stability has been capable of formation.' I was largely responsible for this government's stability but later this same newspaper abused me for keeping the government stable. It is now admitted that from this period onwards, our economic growth developed and Mr Lemass has been praised as the man responsible but I was abused. I lost my seat in the *Dáil* and the Corporation for putting the country before my own interests.

As I said, it was the greatest achievement of my life when I was elected to the *Dáil* under my own steam. I got there in spite of all the begrudging. I was, however, disappointed when I found the *Dáil* to be a dull, boring place.[13] Mr De Valera was the outstanding personality but Mr Seán Lemass was the ablest man in the House. I admired his cool, calculating and business-like qualities. He was the man largely responsible for our economic growth and our present prosperity. In my opinion, he was not a great political leader but a great minister. He was, however, clannish. I was always impressed by Neil Blaney.[14] He was forceful and always made a good case. Charlie Haughey, the Minister for Finance, had personality and drive.[15] He was popular and the victory of *Fianna Fáil* in 1969 was to some extent due to the fact that he was Minister for Finance and Director of Elections for *Fianna Fáil* at the same time. He could and did use his position as Minister for Finance to influence the voters in his 'giveaway budget'.[16] Mr Dillon, the leader of *Fine Gael*, was a man of words rather than action.[17] He was the best orator in the House and always a treat to listen to. I felt he failed as a leader because his strength began and ended in a speech.

The then leader of *Fine Gael* is now *Taoiseach*, namely Cosgrave. He, to me, is too much of a gentleman. He is honest and compassionate but politics is a dirty game and you have to be tough to survive in it, especially to lead a party.[18] This party is conservative and its following, rural. It was 'the Treaty' party that won the Civil War. Its supporters of 'the Treaty' are the backbone of the party. There is always the danger that this party will split with a farmer's party in the offing.

The Labour party never impressed me in my time; it was largely a trade union group. However, I was always impressed by Mr Corish as an honest straightforward type but I find his character lacking in supremacy to lead a mixed gathering like the Labour party.[19] In the general election of 1969, a number of television personalities and intellectuals were elected to the *Dáil* on behalf of the Labour party. I consider Dr Conor Cruise O'Brien the ablest.[20] The trade unions' 'grass-roots groups' and the intellectuals won't mix, so I believe the trade unions will always be the backbone of the Labour party in this country. They have the money and they are like a secret society. They are a tough crowd, having come up the hard way. They can be perspicacious, cunning and will want a price for their support. In regards to television personalities, they will lose their popular image. On television, they could lay down the law while appearing omniscient but they won't get away with that in politics. There is a night of the long knives, every day and every night in the political game. One striking personality is Dr Noël Browne.[21] He is sincere and has been a member of all parties except *Fine Gael*. Another was the late Donagh O'Malley, Minister for Education in the *Fianna Fáil* government.[22]

I believe *Fianna Fáil* will remain a strong virile party for a long time to come and will be in power at least ten years out of every fifteen. *Fine Gael* may split or disappear in time and a strong farmer's party will arise in its place. Labour may yet become the main opposition party but, I am afraid, not for many years and I don't believe that they will ever have an overall majority. This country is conservative and largely agricultural. We will be industrialized within limits and it is only from the latter that Labour can hope to accrue strong support. Whether Labour likes it or not, its only chance of becoming a government or part of one is within the framework of coalitions or inter-party governments.

Women are now clamouring for equality with men. They are as good as men and in some cases better in certain professions but I don't think politics suits them. They may point out certain cases, such as Mrs Gandhi in India, but she was the daughter of the former Prime Minister, otherwise she may not have been a town councillor let alone Prime Minister.[23] Mrs Golda Meir was Prime Minister of Israel but it seems that she was only a compromise leader.[24] Mrs Castle was a British minister but it is obvious that she was elected as a sop to women voters.[25] Some of our people may point to Countess Markiewicz but she was not a minister of a functioning government. She largely owed her importance to the fact that she had an aristocratic title. Over the last 200 years, many of the popular leaders have been members of the British aristocracy or the British ascendancy class. We seemed to have suffered an inferiority complex in our desire to elevate such people. Most of the women in the *Dáil* are widows of former members. I would imagine they were nominated because they were considered good at tugging on the emotions and therefore good for votes. I met several women councillors who were not widows of former members. In all cases I was disappointed. Few of them spoke, and when they did they got their names in the newspapers not because of what they said but because they spoke at all! There was one exception, and she was good within limits.

Politics is a dirty business and does not suit women. Not all women are angels, but when we think of women in politics, we think of women as leaders. Politics, as well as being a dirty business is a very serious business involving grave responsibilities. It is also a business that requires deep thought, much reflection and a tremendous amount of courage at times. With few exceptions women have domestic responsibilities and it is their nature and function to give such matters priority. Politics is a full-time job or should be. Women do not, as a rule, think deeply. Some women councillors on the Dublin Corporation and local bodies were often a great nuisance. They asked silly or irrelevant questions. Other councillors at the meeting would nod, wink and look at the chairman in despair. If a male councillor asked such questions, he would be laughed at, told to shut up or told that he was out of order. Women, although they ask for equality, also expect the red carpet and to be tolerated if they make a nuisance of themselves as well. There will, of course, be the rare exceptions but I am afraid they will be very rare. Women were made to be charming and let us hope they continue to be so. I do not think politics would suit women who desire to retain their charm, as politics is a business that is inclined to make people bitter, sour, long-faced and horse-faced. These qualities are not feminine. Elizabeth Leseur, that saintly and religious woman, said about women: 'I cannot understand why philosophy is not made the crown of feminine education. What a woman so often lacks is true judgement, the habit of reasoning, the steady individual working on the mind. Philosophy could give her all that and free her from so many prejudices and narrow views which she transmits assiduously to her sons to the great harm of our country.'[26] Some women are philosophers, but very few. Ninety-nine per cent of ordinary women have no interest in active politics and never will. My own wife hates politics and she has good reason to. Some ambitious women think that they would be better than men in regards to domestic matters but I do not think so. Most, if not all, male MPs are married and can make a better case than women. These specific matters only take up about 5 per cent of a parliament's time.[27]

NOTES

1   The original chapter title was: 'The *Dáil*'.

2   A quotation from 'An Essay on Man' by Alexander Pope, born 22 May 1688 and died 30 May 1744. Pope is considered one of the greatest English poets of the eighteenth century.

3   Albert Reynolds was born in Rooskey, County Roscommon in 1932. He made a successful career as a businessman before entering local politics in County Longford in 1975. Reynolds was first elected to the *Dáil* for the constituency of Longford/Westmeath in 1977. As Minister for Posts and Telegraphs and Minister for Transport from 1979–81, he revolutionized the telecommunication system which saw the Irish telephone system transformed into one of the best in Europe. As Minister for Industry and Energy in 1982, he developed the National Grid, establishing the gas pipeline from Cork to Dublin. Reynolds was Minister for Industry and Commerce in 1987–88 and Minister for Finance 1988–91. As minister, he reduced all personal tax rates for the first time in twenty years and also successfully marketed the Financial Services Centre resulting in 200 financial firms setting up business there. He was sacked for challenging the leadership of Charles Haughey in 1991 but a few months later he took over as leader of the party and *Taoiseach* in continuation of the coalition government with the Progressive Democrats. At the beginning of 1993, Albert Reynolds was returned to office in coalition with the Labour party. His greatest achievement

was in Northern Ireland and Anglo-Irish relations; he signed the Downing Street Declaration in 1993. It was his determination that gave impetus to the peace process and the establishment of an IRA ceasefire in 1994 followed shortly by a loyalist ceasefire. In a dispute with his coalition partners, the Labour party, the government fell and Reynolds resigned as leader of *Fianna Fáil* and *Taoiseach* in late 1994.

4   As I sit writing this, a headline in *The Irish Independent*, dated Friday 30 September, 2005, p. 9, stares up at me to the effect that Ireland is to face a €21,600 fine for each day it extracts peat from the ground, as it is considered by those who lord it over our affairs to be harmful ecologically. First we are told that we cannot burn some leaves and twigs at the bottom of our garden. Then we are told that we cannot do what we, the Irish, have been doing for as long as the Irish lit fires. And from our climate I would venture to say that that goes back a long way. Mind you, the argument is not the burning of that turf; the argument is directed at the removal of it from the ground. I don't see them having an issue with the practice of extracting coal from the ground or oil for that matter, on the assumption that it is environmentally damaging, which it is, at just about every stage. At least that was the reason put forward when insisting that cars be fitted with catalytic converters among other things, at the motorist's expense. As I write this, countries are queuing up to enter into an alliance with the EU, which, let me make clear, is a good and wholesome aspiration. However, I wonder if they realize the finer details of that alliance. As far as I can see the ones to gain most from this alliance are the politicians. It has widened their field with a cluster of new jobs. How many government ministers who have passed their sell-by date have been shunted over to Europe to take up an even more lucrative job as an EU Commissioner etc., to make way for some political crony back home in the wheeling and dealing that goes on behind closed political doors.

5   This particularly applies to the front benchers.

6   Allowances were not subject to tax.

7   I am aware that De Valera is alleged to have turned *The Irish Press* newspapers into a family business. Should this be so, then he didn't appear to be much of a businessman. Éamon De Valera's will amounted to a mere £2,800.

8   This included the *Ceann Comhairle* or chairman.

9   The foundation and success of a new rural-based party, *Clann na Talmhan*, and the success of the Labour party until its split after the 1943 election, is indicative of the increasing agricultural and urban unrest during the war years in Ireland. See J.J. Lee, *Ireland 1912–1985: Politics and Society* (Cambridge: Cambridge University Press, 1989), pp. 239–41.

10   *Parliamentary Debates, Dáil Éireann*, 'Appointment of *Taoiseach*', vol 192, 11 October 1961, cols 25/26.

11   Both deputies Browne and McQuillan were members of DPD, the Department of Planning and Development. Deputy McQuillan appears to have been quite lively in the House. See *Parliamentary Debates Dáil Éireann* entitled 'Suspension of Member', vol 174, 22 April 1959. *An Tánaiste* states: 'I move that Deputy McQuillan be suspended from the service of this house'. In *Parliamentary Debates Dáil Éireann* entitled 'Business of *Dáil*', vol 120, 11 May 1950, *An Leas-Cheann Comhairle* states: 'Respecting the notice given by Deputy McQuillan of his intention to raise on the Adjournment...he should not be arraigned on the Adjournment. If Deputy McQuillan wishes to discuss the matter, it should be raised by way of specific motion not on the Adjournment.' In *Parliamentary Debates Dáil Éireann* entitled 'Oral Questions: Use of State Car', vol 118, 15

December 1949, *An Ceann Comhairle* states: 'Order. If Deputy McQuillan cannot cease disorderly interruptions, he will have to leave the House.' In *Parliamentary Debates Dáil Éireann* entitled 'Oral Questions: Old Age Pension Claim', vol 203, 19 June 1963, *An Ceann Comhairle* states: 'Order. Deputy McQuillan will resume his seat. Order. Deputy McQuillan will resume his seat. I am calling Question 31.' See *Irish Student Law Review* subtitled *Justice*, vol 3 No. 1, Hilary, 1965; 'The National Emergency: 25th Birthday' by Niall P. Connolly, p. 3. Connolly refers to *Taoiseach* Seán Lemass on 6 December 1960 when he had to answer McQuillan's question about rescinding the State of Emergency Resolution; Lemass stated that he did not think it would be appropriate 'having regard to the present unsettled international situation'.

12   *Parliamentary Debates, Dáil Éireann*, 'Nomination of Members of Government – Motion of Approval (Resumed)', vol 192, 11 October, 1961, col. 73.

13   During Sherwin's time in the *Dáil*, he felt that many of the deputies were frustrated with little to do. This may explain why there were often rows resulting in strong language. Deputies often protested to the *Ceann Comhairle* but he always ruled that if he did not hear anything, he could do nothing. Deputies were seldom in the *Dáil* chamber, the House was often empty. Dublin deputies were seldom in the House in the daytime, when they were attending to their private jobs or business.

14   Neil T. Blaney was born on 1 October 1922 and died on 8 November 1995. Blaney was first elected to *Dáil Éireann* in 1948 as a *Fianna Fáil* TD representing Donegal North-East. Blaney served as Minister for Posts and Telegraphs (1957), Minister for Local Government (1957–66), and Minister for Agriculture and Fisheries (1966–70). In addition to this, he introduced the Planning Act in 1963, was President of the FAI (1968–73) and a patron until his death and an MEP from 1978–84 and 1989–94.

15   Charles Haughey, born on 16 September 1925, died 13 June 2006, was the sixth *Taoiseach* of the Republic of Ireland, serving three times in office: 1979–81, March 1982 to December 1982, 1987 to 1992. He was the fourth leader of *Fianna Fáil* from 1979 until 1992.

16   'The give away budget' gave a substantial increase in social benefits and free travel for old age pensioners and IRA veterans.

17   James Dillon was born in Dublin in 1902. He is considered one of the most outstanding parliamentarians of the twentieth century. His father John Dillon was also active in politics and became leader of the Irish Parliamentary party. Dillon was elected TD for West Donegal in 1932 and between 1938 and 1969, he was TD for Monaghan. Shortly after his election in 1938 he was unanimously elected deputy leader of *Fine Gael* under William T. Cosgrave. The outbreak of the Second World War and *Fine Gael*'s acceptance of De Valera's policy of neutrality brought about Dillon's resignation from *Fine Gael* in 1942. As an Independent TD, he was appointed Minister for Agriculture in the inter-party government (1948–51). He was an outstanding Minister for Agriculture and is remembered for the land drainage and reclamation schemes which he initiated. He also initiated the Island Fisheries Trust. His aim was to make both resources, land and water, productive for the people of Ireland. He was an outstanding orator and his rhetoric in the *Dáil* was exceptional. He died in 1986. See Maurice Manning, *James Dillon: a Biography* (Dublin: Wolfhound Press, 2000).

18   Liam Cosgrave was born on 13 April 1920 and served as fifth *Taoiseach* of the Republic of Ireland from 1973–77. He became a TD in *Dáil Éireann* in 1944 and retained his seat until his retirement in 1981. He acted as Parliamentary

Secretary to the *Taoiseach* and Minister for Industry and Commerce from 1948–51. Cosgrave served as Minister for External Affairs from 1954–57. During his term as minister, Ireland joined the United Nations. He became leader of the *Fine Gael* party from 1965–77. Throughout Cosgrave's leadership, he was considered dour and conservative yet trustworthy and honourable.

19 Brendan Corish was born in 1918 in Wexford and was elected to the *Dáil* in 1945. Between 1945 and 1951, he was Parliamentary Secretary to the Minister for Local Government and Defence and in 1954 became Minister for Social Welfare in the second inter-party government. In 1960, Corish succeeded William Norton as Labour leader. He was *Tánaiste* and Minister for Health and Social Welfare between 1973 and 1977. In 1977, Corish abdicated as leader of the Labour party. He resigned from political life in 1982. Brendan Corish died on 17 February 1990 in County Wexford, aged 71.

20 Dr Conor Cruise O'Brien, former Labour party TD, was born in Dublin in 1917. He entered the Department of External Affairs in 1944 and served as counsellor in Paris (1955–56) and as a member of the Irish delegation to the United Nations 1956–60. He left the diplomatic service in 1961 after representing the UN Secretary General in Katanga in the Congo and was Vice-Chancellor of the University of Ghana between 1962 and 1965 and a professor at New York University 1965–69. He has been pro-chancellor of the University of Dublin since 1973. He was Minister for Posts and Telegraphs from 1973 to 1977 during the *Fine Gael* coalition and served as senator from 1977 to 1979. O'Brien served as editor of *The Observer* between 1979 and 1981.

21 Dr Noël Browne, the son of a RIC man, was born in 1915. He was a TD at various times between 1948 and 1982 for five different left-wing and Republican parties. He was elected in 1948 for *Clann na Poblachta* and became Minister for Health on his first day in the *Dáil*. As minister, he was successful in tackling the tuberculosis problem of the time but came under pressure from the Roman Catholic Church and Irish Medical Organisation for his plans to make State GP care available to all children under five years and their mothers, known as 'the Mother and Child Scheme'. As a result, he resigned from government and from *Clann na Poblachta* but was re-elected as an Independent in the 1951 general election. Browne joined *Fianna Fáil* in 1953. He lost his seat in the 1954 general election and was again elected as an Independent in the 1957 general election. Dr Noël Browne co-founded the National Progressive Democrats in 1958 and held his seat in the 1961 general election. In 1963 both of the party's TDs joined the Labour Party. He lost his seat in 1965 but was re-elected in 1969. At the 1973 general election he was not nominated for the *Dáil* but won a seat on the *Seanad*. In 1977, he was again elected for Labour but left the party and won a seat for the Socialist Labour party in 1981. He retired from politics in 1981 and died in 1997.

22 Donagh O'Malley, a native of Limerick City and affectionately known as 'the School Man', was arguably one of the most dynamic ministers in post-war Irish history. He was born in 1921 and was first elected to *Dáil Éireann* in the 1954 general election in the constituency of Limerick East. He retained his seat at each subsequent election until his death. O'Malley had been Mayor of Limerick before entering the *Dáil* but will be forever remembered for his dynamism as a Minister for Education. While in the office, Patrick Hillery had commissioned the Investment in Education report. In 1966, having succeeded Hillery, O'Malley introduced free secondary school education. He extended the school transport scheme and commissioned the building of new non-denominational comprehensive and community schools in areas where they were lacking.

O'Malley also introduced Regional Technical Colleges (RTCs) now called Institutes of Technology in areas where there was no third-level college nearby. The best example of this successful policy is Limerick, which is now a university. He remained a minister until his death. O'Malley had previously served as Minister for Health (1965–66) before moving to the Department of Education. Donagh O'Malley died in 1968.

23   Indira Gandhi, Prime Minister of India from 1966 to 1977 and 1979 to 1984, the only child of Jawaharlal Nehru, was born in 1917. Her marriage to Feroze Gandhi in 1942 was almost universally denigrated by orthodox Hindus because it was an intercommunal love marriage, not arranged by her parents. Arrested and jailed for nationalist activities shortly after their marriage, Indira was jailed for eight months and Feroze for a year. On her release, Indira became the principal confidant and hostess of her father during the period of Nehru's prime ministership (1947–65). Indira Gandhi was chosen as party leader and Prime Minister by party bosses 'the Syndicate' within the Congress party in January 1966. At first, Indira was pliable and compromising but after the Congress party suffered unprecedented defeats in the 1967 national elections, she became more assertive and opted for a series of choices that pitted her directly against the Congress party high command, which had previously been built by her father. As a consequence of her backing V.V. Giri for the presidency of India in 1969 and her activities in subsequent election campaigns, Mrs Gandhi caused a major split in the Congress party, resulting in the eventual acceptance by the election commission of the official name Congress Party-Indira (or Congress-I) to describe the party led by Mrs Gandhi. Indira's Congress-I gained an unprecedented two-thirds majority in both houses of parliament in the early 1970s and overwhelming victory in the 1971 elections fought under the slogan *garibi hatao* (abolish poverty). In 1971, her New Congress government waged a successful war against Pakistan. Expectations raised by the *garibi hatao* campaign and India's victory over Pakistan in 1971 led to great disappointment and political difficulties in the mid-1970s, owing in part to the severe economic problems associated with a sixteen-fold increase in world oil prices between 1973 and 1975 but also to the inclination of Mrs Gandhi's insecurity in the face of mounting political and economic problems and her open attempts to thrust her sons, Sanjay and Rajiv, forward as successors to her leadership. In June 1975, Mrs Gandhi took the unprecedented but constitutional step of jailing her opponents under emergency provisions of the constitution after she had been convicted in the Allahabad High Court of two charges of electoral impropriety. The so-called emergency lasted until March 1977 when lower castes and minorities deserted the New Congress in a national election and it was defeated by a coalition of parties known as the *Janata Morcha*. Factionalism among the *Janata* partners and their inability to succeed in bringing Mrs Gandhi to trial resulted in the defeat of the *Janata* government in the 1979 elections and the return of Mrs Gandhi's Congress-I to a dominant position in Indian politics. After Mrs Gandhi's return to power, her government was confronted with serious challenges to its ability to maintain law and order as conflicts between religious and ethnic groups broke out in different parts of the country. As a result, Mrs Indira Gandhi became the target of Sikh anger and on 31 October 1984, she was assassinated by Sikh members of her bodyguard.

24   Golda Meir was born on 3 May 1898. She moved from Kiev to Milwaukee with her family in 1906. She married Morris Myerson, moved to Palestine, became an officer of the Histradut Trade Union and was active in politics. In 1948, Meir was

appointed a member of the Provisional government. After independence, she became Israel's Ambassador to the Soviet Union and in 1949 was elected to the Knesset and served as Minister of Labour from 1949–56 and as Foreign Minister from 1956–66. Meir became Secretary General of the new Labour party and on the sudden death of Levi Eshkol in 1969, she became Premier at the age of 70. Golda Meir was Prime Minister of Israel from 1969–74. The Yom Kippur War was fought during her term in office, beginning with the Egyptian and Syrian assaults of 6 October 1973. Meir resigned in 1974 after the end of the war and Yitzhak Rabin assumed the office of Prime Minister. She died in 1978.

25   Mrs Barbara Castle was elected MP for Blackburn in 1945. She held the seat for more than thirty years. Following Labour's defeat in 1970, Mrs Castle held a number of posts on the opposition bench and spent some time on the back benches. Barbara Castle was one of the most impressive politicians of her generation, at the peak of her influence in partnership with Prime Minister Harold Wilson. She was respected for her intellect and feared for her sharp tongue. She was an ambitious, feisty and powerful woman long before Margaret Thatcher arrived on the scene.

26   Elizabeth Leseur was born in Paris in 1866. She led an active social life whilst practising sanctity within her married life. Among her writings was a *Spiritual Journal* in which she prays for the conversion of her atheist husband Felix. She died in 1914.

27   Interestingly, an article dated 10 December 1970 and entitled '*Dáil* should have more Women' was found among Sherwin's papers which included many newspaper cuttings. It was submitted by Veronica Hartland, a peace commissioner in Cobh. Unfortunately the name of the newspaper was not included although it was marked 'H' in blue pen, perhaps referring to *The Evening Herald.*

7

THE TURNOVER TAX

During all of the time that I was a member of the *Dáil*, I never had any discussions with the *Taoiseach* or any other minister regarding my vote for the government. I was satisfied that the government was doing well. The economic position of the country was improving. We were becoming more industrialized and we were exporting more. These were matters that the man or woman on the street does not understand. They take improvements for granted. It takes time however for results to show. Every year there is increased taxation because all improvements must be paid for. Again, the average person does not understand the need for more taxation, and opponents of whatever government is in power, appeal to this lack of understanding. Increased taxation does not matter as long as the standard of living continues to improve and it can be proved that, despite taxation over the years, the standard of living has improved further. Every time there are increased wages, all government employees, e.g. civil servants, soldiers, *gardai*, etc., also get increases as well as approximately 300,000 people on social benefits. All prices go up following an increase in wages so the government and the local authorities have to pay this extra cost. The average person might see this point if it was explained in simple language to him. However, selfishness or lack of awareness suppresses logic, and political opponents of the government are always awaiting the opportunity to misrepresent the government. Christ was asked in Jerusalem by some Pharisees: 'Should the people pay taxes to the Government?' He answered: 'Render unto Caesar the things that are Caesar's and unto God the things that are God's.' He was criticized for giving this advice so what chance has the mere human for being honest and responsible?

The first time that I heard of the turnover tax was in April 1963. I knew that all the Common Market countries we were going to join had this tax system. In fact, it was a condition of membership that this tax system be adopted. At present, the principle Common Market countries are using the new added value tax system and all other members or intending members must adopt this new system. The value added tax is much more severe on the working class than any other system. It benefits the business people at the expense of the workers. The *Fine Gael* leaders have advocated this new system many times and a Labour party sub-committee on finance recommended this new tax but as usual the Labour politicians don't like acting responsibly and all references to taxation is taboo until they get into power.

When the turnover tax was introduced in the 1963 budget, I examined it and found it was a very small tax. Proof of this is that it only produced £11 million, although it was put on everything. The government was in debt to the tune of £6 million because they had not provided for this money in the previous budget, so they were only looking for an extra £5 million, which they intended to give to people on social benefits and milk producers to keep down the price of milk. The government gave increased children's allowances to offset this tax. The tax was a godsend to the opposition, as they knew that the government only held power by one vote. Obviously all of the big moneyed people were against this tax because they were being asked to make up accounts when refunding the tax to the government. They also did not like the idea of paying tax on the interest on their bank account and particularly the fact that the revenue people would know how much they were making. They could not swindle the revenue so easily once their accounts were known. They were the real opponents of the tax. In fact, they had a parade of 8,000 cars from all over the country which passed the *Dáil.* As I said at the time, they were not the old age pensioners or the unemployed. They represented over £100 million: the wealth of the country. To think, that the hypocritical Labour party joined in with the wealth of the country to defeat this tax which could do so much national good, all because they wanted political power. They were prepared to sell James Connolly and their soul for power and position. They realized that if there was a general election with everyone worked up against the government, they and *Fine Gael* could get a majority without needing to depend on Independents or small parties. They also made an all-out effort to bribe or frighten me into withdrawing my support from the government, after realizing my influence following a leading article in *The Irish Times,* where they hailed me as 'the lynch-pin that kept the Government in power'. Threats never frightened me and the more I was threatened, the more defiant I became. Having failed, they and *Fine Gael* decided to slander me.

I saw nothing wrong with the tax. There is an increase in taxation in every country every year. It does not matter if taxation is increased as long as wages and benefits are also increased. The government had to get the £11 million and if there was a change of government, the new government would have to increase taxation by that amount. This tax was small because it was enforced on everything and you only paid according to what you had to spend. The workers paid much less by this tax than they would by any other tax. If income tax was increased, the workers in Dublin would have to pay a lot more than they would under the turnover tax because country people don't pay income tax. Therefore, city workers would have to pay the compatriot's share of taxation. When the turnover tax was introduced by the government, I decided to support the government, not the tax, although I knew that the tax was necessary, albeit unpopular. A *Radio Éireann* compere asked some beer drinkers on an after-dinner show if they would continue to buy pints of stout if the price was increased to eight shillings a pint.[1] The compere was referring to future prices.[2] Some of the people who were obviously mugs, and I am not talking about beer mugs, assured him that they would stop drinking. These are the people, and there are many such people, that politicians love to lobby. They are the kind of people who politicians say would buy O'Connell Bridge. They do not think. They do not reflect. They are pushovers from the word go. Other pint drinkers were not so asinine. They answered that it would not matter as long as wages and benefits increased accordingly. If every member of the public gave such questions a little thought and a little objectivity without prejudice, we would have more responsible, more honest people in public life. The press do their best, but so far radio, and particularly television, have utterly failed. It could be that because they are under government control they are afraid of being objective in their approach because frank discussion about politics would show up the ambiguity that is an essential part of the game. We have had political broadcasts but they are only a rehash of the lying and the double talk in the *Dáil* or at the hustings. During a general election, the parties monopolize the radio and television. Independents, who alone may talk the truth, are barred.

Although I played a vital part in keeping a stable government in power and although I was the most slandered and misrepresented member of the *Dáil*, I never got a single chance to put my point of view across on television. Regularly, people of no consequence and even petty criminals can use television, and these people are much sought after. The turnover tax was a tax of sixpence in the £1 on money spent but there was no tax on rent, bus fares or insurance. For example, a labourer who had about £10 a week in 1963 paid tax on about £8 if he spent all his money. In other words, the tax cost him four shillings weekly, but to offset this tax, all families with children got two shillings and sixpence weekly for the first child and one shilling and one penny and one ha'penny for every child born thereafter. Thus, a couple with one child had only to pay one shilling and sixpence a week, and a family with three children paid four pence ha'penny weekly. A family with five children got five shillings and ten pence ha'penny altogether. They had only to pay four shillings tax a week. Now, because of all the propaganda about the tax, all workers got a wage increase of 12 per cent on their total wage. In other words, the man who paid four shillings tax got an increase of twenty-four shilllings. If he was a tradesman, he probably got about £2 to £3 increase for a tax of about six shillings, and all of this was over and above the increase in children's allowances. So what was all the complaining about? All the workers were making a small fortune out of the tax, at least a small fortune compared to the small tax. Later, many food stores charged no tax so a lot of people got children's allowance and a significant wage increase for little or no tax. They still have this wage increase in their wage structure.

It was the shopkeepers and the big moneyed people who paid most of the tax. The workers had the best time of their lives. On several occasions, prominent members of the *Fine Gael* party, both in the *Dáil* and on television, said that the economy was upset because the workers got too much when they got the 12 per cent increase in wages following the introduction of the turnover tax. If they got too much, then what were they moaning about? Is it that the party politicians are right, that they are chumps one and all? Or is it that the Labour party, who are the mentors of many workers, are more corrupt than other parties because they worked them up to make them think that they were losing rather than gaining? I had two motions on the *Dáil* agenda when the tax was introduced. Motion one: That all disabled people get the same increase as other social beneficiaries and that their account be taken out of the Health Account where they had received nothing for six years and put into the social welfare account. The second motion was very important: That all people on social benefits in future receive increases in proportion to wage increases and that these benefits are increased to a specific level. In the past, these people only got one shilling or one shilling and sixpence or at most two shillings and sixpence and in some years they got nothing. How could I expect the government to accept these motions if I was not prepared to vote the money? Only hypocrites would refuse to vote money. The opposition never had a better chance of annihilating *Fianna Fáil* because almost everyone was worked up to oppose the tax. I alone stood in their way. I received many deputations from business interests who promised me maximum support in the event of an election. The Labour party offered to make me Lord Mayor if I agreed to vote against the tax.

Following a meeting of Dublin City Council on 17 June 1963, I was lobbied by four Labour councillors. Their spokesman was Captain James Kelly, the leader of the Dublin rate payers in the Corporation, who was anxious for an election.[3] With me when the offer was made was Alderman Tom Stafford.[4] I stated the above, giving the names of the two witnesses, Captain Kelly and Alderman Stafford in *The Evening Herald*.[5] My statement was not challenged. I refused their support under such conditions. The outgoing Lord Mayor was Alderman James O'Keefe, TD. It was my vote that made him Lord Mayor. He was the leader of the *Fine Gael* group. He had promised me that he would get me *Fine Gael* support if I was nominated for the mayoralty, but because of the turnover tax issue he told me that he would have to consult James Dillon TD, leader of *Fine Gael* in the *Dáil*. He told me later that Dillon had told him that it would be all right to support me but that it would depend on whether I was going to vote for the tax or not.

There was an organized campaign of blackmail by members of RGDATA and other business people.[6] They induced shopkeepers in my area to send scores of telegrams to my home promising me full support if I voted against the government but opposition to re-election if I refused. They also organized a march to my home to intimidate my family and me. When I voted for the government, the opposition parties were instructed to attack me in the newspapers. I also received many filthy and insulting letters and Oliver J. Flanagan's slander in the *Dáil* was repeated, that being that I took a bribe from the government in exchange for my vote.[7] I received one letter with a 3.03 rifle bullet enclosed and a statement that they should have finished me off in 1922, that they should have murdered me.

NOTES

1   Sherwin is referring to a radio programme which was aired on 25 February 1970. *The Radio Éireann Authority* was set up under the terms of the Broadcasting Authority Act 1960 to provide television and radio services to the Republic of Ireland. The name was changed to the *Radio Telefís Éireann Authority* in 1966. Television services commenced on New Year's Eve 1961.

2   The phrase 'future prices' refers to the prices of 1980.

3   Captain Kelly was later District Justice. There was another James Kelly, a captain in the Irish army who was ordered to go to Belfast to help the IRA with arms. He was said to have discussed 'smuggling' in 1969 and met Gerry Adams in 1970.

4   Thomas Stafford, Councillor and Lord Mayor of Dublin 1967–68. His son is Councillor Tom Stafford of the *Fianna Fáil* party and member of Dublin City Council for the North Inner City local electoral area. He lost his seat in the 1999 local elections but regained it in the 2004 local elections. His other son, Councillor John Stafford, also of *Fianna Fáil*, was Lord Mayor of Dublin (1997–98). In an article written by journalist Isabel Hurley entitled 'Millennium

needle gets Council green light' which appeared in *The Irish Independent* dated Tuesday 2 March 1999, both brothers are referred to. Dublin City Council had given the green light to the controversial £40m stainless steel spike monument for O'Connell Street. Councillor John Stafford had voted for it describing it as 'a beacon of light' whereas his brother, Councillor Tom Stafford, objected, saying it was 'nothing to write home about'.

5   This statement was dated 13 March 1968.

6   RGDATA stands for the Retail, Grocery, Dairy and Allied Trades' Association. RGDATA was formed in 1942 and acts as the representative body for the independent retail grocery sector in Ireland.

7   Oliver J. Flanagan (1920–87) was first elected to *Dáil Éireann* in 1943 as an Independent TD for the Laois/Offaly constituency. He is most remembered for a notorious speech he gave in the *Dáil* in 1943 when he advocated 'routing the Jews out of the country'. In 1973 he joined the Cabinet of Liam Cosgrave as a minister in the national coalition government. He served until 1977 and retired from the *Dáil* in 1987. Flanagan was renowned as a right-wing politician. He famously quoted on the Irish chat show 'The Late Late Show' that there was 'no sex in Ireland before television'. This quotation alludes to the changing social order after the arrival of that medium into Ireland.

8

SLANDER IN THE *DÁIL*

The election of Lord Mayor took place on Monday 25 June 1963. I could have been Lord Mayor that night had I agreed to vote against the government. The mayoralty is worth a few thousand pounds and you live the 'life of Reilly' for twelve months. You also get many presents. In fact, had I voted against the government, I might have been Lord Mayor for several years, as the *Fine Gael*–Labour government, which would certainly have been elected, would have let me continue for a few years. I would have headed the poll in the subsequent general election and perhaps have had my son elected, as they would have wanted my support. I had everything to gain but I refused to play the hypocrite, since I was convinced that you could not help people without money. I was further convinced that the tax was very small and that the workers would gain, as they would get an increase in wages as well as the increased children's allowances. I asked the *Fianna Fáil* members to support me for the mayoralty but the majority refused. They wanted the mayoralty for themselves. They did not care how I voted in the *Dáil*, which goes to show that most party members don't care about their party's welfare and are only using it for their own ends. The vote on the turnover tax was on Tuesday 26 June, the day after the mayoralty vote.

On the night of Tuesday 26 June 1963, a deputation of women from my constituency called on me in the *Dáil*. I saw them in the restaurant. They told me that if I voted against the tax that I would get their support. They then presented me with a testimonial signed by over 1,500 women members of my constituency. I told them that I was an Independent and would use my own judgement and that I would not be bullied. Later, at about 8.30 p.m., I was approached in the *Dáil* bar by a prominent member of the *Fine Gael* party who was also a barrister. He took a large wad of notes from his jacket and told me that it was all mine if I voted against the government. I told him to go away. I moved to another table and he followed me and again pressed me to take the money. I was with Mr Patrick Campbell PC at the time. Campbell had to tell him to leave.

The government won by one vote. Jim Carroll TD, who had voted for Mr Lemass all along, voted against the government. According to several *Fine Gael* deputies, Carroll was watching me closely to see which way I was voting, because if I voted against the government he was ready to vote for the government in order to avoid an election. I am satisfied that the opposition had no interest in the people or the tax. They saw a great opportunity to get back into power and that was their main concern. The people had everything to lose if this happened, as the opposition had no policy and would have taxed the people worse than the government, as they had done previously. The opposition was in power on two occasions. They formed a coalition government comprising several parties. The first was elected on 18 February 1948 and remained in power until 7 May 1951. During the election campaign Deputy O'Higgins, one of the *Fine Gael* leaders ,said in Cork: 'If we are elected, we will reduce taxation.'[1] Mr Liam Cosgrave announced at Dún Laoighaire: 'We will reduce expenditure.'[2] Mr Donnellan, leader of *Clann na Talmhan*: 'We will reduce taxation.'[3] Mr Everett, Labour leader, declared in Arklow that if they were elected, they would remove the means test in the case of applicants for social benefits.[4] Notice how they all promised to reduce taxation. In other words, they were not going to help people in need. On the other hand, Mr Everett promised that there would be no means test, which would have cost £3 million. They were all ministers in the new government but none of their promises was carried out. In fact, taxation increased.

The next coalition government was elected on 2 June 1954 and remained in power until 12 February 1957. During the election campaign, Mr Norton, Labour leader, announced: 'We will reduce prices.'[5] Labour claimed that they would reduce the cost of beer, spirits and cigarettes, give pensions at sixty-five for men and sixty for women, speed up housing, lower interest rates on loans for housing, review income tax, extend health services and amend the Managerial Act.[6] Mr Everett, Labour leader, remarked: 'It is tragic to see all the building workers idle and the mass emigration.'[7] Mr John A. Costello, leader of *Fine Gael*, stated: 'We are never again going to allow the unemployed to be neglected, that they have to lie down on the streets of Dublin, to force a change in government policy which all reason had failed to secure.'[8] Mr Norton, leader of the Labour party said: 'All social benefits will be increased.'[9] The *Fine Gael* election appeal read: 'Your rent and rates are increasing. You don't want to emigrate.'[10] Mr Heffernan, *Fine Gael* leader, declared that, if elected, they would put a stop to emigration.[11] Mr Keyes, Labour, announced: 'There will be work for all.'[12] Mr Costello, leader of *Fine Gael*, affirmed: 'We will reduce taxation and increase social benefits.' None of these promises was carried out. In fact, the country nearly collapsed.

Mr Corish said: 'The vital issues are the cost of living and unemployment. Food prices should be reduced and all social benefits increased.'[13] Corish went on to say at the Labour Annual Conference at Limerick: 'I cannot abolish the means test in the case of applicants for social benefits; it would cost £4 million.'[14] At the same conference Corish answered in reply to a motion by delegates that children's allowances should be allowed in the case of children still at school, up to the age of 18 years. He also stated that allowances should be the same as in Britain and that such a motion would cost £12 million. Notice how the minister is concerned about the cost of everything but the cost is immaterial when out of power.[15] Mr McCabe, a delegate, asked Mr Norton, Labour leader and the Minister for Industry and Commerce, about his promise to reduce prices. He received no answer. Notice how Mr Everett, the then Minister for Justice, had previously promised that the means test would be abolished. Mr Jim Larkin, Labour, asserted: 'Labour is pledged to reduce food prices.'[16] Mr Noël Browne, TD, who became a leader of the Labour Party but then a *Fianna Fáil* candidate in the 1954 general election, announced: 'If prices were to be reduced to the 1951 level it would cost £18 million. Where would the government get the money?'[17] He was a member of a responsible party then so he faced up to realities. However, he does not do that now. He talks about increased benefits, but like all of his former Labour colleagues, never mentions the heinous yet necessary words: increase taxation to achieve results. Mr Norton, Labour leader declared: 'We aim to bring down prices and reduce unemployment.'[18] Norton went on to say: 'Our terms for joining the Coalition: prices must come down. Unemployment must come down.'

The coalition's first budget of 1955 increased taxation by £1 million. Only non-contributory old-age pensioners got two shillings and sixpence. There was no reduction in prices. Their second budget of 1956 increased taxation by £6.5 million. They increased cigarettes by five pence on twenty and sixpence on an ounce of tobacco, they added sixpence to a gallon of petrol, a ha'penny to a box of matches, and a 10 per cent betting tax; and they re-introduced the tax on dancing, a tax on minerals and an extra £500,000 increase on postal charges. The five pence on cigarettes was like one shilling in 1972 and they had promised to reduce prices. The plain truth is, if there is no increased taxation, there can be no increased benefits unless you get a loan of money but loans have to be paid back with interest. When the coalition government was in power in 1949, they had a deficit of £9 million at budget time. To avoid large-scale taxation, they raised a loan of £12 million to pay their way. This policy could lead to bankruptcy. People are selfish or perhaps uninformed. You have to be a hypocrite to get their support or, as Dan Breen said: 'You must be a crook.' There will always be an army of hatchet men in politics who are not interested in telling the truth, if they are to survive.

One of the chief reasons Christ was crucified was the fact that He was not on the side of the political religious *Sanhedrin*.[19] The party hatchet men worked up the mob against Him, although Pilate, the Roman governor, held that He was innocent of any crime. It is the same in politics. You are a villain if you are on the other side and you are no use if you are not on their side. When he was an Independent Dr Noël Browne said on television that no matter how you voted in the *Dáil*, you were attacked by the other side. Speaking of taxation; when the British government decided to give old-age pensions for the first time in 1909, they increased beer prices to help pay for it. As the British Parliamentary Party got a lot of their funds from publicans and the breweries, they voted against the budget. This was hypocrisy but considered good politics. In Victor Lasky's *John Fitzgerald Kennedy: the Man and the Myth*, Kennedy is quoted as saying that no matter how you vote, somebody is happy and somebody is unhappy.[20] If you vote against enough people you are dead politically. If you vote for everybody but against the tax to pay for it, you might as well be dead politically because you are useless. Dr Hjalmar Schacht, German Finance Minister to Hitler and economic expert who helped Hitler to finance the war, said that within a national economy, one man can enrich himself at the expense of another.[21] They lose what the other gains. Taxation legislation sees to it that inequality between rich and poor does not become too great but it is impossible to distribute more than is produced. It is said that this home truth has to be repeated continuously. Cardinal Richelieu, who was Prime Minister of France, stated that he felt sorry for the poor but as he wrote philosophically he remarked that only God can make something out of nothing and he was not God and taxation ... that which is intolerable in their nature, becomes excusable and necessary.[22] You can neither do anything nor give anything without taxation and those who talk about reliefs while at the same time singing dumb about taxes to pay for them are liars and hypocrites of the first order. The late Senator James Dunne, Labour, was quoted in *The Irish Times* as saying that it is not the fault of the workers that the economic facts of life ... have been made almost unintelligible to them.[23] The fact of the workers being ignorant of the economic facts of life is the Labour party's fault – they have a stake in workers' ignorance. They can promise the workers the moon and never mention the cost. They are satisfied that the workers will forget to ask that question.

In view of the many irresponsible promises to get votes in the 1954 general election, let's see what happened. The old-age pensioners got only two shillings and sixpence in 1955 and nothing in 1956. The Provisional United Trade Unions complained that they were alarmed at the rise in unemployment.[24] The Dublin Trade Union Council demanded a meeting of the *Dáil*,[25] stating that the government had no policy and has failed ignominiously to carry out its programme: 'Four hundred unemployed hold protest meeting at the Labour Exchange, Werburgh Street.' Another statement read: 'Four hundred workers on short-time at Waterford.'[26] The Transport Union declared: 'Registered unemployed now 100,000.'[27] The municipal authorities of Ireland stated: 'This is the worst emergency ever.'[28] The unemployed march in O'Connell Street carrying banners stating: '16,000 live in slums and no work.'[29] The Dublin County Council manager stated that: 'Loans under Small Dwelling Act are suspended because of scarcity of money.' Victor Carton, chairman of the Housing Committee declared: 'The building trade in the country is ghastly. Building has almost come to a standstill.' Prices increased, taxation increased and old-age pensioners got only two shillings and sixpence in two years. Emigration rose to almost 100,000 in 1956 and the figure for registered unemployed was 100,000 in January 1957, with half of the building workers sitting idle. I mention all of this to show how politicians will make outrageous promises while keeping silent about taxation with a view to deceiving voters, especially workers, who, as Senator James Dunne said, 'don't know the economic facts of life'.

During the discussion on the turnover tax, Oliver J. Flanagan TD accused the government of doing a deal with a millionaire ice-cream merchant to introduce the tax.[30] Brian Lenihan, a parliamentary secretary, shouted: 'Perjurer!'[31] He was referring to evidence that Flanagan had given in a court case which three judges had refused to accept. Mr Lenihan later exclaimed: 'You have the dirtiest tongue in Irish public life. That is well known.'[32] He again shouted: 'Dirty Pup!'[33] Mr MacEntee, Minister for Health, proclaimed: 'Did not three judges find that Deputy Flanagan was a perjurer?'[34] Flanagan then uttered: 'Surely the Minister for Finance heard the rumours afloat in this city that both Deputy Sherwin and Deputy Leneghan got £3,500 cash for their votes.'[35] He also declared that there was a rumour in the House that Deputy Sherwin got an IRA pension and four or five years' back money to vote for the tax.[46] Mr Lenihan, a parliamentary secretary, again shouted at Flanagan: 'You are the lowest thing in Irish public life today!' Dr Ryan, Minister for Finance added: '...and the most cowardly!'[37] I was not in the House at this time but when I was told, I made for the *Dáil* chamber and shouted at Flanagan: 'That is a lie!'[38] I asked the *Ceann Comhairle* for time to answer Flanagan. The *Ceann Comhairle* told me that if I gave notice, I would be allowed to make a statement. I told the House that Flanagan represented the *Fine Gael* party who had crippled me for life in 1922. I called them a lot of murderers. I had never been personal in the House and I never referred to the Civil War but here was a deputy, known to be a slanderer and a thug, accusing me of getting a pension for voting for the government when, in fact, I had been suffering for forty years and lost a fortune because those whom Flanagan represented had tortured me five times when I was arrested and kept me in several jails for twenty months. I saw red! So would anyone had they been in my position.

On 19 July 1963, I explained to the House that there was no truth in anything that Flanagan had said. I called him a 'Dirt-Bird' which was true, because he was always slandering or abusing people. Some years before, he had given evidence on oath in the famous Locke Distillery case. When the three judges were summing up, they affirmed that they did not believe Flanagan's evidence. When Mr Lenihan shouted 'Perjurer!' he was referring to this case. Flanagan replied that *Fianna Fáil* had bribed the three judges. Although Flanagan maintained there was a rumour in the House, no other deputy admitted that they had heard such a rumour. No other deputy supported Flanagan. In fact, several *Fine Gael* deputies, including Maurice Dockrell, a prominent member of *Fine Gael*, said to me that same night that Flanagan should be thrown out of the *Fine Gael* party.[39] Flanagan never repeated this slander outside the confines of the *Dáil*, where anything, including slander, is privileged, thus depriving me of the chance to take him to court.

The pension that Flanagan referred to was a disability pension. Such pensions are granted by a medical board and not by ministers or governments. I actually refused to accept this same pension in 1937 and in not accepting it I sacrificed several thousand pounds. I originally asked for the pension under the Pension Act of 1932 but was told that I could only succeed under the Pension Act of 1937, so on principle I refused to apply. I applied under the Pension Act of 1937 in 1962 and was awarded a wound pension of 50 per cent. Later the Medical Board increased this disability to 100 per cent as they found other injuries. I had been examined in 1933, 1942, 1960 and again in January 1963 by medical boards. Electric plates were applied to all of the nerves of my fingers, arms, legs and other parts of my body. There was no reaction to electrical tests in many parts of my body, including my right hand. The chief medical officer was Dr Hogan, who had been on the board for thirty years and was an officer of the Free State Army, which had fought against the Republicans in the Civil War. The pension was small, not worth talking about. I did not accept it until I lost my seat in the *Dáil* in 1965. The full pension was three pounds and five shillings a week. The rate then paid to families on unemployment assistance was four pounds two shillings and sixpence a week for a man and his wife and four dependent children. I had a wife and four dependent children when I lost my seat in the *Dáil* so I had seventeen shillings and sixpence less than a man on the dole who had no stamps, and I had no other income as I had no job or business. It would have paid me to tell the Pension Board to keep their pension, as I could have drawn the dole and got seventeen shillings and sixpence more, plus other amenities. Flanagan asserted that I had got four or five years' pension retrospectively, which was another lie. It is on record that I got six weeks' pension retrospectively and to get this small pension, I was suffering hell from physical weakness while others who never served the country and who were not suffering any ill health were getting seventeen shillings and sixpence more.[40] It's ironic, when you think of it!

Fianna Fáil never gave me the itch and I never had any consultations with them. As I have said, I acted on principle but many deputies, including *Fianna Fáil* deputies, told me that I was a fool. They said that I should have run with the crowd. They said that they would have run with the crowd had they been in my place, even if the crowd were wrong and ignorant. You can judge the morality of politics by the following report which appeared in *The Irish Times*:

> It has been said yesterday in Leinster House, that even if Sherwin and Lenihan had been absent when the vote took place, that arrangements had been made for certain opposition deputies to be absent as they did not want a general election.[41]

This was the feeling among the ordinary deputies but the 'brass-hats' wanted an election because they were certain to be returned and they were also certain to be ministers. An *Irish Times* 'leader column' claimed: 'The tax is a God-send to the opposition group. They would be more than human and less than political if they did not fan the flames of discontent.'[42]

On 2 May 1963, the front page of *The Irish Times* announced: 'Bankers alarmed: Large numbers of depositors are withdrawing their money because they will have to pay turnover tax on their bank interest. They also object to the revenue people knowing how much money they are banking.' During the debate on the turnover tax,

8,000 cars from all parts of the country representing the wealth of the country passed the *Dáil* as a protest against the tax. In other words, the so-called Labour party joined hands with the wealthy people of the country to defeat the government so that they would become ministers in a government. The wealthy people and the business people know the economic facts of life. They knew that they were going to lose by the tax. On the other hand, the workers do not know the economic facts of life; at least they do not understand economics. They depend on the advice of people like those in the Labour party. Dr Schacht, the German economic expert said: 'One section of the community loses what the other section gains', and that is a fundamental truth. So if the people with the bank accounts and all the business people were going to lose, then the ordinary people stood to gain. *The Irish Times* 'leader column' stated:

> We have said that we believe Mr Dillon, leader of *Fine Gael*, has not put before the country any programme which reflects serious thinking in the light of the times. There is a measure of justice in Mr Lemass's charge that *Fine Gael* has offered to improve the condition of everyone without making it clear to which the bill is to be presented.[43]

The Irish Independent read: 'Taxation would benefit old-age, widows, the blind and other social welfare services. However, it could not be done without adjustments in taxation.'[44] Mr Corish exclaimed at Mallow, Cork: 'Some of Labour's aims are not possible for twenty years.' He continued: 'Labour would not say where the money would come from until they got into office.' You can judge the opposition by *The Irish Times'* view of Mr Dillon's policy and Mr Corish's statement at Mallow. It was like asking the price of a suit or dress and being told: 'You will be told the price after you have bought the article.' Few people would buy under those conditions, not even the most ignorant, but in politics they are buying 'a pig in a poke' every day of the week.

Mr Oliver J. Flanagan was a baffling character. He was once secretary of a *Fianna Fáil Cumann*. He later stood as a monetary reform Independent candidate and was elected to the *Dáil*. When I was chairman of a debating society in about 1945, I invited him to speak about monetary reform. He admitted that he knew little about the subject and I am not aware that he ever spoke about it in the *Dáil*. He later joined *Fine Gael* and became a parliamentary secretary. He is a TD for Laois/Offaly and received the highest vote ever – 19,000 on one occasion, although he used numerous political tricks to advance himself politically. He was always in contact with his constituents, who included priests and nuns, but unfortunately he was forever attacking political opponents and was always personal. He posed as an honest representative, but would stop at nothing to achieve his own ends. He was a true disciple of Machiavelli. He uttered profanities and in his slanderous and personal attacks on people appealed to a like-minded level of the electorate, who in turn influenced weak-minded people among the working class. *The Irish Independent* 'leader' referring to Flanagan's slanderous statement asserted: 'Most of what was said was slanderous. Only parliamentary privilege prevents it from being otherwise.'[45] An *Independent* reporter proclaimed: 'One of the great problems is to protect deputies from unsubstantiated allegations and charges hurled across the floor and these charges are often believed by people outside.'[46]

Flanagan had bribery on the brain on the day that he started this trouble, the date being 17 July 1963. He inferred that the government was bribed by a millionaire ice-cream merchant. He also maintained that the purpose of the turnover tax was to put many shopkeepers out of business, and that this would enable the millionaire to open more ice-cream shops in O'Connell Street, Dublin, on the cheap.[47] Later, in answer to Mr MacEntee, Minister for Health, who had said that three judges had found Deputy Oliver J. Flanagan to be a perjurer, Flanagan answered that the three judges were bribed by Mr De Valera and Gerry Boland, Minister for Justice.[48] Later Flanagan alleged that there was a rumour in the city that Deputy Sherwin and Leneghan got £3,500 each to vote for the turnover tax, but when asked for evidence he answered: 'It was only a rumour.'[49] He later suggested that: 'there is a rumour widely circulating in the House that Deputy Sherwin has been given an IRA pension which is retrospective for the past four or five years'.[50] There was no rumour in the city or the House: it had been invented by Deputy Oliver J. Flanagan. Not one of the 143 deputies said that they had heard any such rumours.

In 1966, after I lost my *Dáil* seat, Flanagan made the mistake of slandering people outside the *Dáil.* He told *The Evening Press* that Mr Richard Deasy, Sean Healy, Secretary of NFO and six members of the committee took bribes from the Minister for Agriculture to call off a big protest march against the government.[51] He realized his mistake and agreed to apologize, pay a sum into a charity and pay all expenses. The miscreant never apologized for anything he said in the *Dáil* because he knew that he could not be got at there. If he ever repeats his slander against me in public he will be in court quick enough. Later Mr Oliver J. Flanagan suggested on Irish television that he believed in jobbery. In other words, he believed in giving priority to those who helped him or his party, i.e. securing jobs for them in front of others. Many of his colleagues called on him to resign from the party but he did not, nor was he expelled. Later again, when some Germans were attacked because they bought some land in this country, he supported the attacks and had the nerve to ask the German Consul to advise his countrymen not to buy land here. The land they bought was small and their capital and techniques were of benefit to this country. If this line was followed to its logical conclusion, then Enoch Powell,[52] the outspoken British Conservative MP, who said that all 700,000 Irishmen in Britain who claimed that they were Irishmen or citizens of the Irish Republic should be treated as foreigners and lose their privileges, would be justified. Oliver J. Flanagan's election, with such a high vote, is a reflection on the common sense of the people of Laois/Offaly and shows thoroughly bad taste.

NOTES

1   *The Irish Independent*, Monday 12 January, 1948, p. 7. Dr Thomas F. O'Higgins, brother of Kevin O'Higgins, was founder and first leader of the quasi paramilitary Army Comrades Association or 'Blueshirts'. O'Higgins served as TD for Laois-Offaly from 1932–54. He was leader of *Fine Gael* in the *Dáil* in 1944 while the Blueshirts' leader Richard Mulcahy was a member of the *Seanad*. O'Higgins served as Minister for Defence during the first inter-party government before becoming Minister for Industry and Commerce in March 1951.

2   *The Irish Independent*, Tuesday 3 February, 1948, p. 6.

3   Michael Donnellan (1900–64) was born in Dunmore, County Galway. He joined Sinn Féin after the Easter Rising and was elected as a councillor on Glenamaddy District Council in 1917. Donnellan served as a member of Galway City Council from 1927–45, originally as a member of *Fianna Fáil*. He became disenchanted with the party in the mid-1930s, as did many supporters in the Connacht province. He founded *Clann na Talmhan* in 1938, essentially a pressure group. However, in that same year a by-election was called in the constituency of Galway West and his supporters persuaded him to stand. Donnellan won 30 per cent of the votes cast. He was elected to *Dáil Éireann* as a TD for Galway West in the 1943 general election. However, he proved too radical for the party members from the province of Leinster and was soon replaced as party leader by Joseph Blowick. He made the decision to abstain on old party leader Éamon De Valera's nomination for *Taoiseach* in 1943. Donnellan served as a parliamentary secretary to the Minister for Finance from 1948–51 with responsibility for the Office of Public Works.

4   *The Irish Independent*, Monday 26 January 1948, p. 6. James Everett, Labour party TD for Wicklow, was first elected in 1923 and was re-elected at every subsequent election until his death in 1968. He became a founder member of the National Labour party in 1944 and was made its leader. Everett was elected twice for National Labour in 1944 and 1948 and led National Labour into the first inter-party government in 1948 during which he became Minister for Posts and Telegraphs. The National Labour party merged with the Labour party in 1950. Everett served as Minister for Justice in the government of the Fifteenth *Dáil* (1954–57).

5 William Norton (1900–63), former *Tánaiste* and leader of the Labour party, was first elected to the *Dáil* in 1932. He became leader of the Labour Party that year as Thomas O'Conner lost his *Dáil* seat. Norton led Labour into the first inter-party government in 1948, becoming *Tánaiste* and Minister for Social Welfare. During the government of the Fifteenth *Dáil* from 1954–57, Norton became *Tánaiste* again, this time as Minister for Industry and Commerce. He retired as Labour leader in 1960 and was replaced by Brendan Corish. Norton died in 1963.

6 *The Irish Independent*, Monday 5 April 1954, p. 8.

7 *The Irish Independent*, Friday 30 April 1954, p. 8.

8 *The Irish Independent*, Monday 3 May 1954, p. 8. John Aloysius Costello was born on 20 June 1891 and died on 5 January 1976. He acted as Attorney General of Ireland from 1926 to 1932, Parliamentary Leader of Fine Gael from 1948–59 and *Taoiseach* from 1948–51 and 1954–57.

9 *The Irish Independent*, Wednesday 5 May 1954. See page 12.

10 *The Irish Independent*, Wednesday 5 May 1954, p. 14.

11 *The Irish Independent*, Tuesday 17 May 1954, p. 10. Sherwin was referring to Michael Heffernan, TD for Tipperary and leader of the Farmers' Party or Farmers' Union, a political party in the Irish Free State between 1922 and 1932. Upon the Farmers' Party's decline, Heffernan joined *Cumann na nGaedheal* and contested in the 1932 General Election. *Fine Gael* was formed in 1932 when *Cumann na nGaedheal* merged with the National Centre Party of James Dillon and the National Guard (the quasi-military Blueshirts). However, upon inspection of the newspaper article, the party referred to is *Cine Gael* not *Fine Gael*. The *Cine Gael* Party was formed by a group of Republican ex-prisoners who felt that the voice of the younger generation had not been heard.

12 Michael J. Keyes, former Labour Party TD, Minister and Mayor of Limerick. Keyes was elected to *Dáil Éireann* in June 1927 but lost his seat in the September election of that year. Winning back his seat in Limerick in the 1933 general election, he was re-elected at every subsequent election until his retirement. During the first inter-party government, Keyes became Minister for Local Government following the death of Timothy Murphy in April 1948 and was subsequently appointed to the Cabinet from Limerick. Keyes was proposed by P.J. Donnellan to a vacancy in the Limerick Corporation following the death of Alderman Dan Bourke TD. He was withdrawn when it became apparent from the trend of the debate that he was unlikely to succeed. Joseph Patrick Liddy of *Fianna Fáil* was elected on the night of 17 May 1952. See 'Fifty years today', *The Limerick Leader*, Saturday 18 May 2002. Keyes became Minister for Posts and Telegraphs in 1954 during the government of the fifteenth *Dáil*. Keyes did not contest the 1957 general election and retired from public life. Keyes is the granduncle of Councillor Joe Leddin.

13 *The Irish Independent*, Friday 30 April 1954. Corish later became leader of The Labour Party, *Tánaiste* and Minister for Social Welfare.

14 *Ibid.*, Saturday 30 April, 1955. The cost here would equate to £10 million at the time of writing circa 1972. See column entitled: 'Social system changes urged: Labour leader deals with problems', p. 12.

15 *Ibid.*, Saturday 30 April 1955. Corish was then Minister for Social Welfare.

16 *The Irish Independent*, Friday 14 May 1954. See page 10. William Norton was leader of the Labour Party from 1932–60. Sherwin refers to 'Mr Jim Larkin, Labour leader…'. James Larkin Sr or 'Big Jim Larkin' joined with James Connolly in forming the Irish Labour Party in 1912. James Larkin Sr died in

1947. See note 6 p. 52. His son, Jim Larkin Jr, contested in the 1954 General Election and was a member of the fifteenth *Dáil* representing Dublin South Central. Upon inspection of the newspaper article, 'Mr Jim Larkin, Labour leader...' is incorrect. It should read 'Mr Jim Larkin, Labour...'.

17 The cost here would equate to £40 million at the time of writing c. 1972.

18 *Ibid.*, Friday 30 April 1954.

19 The *Sanhedrin* refers to the Jewish Parliament or council that controlled Jerusalem during the time of Christ.

20 Victor Lasky, first lieutenant in the United States army, newspaper journalist, long-time reporter and former syndicated columnist who lectured and wrote for *Accuracy in Media*, a watchdog organization in the late 1980s, was born in 1918. A native of Liberty, New York, Lasky was noted for his vocal criticism of communism and journalistic misconduct. Lasky began his journalistic career in 1940 as a copy boy at *The New York Journal American*. Later, he was a reporter for *The Chicago Sun*. In 1955, he wrote for RKO Radio. From 1956–60, he was Public Relations Executive with Radio Liberty in New York. He wrote a column for North American Alliance between 1962 and 1980. An anti-communist activist, co-founder and first Vice-President of the Council Against Communist Aggression, Lasky wrote on communist subversion and aggression from the Korean War to the Vietnam War. See *John Fitzgerald Kennedy: the Man and the Myth* (New York: Macmillan, 1963). Lasky is also the author of *Robert F. Kennedy: the Man and the Myth*.

21 Dr Horace Greely Hjalmar Schacht was born on 22 January 1877 in Tinglev, Germany. His mother, a Danish baroness, partially named him after American journalist Horace Greeley. Schacht became one of the directors of the Reichsbank in 1916 and in 1923 became currency commissioner for the Reich. Schacht was appointed President of the Reichsbank after his economic policies helped reduce inflation and stabilize the German *Mark*. He collaborated in the Young Plan to modify the way that war reparations were paid after Germany's economy was destabilizing under the Dawes Plan. Though never a member of the Nazi party, Schacht became influenced by Adolf Hitler after reading *Mein Kampf* and helped to raise funds for his Nazi party after meeting with him. Schacht organized German industrialists to sign a petition calling for President Paul von Hindenburg to appoint Hitler Chancellor of Germany in 1933. In August 1934, Hitler appointed Schacht Minister of Economics. He was appointed General Plenipotentiary for the War Economy in May 1935 and was awarded honorary membership of the Nazi Party and the Golden Swastika in January 1937. Schacht resigned as Minister of Economics and General Plenipotentiary in November 1937 due to his disapproval of Hitler's war aims and excessive military spending because he believed it would cause inflation, as well as conflicts with Hermann Göring, but was re-appointed President of the Reichsbank until he was dismissed from the position by Hitler in January 1939. Schacht instead held the title of Minister without Portfolio until he was fully dismissed in January 1943. Schacht was falsely accused of being involved in the 20 July 1944 plot to assassinate Hitler. He was arrested and sent to Dachau concentration camp as a 'special prisoner' until it was liberated in April 1945. He was arrested by the Allies and accused of war crimes at the Nuremberg Trials but was acquitted and released in 1946. He was again arrested by Germans, tried in a denazification court and sentenced to eight years in a work camp but was released early in September 1948. He formed the Düsseldorf Bank after his release and became economic and financial advisor for developing countries. Schacht died in Munich, Germany on 4 June 1970.

22 Cardinal Richelieu, 1585–1642, dominated the history of France from 1624 as Louis XIII's Chief Minister.

23 *The Irish Times*, Saturday 7 March 1970. Incidentally, a column entitled 'Inside politics' on p. 12 and 'A critical look at housing' by Kevin Delaney on p. 16 may be of interest

24 *The Irish Independent*, Saturday 14 December 1957, p. 9.

25 *The Irish Press*, Wednesday 2 January 1957, p. 5 entitled: 'Summon *Dáil*, say Unions.'

26 *The Irish Press* reports dated Thursday 10 January 1957, p. 5 entitled: '400 workers put on short-time in Waterford', and p. 6, article entitled 'Meetings of Dublin's unemployed'.

27 *Ibid.*, Wednesday 30 January 1957, p. 1 entitled: 'General election demand. *Fianna Fáil* tables a "no confidence motion"'. Another column was entitled: 'Union tells TD members "don't support Coalition"'.

28 *Ibid.*, Thursday 17 January 1957, p. 1. The article is entitled: '*Taoiseach* on unemployed', it continues on p. 7. Also on p. 7 there is an article entitled: 'Unemployed marched in protest.'

29 *Ibid.*, Tuesday 17 January 1956.

30 *Parliamentary Reports, Dáil Éireann*, 'Finance Bill 1963 Fifth Stage (Resumed), vol 204, 17 July 1963, col. 1296/7. 'I venture to say there are thousands of small shopkeepers in business today who will close down as a result of this tax. It will put them out of business. Mark you, the Government are out to close up the small shopkeeper and put him out of business. This tax was designed by the friend of the millionaire ice cream merchant for no other reason than to put the shopkeeper of Dublin and of the country generally out of business. The more shops there are for sale in O'Connell Street, the cheaper the ice cream merchant will get them.'

31 *Ibid.*, col. 1297. Brian Lenihan was born in Dundalk, County Louth in November 1930. He was first elected to *Dáil Éireann* in 1961 for the constituency of Roscommon, later Roscommon/Leitrim. He had been a candidate in the 1954 and 1957 general elections in Longford/Westmeath and Roscommon respectively. He served as Senator from 1957–61 and was Minister for Justice from October to November 1964 and from 1964–68; Minister for Education 1968–69 and Minister for Transport and Power 1969–73. Brian Lenihan lost his seat in the 1973 general election, having served as Minister for Foreign Affairs in the outgoing government. Following a term as Leader of *Seanad Éireann* from 1973–77, he contested the 1977 general election for the constituency of Dublin West and was re-elected at each subsequent election until his death. He was MEP and Leader of the *Fianna Fáil* delegation 1973–77; Minister for Forestry and Fisheries 1977–79; Minister for Foreign Affairs 1979–81; Minister for Agriculture from March to December 1982; deputy leader of *Fianna Fáil* from 1983–89; *Tánaiste* and Minister for Justice from 1989–90 and Presidential Candidate in 1990. Brian Lenihan died on 1 November 1995.

32 *Parliamentary Reports, Dáil Éireann*, 'Finance Bill 1963 Fifth Stage (Resumed), vol 204, dated 17 July 1963, col. 1300. Flanagan responded: 'There is no Deputy or Minister in this House will silence me, or muzzle me either – not the *Tánaiste*, the *Taoiseach* or Minister for Finance, and least of all, the Parliamentary Secretary, Deputy Lenihan' to which Seán MacEntee spurted: 'It is hard to muzzle an ass.'

33 *Ibid.*, col. 1303.

34 *Ibid.*, col. 1298. Seán MacEntee was born in Belfast in 1889. From a republican

background, he joined the Irish Volunteers and remained with the minority led by Eoin MacNeill who opposed fighting for Britain in the First World War. He took part in the Easter Rising and was imprisoned until 1917. He was elected an abstentionist Sinn Féin TD for Monaghan South at the 1918 general election. He was elected to the Second *Dáil* and during the Treaty debates he adopted an anti-Treaty position. He was one of the few TDs to voice concern over the partition of the country and the independence of the proposed Boundary Commission. He contested the 1923 general election as a Republican but failed to be elected. He became a founder member of *Fianna Fáil*, leaving the Sinn Féin *Ard Fheis* along with Éamon De Valera. He was elected a *Fianna Fáil* TD at the 1927 general election and he retained his seat at each subsequent election, for a number of Dublin constituencies until he retired from the *Dáil* before the 1969 general election. De Valera appointed him Minister for Finance (1932–39) in his first government and he remained a minister throughout De Valera's time as *Taoiseach*. He served as Minister for Industry and Commerce (1939–41); Minister for Local Government (1941–48) and Minister for Finance (1951–54). After Seán Lemass succeeded De Valera, MacEntee, along with Frank Aiken and Dr Jim Ryan, were the only three Cabinet members retained. MacEntee served as Minister for Health (1957–65); Minister for Social Welfare (1957–61) and *Tánaiste* (1959–65). He resigned as *Tánaiste* and Minister for Health after the 1965 general election, remaining a senior member of the party. Together with Frank Aiken, he supported George Colley against Jack Lynch after Lemass retired. He became a loyal supporter of Jack Lynch and was opposed to Charles J. Haughey. The last surviving member of the First *Dáil* and of De Valera's first Cabinet, Seán MacEntee died in Dublin on 10 January 1984.

35   *Parliamentary Reports, Dáil Éireann,* 'Finance Bill 1963 Fifth Stage (Resumed), vol 204, 17 July 1963, col. 1298 to which Lenihan shouted: 'He [Flanagan] is a contemptible little man!'

36   *Ibid.,* col. 1303.

37   *Ibid.,* col. 1303. A Deputy shouts: 'Dirt, Dirt, Dirt.'

38   *Ibid.,* col. 1303.

39   Maurice E. Dockrell, *Fine Gael* TD, was elected to the Eleventh and Twelfth *Dáil Éireann* (1943–44) representing Dublin South. He represented Dublin South Central in the Thirteenth to Eighteenth *Dáil* (1948, 1951, 1954, 1957, 1961 and 1965) and Dublin Central in the Twentieth *Dáil* in 1973.

40   All applicants for a pension under the Military Service Pensions Act, 1934 were required to submit an application containing an account of activities claimed. Each application was investigated by a Referee. The Referee was a member of the Judiciary and appointed by the Minister of Defence. The Referee had statutory powers to interview applicants and witnesses under oath. The sworn evidence, together with any supporting statements supplied on behalf of the applicant by his former officers was considered by the Referee, who furnished his findings to the Minister. The records in respect of Francis Sherwin, formerly of 11 Linen Hall Street, Dublin show that he applied in 1935 for a pension under the Military Service Pensions Act 1934, but following the normal detailed investigation, his application was unsuccessful. The records also show that Frank Sherwin applied in 1933 for a disability pension under the Army Pensions Act 1932, but the Army Pensions Board reported that he was not suffering from any disability attributable to service. He appealed this decision in 1943 and again in 1960 but the appeal was unsuccessful. Following the enactment of the Army Pensions Act 1962, his case as considered again and the Board reported in 1963

that Mr Sherwin's disability was attributable to his military service and he was awarded a disability pension payable from January 1963. However no payment was made as Mr Sherwin was not satisfied with the commencement date of the award and refused to accept the pension.

41   *The Irish Times*, Thursday 27 June 1963, p. 15: 'Turnover tax to meet more opposition'. Incidentally, most of this date's coverage was devoted to President JFK's visit to Ireland.

42   *Ibid.*, Tuesday 21 May 1963, p. 1 entitled: 'National protest against turnover tax planned'. See the Editor's Comment on p. 7 entitled: 'Unpsychological Tax'.

43   *Ibid.*, Thursday 13 June 1963, pp. 1 and 6.

44   *Ibid.*, Monday 5 April 1965, p. 11: 'Frances Condell's Monday chat about life in general'.

45   *Ibid.*, Thursday 18 July 1963, p. 13.

46   *Ibid.*, Friday 19 July 1963, p. 10.

47   *Parliamentary Reports, Dáil Éireann,* 'Finance Bill 1963 fifth stage (Resumed), vol 204, dated 17 July 1963, col. 1296/7.

48   *Ibid.* col. 1298. Oliver J. Flanagan stated: 'The three judges that Gerry Boland and De Valera bribed and got at.'

49   *Ibid.*, col. 1302. Oliver J. Flanagan answered: 'I said I heard rumours.'

50   *Ibid.* column 1303.

51   Flanagan is alleged to have made this remark to *The Evening Press* on Sunday 27 February 1966. Richard Deasy was President of the NFO (the National Farmers Organisation). It was founded in the mid-1950s to get a better deal for farmers when conditions on the land were dire. During the 1960s, the association came into strong conflict with the then *Fianna Fáil* government. Following a collapse in farm prices, Richard Deasy led a march from Bantry in County Cork to the capital.

52   John Enoch Powell MBE, poet and politician, was born in Birmingham on 16 June 1912 and died on 8 February 1998. At the outbreak of the Second World War, Powell enlisted in the Royal Warwickshire regiment and rose through the ranks from private to brigadier. He acted as political researcher to the Conservative party and was elected MP for Wolverhampton South-West in 1950 and held the seat for the next twenty-four years. He was sacked from the shadow Cabinet following his famous *Rivers of Blood* speech in Birmingham in April 1968 in which he challenged what he considered disastrously lax immigration policies. He was also firmly against joining the European Common Market, a part of the Conservative party manifesto. He dramatically quit his party, re-entering Parliament as a Unionist MP for the constituency of Down South, Northern Ireland, which he continued to represent until losing his seat in 1992.

9

THE IRISH TIMES LIBEL ACTION

The scenes in the *Dáil* took place on 17 July 1963. On the following Sunday, 21 July, *The Sunday Review*, a pictorial sensational type of newspaper, devoted the front page to the *Dáil* scenes.[1] They especially pinpointed my claim that I was crippled, implying that I was no cripple. They published two pictures of me – one cycling and another walking smartly into Leinster House.[2] The newspaper also referred to the fact that I had nine children and that I posted up my own election bills like an expert. The editor called himself 'Backbencher', a well-known reporter and writer by the name of John Healy who was also chairman of the Irish television programme *Hurlers on the Ditch*. He was later described by my counsel, Mr S. Heavey SC as 'a key-hole reporter'. He claimed to be a political expert and his column in *The Sunday Review* was entirely devoted to politics. He was prejudiced against the *Fianna Fáil* government and all those who supported that government. He was obviously *Fine Gael* in politics and a fan of Oliver J. Flanagan TD. He specialized in attacks on politicians and the scenes in the *Dáil* on 17 July were 'meat for his grinder'.

The Irish Times newspaper is considered a serious and objective paper but on 31 July 1963, in an article by the late Seán O'Riada entitled 'Plain Words', he implied that I took a bribe to vote for the government.[3] I instructed my solicitor Con Lehane to demand an apology from *The Irish Times* but they refused to oblige.[4] I took an action against *The Sunday Review* and *The Irish Times* and the case was heard in the High Court on 2 November 1964. At that time many were prejudiced against me because I had voted for the government on the turnover tax issue, especially business people or those with money in the bank. The opposition had worked the ordinary people up against me because they saw a chance of getting into power and I was the man who had prevented it. Under the existing circumstances, the jury was also likely to be prejudiced against me. I later found out that one of the jury was an ex-Free State officer who took an active part against the Republicans in the Civil War in 1922. Another member of the jury was a director of a bank that had shares in *The Irish Times*. I am satisfied that the majority of the jury were prejudiced against me. In political cases, and my case was one of those, there should be no jury. The case in the High Court lasted five days. The judge was Mr Justice Henchy; counsel for *The Irish Times* was Mr Kenny SC, Mr Crivon SC and Mr Fahy, instructed by Messrs. Hayes and Sons. My counsel was Mr T. Doyle, Mr S. Heavey SC and Mr Hamilton, instructed by Messrs. Lehane and Hogan. Before the action was heard in the High Court, the following correspondence took place between our respective solicitors:

1, Upper Ormond Quay,
Dublin 7.

1 August 1963.

Messrs. *Irish Times* Ltd,
31, Westmoreland Street,
Dublin.

Dear Sirs,
We act as solicitors for Mr Frank Sherwin, *Dáil* Deputy, 11 Linenhall Street, Dublin, at whose request we write you.

According to our instructions the weekly newspaper, *The Sunday Review* is published by your company. In the issue of 21 July of the said *Sunday Review* there was published on page two thereof an article entitled 'That was the week that was – Inside Politics', by 'Backbencher'.

This article which is headed by two photographs of our client contains a number of statements highly defamatory of our client which libel him in a most gross and cruel fashion. The article contains in its text the clear innuendo (a) that Deputy Sherwin lied to *Dáil Éireann* and misled it by suggesting that he was crippled for life when in fact he was not so crippled (b) that as a *Dáil* deputy he voted for the Turnover Tax not in accordance with his convictions but in order to obtain an IRA pension retrospective for five years (c) that he was a person who would attempt or had attempted to obtain a pension to which he was not properly entitled (d) that he was a dishonest and untruthful person and unfitted to be a member of *Dáil Éireann* (e) that his conduct in *Dáil Éireann* merited condemnation and reprobation by the Irish people.

The whole tenor of your contributor's article reeks with malice against our client and our instructions are that unless you are prepared to publish a complete withdrawal and apology <u>in terms to be settled by us</u>, proceedings against you for libel will be instituted without further notice.

We do not propose nor do our instructions permit us, to enter into any correspondence in connection with this matter. Unless we have your unqualified assurance that you will publish the recantation and apology above referred to, proceedings must issue forthwith.

Yours faithfully,

<u>LEHANE & HOGAN</u>

15, St Stephen's Green,
Dublin 2.

25 February, 1964.

Messrs. Lehane & Hogan,
Solicitors,
1 Upper Ormond Quay,
Dublin 7.

<u>SHERWIN -V- IRISH TIMES LTD</u>

Dear Sirs,
We would be obliged if you would, within four days from the date of receipt of this letter, furnish us with full and detailed particulars of the following matters referred to in the statement of claim herein, *viz*:

1.

(a) The date on which the Plaintiff alleges that he was tortured and crippled for life on each of the five occasions alleged by the Plaintiff.

(b) The place on and in which the Plaintiff alleges that he was tortured and crippled for life on each of the five occasions alleged by the Plaintiff.

(c) The nature and duration of the alleged tortures on each of the alleged five occasions.

(d) The names of each of the alleged torturers.

2.

The nature and respect in which the Plaintiff was crippled for life, specifying the nature of the alleged crippling and its effects upon the Plaintiff.

3.

(a) Each date upon which the Plaintiff made an application or renewed an application for an IRA pension.

(b) Whether such application was made in writing or verbally. If in writing: a copy of each such application should be furnished, together with a copy of the reply thereto. If made verbally, the name and address of the person to whom application was made should be furnished.

4.

The ground or grounds on which the Plaintiff is alleged to have been refused an IRA pension.

5.

(a) (If in receipt of an IRA pension) the date on which such pension was granted and the amount thereof.

(b) If not yet in receipt of such pension, when it is expected that the pension will be granted.

Your early reply to the above will oblige and will obviate an application to the court to compel delivery thereof.

Yours faithfully,
HAYES & SONS.

Bank of Ireland Chambers,
1 Upper Ormond Quay,
Dublin 7.

9 March, 1964.

Messrs. Hayes & Sons,
Solicitors,
15, St Stephen's Green,
Dublin 2.

RE: SHERWIN -V- IRISH TIMES LTD

Dear Sirs,
The following are the particulars requested in the letter of 25 February:-

1. (a) 8 November, 1922, on four occasions on that day and on about 1 December 1922, one occasion.
(b) Griffith Barracks formerly Wellington Barracks on the first four occasions and Portobello Barracks on the fifth occasion.
(c) On the first occasion Plaintiff was kicked and punched for a period of fifteen minutes. On the second occasion Plaintiff was stripped naked, placed across a table, his arms were twisted and he was beaten across the spine and back. Plaintiff does not know how long this lasted as he lost consciousness. On the third occasion some two hours after the last immediately referred to occasion Plaintiff was again brought to the Intelligence Office room and was again punched and beaten on the head and kicked for about twenty minutes. On the fourth occasion about an hour later he was again brought to the room of the intelligence officer, Wellington Barracks. He was jammed in a corner and struck with a rifle butt and an attempt was made to force the muzzle of a rifle into his mouth. On the fifth occasion some three weeks later he was brought to Portobello Barracks and he was beaten and kicked in the Intelligence Room there.
(d) As to (a) I, by Joseph Dolan and Frank Bolster and two others unknown to him. As to (a) II (a) III (a) IV by Joseph Dolan alone. As to (a) V, an officer named Dalton who appeared to the Plaintiff to be in charge of intelligence at Portobello Barracks.

2. As a result of the beatings on the spine Plaintiff's nervous system was affected, he lost the use of his right arm and his right

leg and his kidneys were affected. His whole nervous system was affected and he suffers from acute neurasthenia.

3. (a) There is no pension known specifically as an IRA pension.
(b) See above.

4 and 5

Without prejudice to the foregoing replies:-
Plaintiff made an application under Section 10 of the Army Pensions Act. 1932, for a disability pension some time in 1933 in writing which was refused on 13 November 1933. A request for reconsideration of said application was refused on 28 July, 1944. A further application was made on appeal in October, 1960 and was refused on 22 December 1960. In August, 1962, Plaintiff again applied under the provisions of the Army Pensions Act. 1962 and in February, 1963, Plaintiff was awarded a disability pension – under Section 29 of the 1937 Act of £118 per annum plus a marriage allowance of 7/- per week. The grounds on which the Plaintiff was previously refused a disability pension were that the Plaintiff had not satisfied the Pensions Board that the disability from which he suffered was attributable solely to military service.

Yours faithfully,
LEHANE & HOGAN.

The Irish Times' case was that they only reported what was said in the *Dáil* and that anything they said in *The Sunday Review* and *The Irish Times* was fair comment. My case was that they added to what had been said in the *Dáil* and implied that what was said in the *Dáil* was true. They implied by pictures and statements that I was not a cripple and that if I got a disability pension that it was as a result of a deal to vote for the government on the turnover tax. *The Irish Times* counsel tried to prove that I was not disabled but they were surprised at the mountain of medical evidence produced to the contrary. In fact, only a quarter of the medical evidence was stated when they switched their defence to one of no malice because I did not look a cripple and ordinary people would hold the same view as themselves. I was on the stand all day and was asked 620 questions. I had evidence from nine hospitals and ten doctors going back to 1925. I had many witnesses in court who could give evidence regarding my physical condition before and after my arrest in 1922.

There were several witnesses who saw the condition of my body after I had been tortured four times at the Intelligence Office, Wellington Barracks in 1922, including Clarke who was actually in the Intelligence Office when I was naked across a table and beaten by four officers. He witnessed me receiving hundreds of blows including blows on the head with revolver butts.

My counsel had my file from the Pension Board comprising numerous signed statements by witnesses over the years, many of whom were dead at the time of the court action, including medical evidence and hospital attendance cards. Mr Michael Healy, representing the Army Pension Board, gave evidence. The following are answers to questions from the transcript of the evidence. Mr Healy conceded that I was awarded a disability pension which was operative from 21 January 1963.[5] I had applied in July 1962. Mr Healy added that I had not accepted the pension.[6] He continued: 'I don't think there could be any objection to saying that the Plaintiff has held at all times that he is entitled to a pension in respect of disablement fully attributable to his service but this pension is not. Therefore he refused to accept it. This pension is granted on a finding that a disability exists but it is aggravated only by his military service.'[7] He also added: 'It is a pension that, having commenced on 21 January 1963, is subject to review on or before 31 January 1966.'[8]

I have always held that I was in perfect physical health prior to my arrest and that is the reason I claimed that I was a case under the 1932 Act. I first applied for a disability pension in 1933. I again applied in 1943 and again in 1960. I did not suffer from gunshot wounds and that could be the reason I was not allowed a pension under the 1932 Act. I suffered from spinal injuries resulting from five beatings in jail in 1922. I also suffered from the hunger strike. I could not work after I came out of jail and I have never worked since. The government brought in the 1937 Act to meet such cases. I, however, refused to apply or accept a pension under this Act. In doing so, I lost several thousand pounds as I could have had my present pension since 1937, had I applied. I agreed to accept this pension in 1962 as I was getting on in age and I realized that I would not always be a member of the *Dáil*, unless I acted dishonestly and I had no intention of doing that. It can be seen from the above evidence how much I was slandered by Oliver J. Flanagan TD. All of his talk about bribes was lies and don't forget that he never came near the court nor did he ever again repeat these slanders. All of the opposition outside and all of the malevolent-minded people had a field day, just as they had a field day when Senator Ted Kennedy was involved in the unfortunate drowning accident which resulted in the death of Mary Jo Kopechne.[9] They always think the worst, especially in the case of celebrities or well-known people.

James Clarke was sworn to give evidence. He was an actual witness to the tortures inflicted on me. He was in the Intelligence Room when I suffered my worst beating. Mr Heavey, my counsel, asked Clarke what happened: 'We were taken out of the place [Doody's] and brought to Wellington Barracks.'[10] Mr Kenny, who represented *The Irish Times*, already knew from the evidence that he had lost his case in trying to prove that I was not disabled and therefore entitled to a disability pension. He interjected and said: 'Again, I don't want to shorten any matters that the Plaintiff wants to bring out. There is no controversy in this case as to any injury suffered by Mr Sherwin in 1922.'

Mr Justice Henchy: 'Is it necessary [for Clarke to give evidence]?'

Mr Heavy: 'I understand the controversy is whether those injuries had any effect on him. Is it agreed he is crippled?'

Mr Kenny: 'Your lordship is well aware of the conflict in this case as to whether these words are to be taken literally or. . . '

Mr Justice Henchy: 'Do you concede he did suffer the beating up in 1922 and was injured?' Mr Kenny: 'For all purposes.'

Mr Heavey: 'It would save an awful lot of time. Is it conceded that Mr Sherwin as a result of his injury was and is disable[d] sufficiently to qualify for a disability pension?'

Mr Justice Henchy: 'It doesn't lie with anybody to question the award he got.'

Mr Heavey: 'I thought that was the whole issue in this case[?]'

Mr Justice Henchy: 'It is conceded that there was an award.'

Mr Kenny: 'Of course it is.'

Mr Justice Henchy: 'Mr Crivon's cross-examination was a bit ambiguous.'[11]

Mr Kenny: 'The question as to whether that is properly described as crippling for life is still in the case.'

Mr Heavey: 'If it is conceded that Mr Sherwin's description of his inabilities, his own disability, if that is conceded and if it is only a question of whether that is properly described as being crippled – I thought it was still in issue – if I may take it that Mr Sherwin's evidence is not questioned on his physical limitations.'

Mr Justice Henchy: 'I take it that is correct.'

Mr Heavey: 'Very good.'

Mr Justice Henchy: 'You don't wish to pursue the examination of this witness?'[12]

Mr Heavey: 'No.'[13]

Doctor Slein was sworn in and examined by Mr Heavey. Mr Heavey: 'I wish you to give your opinions of your findings?'

> Dr Slein: 'The above signs are only consistent with injury to the nerve roots at their points of exit from the spinal vertebrae on the right side, the upper spinal vertebrae on the right side. This explains the muscle disability found on examination. No degenerative organic muscle condition would cause the specific and unrelated signs outlined above.'
>
> Mr Heavey: 'What sort of trauma would be consistent with these signs?'
>
> Dr Slein: 'When I questioned Mr Sherwin he described his spinal injury in the lower region and the upper chest and that relates to having been beaten in prison. This, I think, is the cause of it, that he was beaten with sticks and rifles.'
>
> Mr Heavey: 'In your opinion a beating such as that could produce the damage and the whole condition you found?'
>
> Dr Slein: 'Yes.'[14]

Mr Richard J. Dowling, political correspondent for *Telefís Éireann* was then sworn in.

> Mr Kenny: 'I was asking you whether you would agree that an unbiased observer might reasonably hold the view that Mr Sherwin is occasionally extravagant in his language?'[15]
>
> Mr Dowling: 'It depends on what you mean by extravagance.'
>
> Mr Kenny: 'What I mean by extravagant, I suppose, is whether the reason you gave a moment ago or not, inclined to use words which may be, perhaps, an exaggeration?'
>
> Mr Dowling: 'He is inclined to get excited sometimes.'
>
> Mr Kenny: '...and use words which would amount to an exaggeration? I am not asking your own view. I am saying an unbiased observer? [*sic.*]'
>
> Mr Dowling: 'I think he is a very astute politician. He may get excited but he doesn't make any mistakes.'[16]

Mr John Healy, otherwise known as the 'Backbencher' of *The Sunday Review*, was sworn in.[17] Mr John Healy, next to Oliver J. Flanagan TD, took delight in making little of politicians, especially those who supported the government. It was his job to make me look fit physically and to question my credibility as a politician. He was asked by Mr Crivon: 'Did you know Mr Sherwin?'

Mr Healy: 'I have had quite a number of years' experience of reporting Mr Sherwin as a reporter. I think the first I had was when I was with *The Evening Press* and became *The Evening Press*'s first City Hall correspondent and at that time my full-time job was to cover local authority meetings in the Corporation and especially the works of the committee and so watched Mr Sherwin very closely at that stage because to my mind I found him to be one of the most active of the members of the Corporation in the matter of attending the Corporation meetings, although the committee meetings were not open to the press. Certainly there was all the evidence that he was a very close attender [*sic*] at those meetings.'[18]

Mr Crivon: 'Was there any feeling of personal animosity or spite against Mr Sherwin?'

Mr Healy: 'No, as I have conveyed, I have a fair admiration for Mr Sherwin because I have taken him very seriously and the one occasion on which my admiration for his activities as a good politician was aroused was the fact that he managed in – and, I think the records will prove this – he conducted a campaign in the Corporation to have a differential when the Corporation sought to place an extra 3d. a room increase in the rent. He fought this very successfully and if I remember my facts rightly, succeeded. This, to me, was very good evidence of his activities as a public representative. For this reason I say I have the highest respect for him.'[19]

Mr Crivon: 'Did you honestly believe what appeared in the column?'

Mr Healy: 'I was utterly amazed that he should say that he was crippled for life in 1922.'[20]

Mr Heavy: 'Are you satisfied from your observation of Mr Sherwin over all the years that he is a man of the greatest honesty in his career?'

Mr Healy: 'The question, the interpretation of honesty, I am satisfied that he himself is honest in what he does when he says he represents the poor man. Yes.'[21]

Mr Heavey: 'Did you ever detect him in a lie?'

Mr Healy: 'In the context of politics and political speech, there are tales that one would say are possibly untrue. I think there is this political definition of what is a broad honesty if you wish.'[22]

Mr Heavey: 'Did it ever occur... Surely you would remember in your mind whether the man was known to you as a truthful man or a liar at the time this article was written? Would you regard Mr Sherwin as a man with an unusual addiction for the truth?'

Mr Healy: 'I have said in the beginning that I regarded him as being broadly honest in the matter of politics.' Mr Heavey: 'Broadly honest sounds a very odd remark. Are you looking to wound but yet afraid to strike?'

Mr Healy: 'I don't mean that.'[23]

Mr Seán O'Riada, having been sworn in, stated that he was a Bachelor of Music and a leader of a folk orchestra. He was examined by Mr Fahy on behalf of *The Irish Times*.[24]

Mr Fahy: 'Did you ever meet or speak to Mr Sherwin?'

Mr O'Riada: 'No.'[25]

Mr Fahy: 'You read these Debates?'

Mr O'Riada: 'I read *The Irish Times* report of the Debates.'

Mr Fahy: 'Did you, having read them, write this article entitled 'Plain Words'?'

Mr O'Riada: 'Yes, I did.'[26]

Mr Doyle: 'I put it to you that you were there reinforcing the suggestion made against Mr Sherwin which had already been made in the Back Bencher [*sic*] article.'

Mr O'Riada: 'Well, my answer is that I had no intention of re-enforcing anybody's suggestion but my own.'

Mr Doyle: 'Were you raking over the mud again?'

Mr O'Riada: 'My Lord, may I object to this particular question[?] It puts me in the light of a mud-raker. A mud-raker is not my function nor my profession. I did not intend to rake any mud. I was merely concerned with writing something which my readers would find entertaining and amusing.'

Mr Doyle: 'Did you think when you were writing that that it might have been hurtful to Mr Sherwin?'

Mr O'Riada: 'It did not occur to me.'

Mr Doyle: 'Did you think it might be damaging to Mr Sherwin?'

Mr O'Riada: 'It did not and may I add that my feeling in the matter of this particular kind of thing is, if a man exposes himself to public life he must, as somebody said in the course of this trial, take the rough with the smooth.'

Mr Doyle: 'You think if somebody is a member of *Dáil Éireann* that he is fair game?'

Mr O'Riada: 'When you say fair game you are using a metaphor. I would complete it by saying fair game within the season.'[27]

Mr Doyle: 'Do you accept now, Mr O'Riada, as apparently your employers accept, that is to say *The Irish Times*, that Mr Sherwin did not get a bribe?'

Mr O'Riada: 'I have heard a great deal about this in court but at times I wasn't paying very close attention.'

Mr Doyle: 'What is in your mind? Do you accept it that Mr Sherwin did not get a bribe?'

Mr O'Riada: 'I am sure he did not get a bribe. The thing is immaterial to me. I couldn't care less.'

Mr Doyle: 'Are you satisfied he was seriously disabled during most of his life?'

Mr O'Riada: 'He must have been. This again – my attitude is the same. It is nothing to do with me.'[28]

The photographers, Mr Tom Collins and Mr Bordon Standing, were then sworn in.[29] I claimed that both pictures were posed at the request of the photographers.

Mr Crivon: 'How did he remount the bicycle?'

Mr Collins: 'He walked out of the precinct of *Dáil Éireann* and came back in again on the bicycle. I did not see him remount the bicycle outside.'[30]

Mr Crivon to Mr Standing: 'In what circumstances was this photograph taken?'

Mr Standing: 'It was taken when Mr Sherwin arrived at Kingsbridge Station to go on a tour to Shannon with some other deputies.'

Mr Crivon: 'Mr Sherwin said in evidence that this was a posed photograph.'

Mr Standing: 'That is correct.'

Mr Crivon: 'Did you ask him to stop and walk or what was [*sic*] the circumstances?'

Mr Standing: 'He in fact was late and the other deputies had gone and I put my equipment away and was leaving the station when I saw him arrive. I asked him if he would wait until I got my equipment out again and walk towards me.'

Mr Crivon: 'How did he walk?'

Mr Standing: 'Briskly.'[31]

My counsel Mr Heavey then cross-examined Mr Standing:

Mr Heavey: 'He [Sherwin] was going to take the train to Limerick Junction and catch up in some way. What I want to suggest to you is that Mr Sherwin was actually sitting in the carriage when you asked him and he actually got up and left the carriage?'

Mr Standing: 'That is correct.'

Mr Heavey: 'Is it also correct when he tells me that you told him the shot or photograph you would like to be one showing him in a

hurry to catch the train?'
Mr Standing: 'That is correct.'[32]

Mr Justice Henchy, when charging the jury, pointed out that *The Irish Times* published Oliver Flanagan's statement in the *Dáil* that Mr Sherwin got a pension with four or five years' back money which was denied by Mr Sherwin. This denial was not published by *The Irish Times*. He also pointed out that Mr Healy representing *The Irish Times* knew on the Saturday morning, that is Saturday 21 June 1963, when this article was being passed for publication on the Sunday, that on the previous day, Friday 20 June, Deputy Sherwin had repudiated the truth of the rumour and Mr Healy accepted the truth of the repudiation. That seems to mean that *The Irish Times* in that passage was reporting as a rumour a statement that Mr Sherwin had accepted a bribe from the government in return for voting for them and that *The Irish Times* knew that rumour was false. He declared: 'Now, it is a question for you to determine whether that report in *The Sunday Review* of the 21 June, 1963 is a fair and accurate report. It is, I suggest, accurate but is it fair? Should, in the interests of fairness as well as accuracy, there have been added a statement to the effect that this was only a rumour and that as far as *The Irish Times* is concerned, as far as Backbencher [*sic*] was concerned, it was baseless.'[33] Mr Justice Henchy continued: 'In 1922 he [Sherwin] was maltreated in the way that he described here. He suffered injuries which, apparently, are with him still.'[34] 'Then you had the evidence of Dr Slein with regard to Mr Sherwin's incapacity. I need not go into it. It establishes without contradiction that he has diminution of power and tone in certain muscles and that his injuries are consistent only with injury to the nerve roots of the spine, that is is [*sic*] consistent with the beating he got in 1922.'[35]

The jury decided against me, obviously, because they were prejudiced. Their decision was that *The Irish Times* and *The Sunday Review* only reported what was said in the *Dáil.* My case was that they added to what was said and that while reporting the slander in full, they did not report my denial. A person who has anything to hide seldom takes action in court because in the course of proceedings the opposition can go back to the past and use anything to damage your reputation. In my action against *The Irish Times* they proved nothing against me. In fact, all of the evidence was that I was honest and never did a dishonourable thing in my life. I received many letters of sympathy and shock at the jury's verdict, including one from Mr Seán McEntee TD *Tánaiste* and from Mr Charles Haughey, Minister for Justice.[36] I received the following letter from Dan Breen, TD.[37]

67, Ballytore Road,
Rathfarnham Road,
Rathfarnham,
Dublin 14.

Dear Deputy Sherwin,

The jury found against you. I am very very sorry. If there is anything
I can do to help you, don't stall me. It is a damn raw deal for you.
Keep your heart up. My best of good wishes.

Dan Breen.

Mr MacEntee's letter:

9, Leeson Park,
Dublin 8.
7 November, 1964.

Dear Frank Sherwin,

May I say how shocked I have been by the verdict in your action. In
my opinion, though only as a layman, it was perverse, contrary to
the law of facts. How twelve normal human beings could hold that
the attacks on you and the words used and applied to you were not
defamatory passes my comprehension.

It is in the national interest that the licence which some journalists
have abrogated to themselves in their references to public men
should be curbed.
Your fight was for all of us.

Very Sincerely,
Seán MacEntee.
(*Tánaiste* and Minister for Health)
PS I am sending this by hand because I want you to know as soon as
possible that you are not without friends,
Seán MacEntee.

I decided to appeal to the Supreme Court against the High Court
decision. The Supreme Court decided in my favour and ordered a new
trial. I don't like courts; I don't like the legal profession, with
exceptions. Most of them are politicians. They are experts at double-
talk. I told my solicitor that I would be prepared to settle with *The Irish
Times* if they paid all expenses and made a public apology. *The Irish*

1.   Frank Sherwin's parents, Christopher Sherwin (photo taken in 1932) and Mary Jane (née Ford)

Flanna-eireann.

Vice-Brigadier ALF. COLLEY,   Commandant SEAN COLE,

Murdered by the enemies of the Irish Republic

at

THE THATCH, DRUMCONDRA.

26th August, 1922.

R.I.P.

(2)   Alfred Colley and Sean Cole were murdered at Whitehall on 26 August 1922.

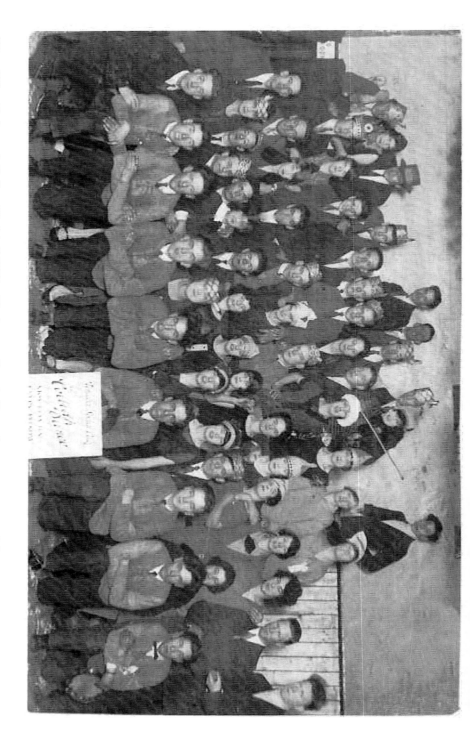

(3) 'The Cole and Colley Club' (1926). Chairman Frank Sherwin on extreme right.

(4a) A wedding photograph of Frank Sherwin and Rosie (neé Kinsella). Photo taken in 1937.

(4b) Frank Sherwin the family man with four of his six sons. From left Vincent, Liam, Alan and Eamon. Photo taken in 1960.

(5)   Frank Sherwin's famous picture 'Outside the
        Housing Department' used to good effect on his
        election posters below the caption 'Action Speaks
        Louder than Promises'.

(6a) Frank and Rosie in the Mansion House holding up The Sam
      Maguire Cup, 'a prize Irish football trophy', with Cllr Michael
      Collins, Lord Mayor of Dublin, 1977–1978.

(6b) Frank Sherwin and Rosie being presented by Lord Mayor Jim
      Mitchell (1976–77) to Queen Margrethe II of Denmark, at a
      function in Dublin's Mansion House.

(7) Frank Sherwin at an Old IRA parade.

(8)   Four old warriors. Frank Sherwin, second from right.

(9)   Five of Frank Sherwin's children follow in their mother's footsteps – Christy, Marie, Vincent, Frank Jr and Kathleen.

(10) Mrs Rosie Sherwin watches as the Lord Mayor cuts the ribbon officially opening the newest bridge to span the River Liffey at Dublin's Heuston Station.

Times agreed to pay all expenses and to put a statement in all the daily newspapers that they did not, nor never did, question my honesty in political life. Consequently, a statement appeared in all of the daily newspapers on the 27 and 28 October 1966. Mr E.C. Micks for *The Irish Times Ltd* said that now that the action had been disposed of, he would like to take the opportunity of saying that while *The Irish Times Ltd* never conceded that the matters in dispute were capable of imputing any dishonesty to Mr Sherwin, it had never been their intention to impute to him any dishonesty or to impugn his motives. The miscreant that started all of the trouble, Mr Oliver J. Flanagan TD, never came near the court, nor did Flanagan ever repeat the slander or give me a chance to bring him to court, as anything said in the *Dáil* is privileged, but his slander has been repeated by birds of a feather amongst the public, which seems to have been his purpose in making the slander in the first place.

NOTES

1 *The Sunday Review* was an *Irish Times* publication.
2 Leinster House is another name for the *Dáil.*
3 Seán O'Riada (1931–71) was a journalist and renowned Irish traditional composer. Some of his compositions include musical scores for the films *Mise Éire* (1960), *The Playboy of the Western World* (1962) and the O'Riada Mass.
4 Lehane was a former Corporation councillor.
5 *The High Court: Transcript of Evidence, Volume One:* 'Action heard before Mr Justice Henchy and a Jury on November 2, 3, 4, 5 and 6 1964 re. Frank Sherwin (Plaintiff) and *The Irish Times Limited* (Defendant)', item 1075.
6 *Ibid.* item 1076.
7 *Ibid*, items 1077 and 1078.
8 *Ibid.* item 1080.
9 Edward Moore Kennedy was born on 22 February 1932 in Brookline Massachusetts. He is a Democratic US Senator from Massachusetts. He is known as one of America's leading liberal politicians. After his brothers John and Robert were assassinated in 1963 and 1968 respectively, he became surrogate father to their children. Ted Kennedy was elected to the Senate from Massachusetts in 1962 to fill the seat left vacant by his older brother John F. Kennedy upon the latter's election as President of the United States. He has successfully run for re-election in 1964, 1970, 1976, 1982, 1988, 1994 and 2000. Ted Kennedy is one of the longest-serving members of the Senate. According to the Almanac of American Politics, he has served longer than all but four other senators in US history. According to NPK, Kennedy plans to run again in 2006. If he wins and serves out his full six-year term, he will have served in the US Senate for fifty years, the longest service of any Senator to date.
10 'Doody's' refers to Doody's Dairy.
11 Crivon was counsel for *The Times.*
12 The witness referred to here was James Clarke.
13 *The Transcript of Evidence*, items 829–31.

14   *The Transcript of Evidence*, items 1099–101.
15   Kenny represented *The Irish Times*.
16   *The Transcript of Evidence*, items 1155–57.
17   *The Sunday Review* was an *Irish Times* publication.
18   *The High Court: Transcript of Evidence*, Vol. 2: 'Action heard before Mr Justice Henchy and a Jury on November 3, 4, 5 and 6 1964 re. Frank Sherwin (Plaintiff) and *The Irish Times Limited* (Defendant)', item 1184.
19   *Ibid.*, item 1194.
20   *Ibid.*, item 1195.
21   *The Transcript of Evidence*, counsel for Sherwin, item 1198.
22   *Ibid.*, item 1199.
23   *Ibid.*, items 1228–29.
24   Mr O'Riada wrote a column in *The Irish Times* and Sherwin claimed that he was libelled in this column.
25   *The Transcript of Evidence*, items 1615–17
26   *Ibid.*, items 1618–19. '... these Debates' here refer to the debates in the *Dáil.*
27   *Ibid.*, items 1715–19. Doyle was counsel for Mr Sherwin.
28   *Ibid.*, items 1766–68.
29   Collins and Standing were employed by *The Irish Times* and the evidence they proposed to give was to demonstrate by photos that Sherwin was able and fit because he walked briskly into a train carriage at Kingsbridge and also cycled into Leinster House.
30   *The Transcript of Evidence*, item 1784.
31   *Ibid.* items 1801–4.
32   *Ibid.* items 1810–11
33   *The High Court: Transcript of Evidence*, Vol. 2 'Action heard before Mr Justice Henchy and a Jury on November 3, 4, 5 and 6 1964 re. Frank Sherwin (Plaintiff) and *The Irish Times Limited* (Defendant)'. The Jury were then charged by Mr Justice Henchy. See pp. 217–18.
34   *Ibid.*, p. 226.
35   *Ibid.*, p. 229.
36   *Tánaiste* is equivalent to Deputy Prime Minister.
37   Dan Breen was the man who was accredited with starting the War of Independence.

10

BRIBERY AND THUGGERY

The confidence vote tabled by the opposition took place on 30 October 1963. It was high drama. *Fianna Fáil* deputy Galvin had recently died and the government seemed certain to be defeated. Mr James Dillon, leader of the opposition, said in a speech that if the government was beaten and his party was elected, he would abolish the turnover tax. It was not yet in operation.[1] Eighteen months later, however, when he thought that *Fine Gael* might be returned, he said that he could do nothing about the tax. He wanted the money; otherwise, he would have to introduce heavy taxation in other areas. After one hour before the vote, I was in my usual seat. Deputy Carroll sat about two seats in front, to the left. Carroll stood up and made the following speech.[2]

> I reiterated that I was not opposed to taxation or purchase tax provided it was not a tax on food. I pointed out that if it were a tax on food, I would oppose it, irrespective of the consequences. Those are my words. I reiterated that sentence even tonight...I am considering the people...I repeat as I said in June, that I am losing confidence in our Minister for Finance, or in the cabinet itself... Some years ago, I had the temerity to label myself as 'Honestly Independent'. I trust that whatever happens tonight, it will be just another indication that I am honestly independent. If any action of mine tonight should help to terminate the life of this government, I know that many people will express their dissatisfaction.

After making his speech he stood up and tapped Deputy Sheridan, who was in front of me, on the shoulder. They both left the *Dáil* chamber as if it had been all arranged. About three-quarters of an hour later they both came back and sat in the same seats. When the bell rang to vote, Carroll and Sheridan voted for the government. This led to an uproar of recriminations from the opposition. *The Irish Times* political correspondent described the scene in his newspaper, 31 October 1963. It was entitled 'Real drama was behind the scenes'. It read:

The fortunes of the Government swayed back and forth during the hours of the debate but the real drama was not in the *Dáil* Chamber but in the lobbies, restaurant and bar. There, groups of deputies and ministers were in huddles of discussion but up to about nine o'clock there seemed to be gloom in the government camp and many were saying that the *Taoiseach* would dissolve the *Dáil* if his majority depended on the *Ceann Comhairle*. Suddenly, the atmosphere cleared and one could hear a sigh of joy or disappointment in the restaurant as a Minister and an Independent strolled slowly in together for a meal. Shortly afterwards it became known that another Independent would vote with the Government. These two votes made a change of four. Two came off the opposition vote and went on to the Government vote. Not many were aware of the change however and the tension was high as 10.30 p.m. approached for the vital vote. As Deputies Carroll and Sheridan were seen to go into the Government lobby there was swift movement in the press gallery as reporters phoned the result, now known as 73–69. The drama was over for the deputies and for the *Ceann Comhairle*, Mr Hogan, whose party had called on him to vote against the Government. In the event, he did not need to vote at all. The result means, in effect, that the government now had a bigger majority than ever before, for in the view of members, the two Independents are almost certain to vote in future with the government.

Deputy Carroll told me later that the government gave him and Deputy Sheridan an assurance that there would be no general election for two years if they voted for the government on the confidence vote but the Government lost two by-elections early in 1965. Mr Lemass had stated that if he lost the two by-elections that he would go to the country. A general election was declared in May 1965, five months earlier than the alleged promise to wait for two years. I knew that I was up against it but I thought that I would get by. I could have joined *Fianna Fáil* and held on to my seat, as the party held two seats in my area but I decided to fight alone. I was always Independent in spite of all of the talk to the contrary. My worst enemies were the Labour party, although I was more Labour than they were as all of my work was on behalf of the workers and those who depended on social benefits. In politics, the more honest you are the more likely you are to be misrepresented because you must be singled out for special treatment so as to detach voters who until then had a good opinion of you.

The Labour party, expecting a general election, invited Miss Susan Bowler, the Independent councillor, to join their party. Their purpose was to exploit her, as they had no time for her otherwise. They looked upon her as a rich woman who was in touch with many of the corporation tenants because she was a solicitor and represented many of them in court as many of them were street dealers who were often in trouble with the law. These were the people that I had worked for and I was largely depending on them as I was a corporation tenant and always defended the tenants against rent increases, etc. The Labour party worked up a campaign of lies and slander against me. They assaulted some of my supporters and tore down or covered over my posters. They imported a crowd of college students into the area, some of them foreigners, to misrepresent me. They were associates of Michael O'Leary, a Cork man of whom nobody had ever heard. He had been put up as a candidate in my area.[3] Although the Labour party brought in Miss Bowler to use her to split my vote, she in turn joined the Labour party to use it for her own advantage. The Labour party machine was used exclusively to help O'Leary and Miss Bowler organize a party of her own with headquarters in Rory O'Connor House, a council estate. Miss Bowler had a caravan touring the estates giving out tea, cakes and sweets. This was all directed against me and aimed at my supporters who were largely poor people. I bribed nobody. I counted on the mountain of work that I had performed as an alderman and TD. The Labour party organization spent all of their time lying about me on behalf of a stranger from Cork. They said that I had two corporation houses while thousands of homeless families had none. This was a lie. I have lived in a small three-roomed corporation house since I was a child and at the time of this election that house was over-crowded. There were eleven in my family. They also said that my daughter Roseleen had a corporation house at Coolock, although she had no children. This was another lie. My daughter had one room in a private house at Coolock, for which she was paying £2 a week. She never had a corporation house dwelling. All these lies were aimed at the voters who needed dwellings. They hoped to antagonize these people against me.

Everyone knew that I was the most active public representative in Dublin. Due to my spinal injuries, I could not work nor could I engage in business, so I was a full-time representative and as far as I was aware, the only one in Dublin. I was on hand every day to counter this mountain of work they said I did because I got backhanders. All the thousands that came to see me knew that this was a lie. The Labour party expected that those who did not know me or were sufficiently malevolent would believe it, just as they hoped that Flanagan's slander in the *Dáil* would be believed. I lost my seat because of all the misrepresentation. I was given no chance to make a case on television. My first preference vote dropped from 5,356 to 1,615.

The Labour party was supposed to be the party of James Connolly, the great socialist writer. If Connolly could speak, I know that he would be proud of me, as no other worked as hard for those in need as I did and all the Labour people knew it, but in politics it would not matter if you were Christ reborn. If you are not on their side, you are there to be misrepresented. When Noël Browne was forced out of the inter-party government in 1951, he joined the *Fianna Fáil* party and was a candidate in the 1954 general election. He was attacked by Mr Norton, the then leader of the Labour party who said on 29 April: 'That turncoat Dr Noël Browne is attacking the Labour party! He is supporting *Fianna Fáil* who increased the cost of food.' Later Dr Browne became a leading member of the Labour party but has since lost the 'party whip'. He is the type that wants to lead. He will not be led. As I have said, Miss Susan Bowler was accepted into the Labour party, but only to be manipulated. During the election campaign of 1965, when I lost my seat, she got more number one votes than Michael O'Leary. I accused the Labour party of large-scale bribery in the corporation estates. I said that tea, cakes, sweets and drink were distributed to adults and children. In a press statement O'Leary denied my accusations but this was a fabrication. Some weeks before the local elections of 1967, Miss Bowler was to be a Labour candidate but she objected to O'Leary wanting to boost himself in Labour literature as he was not a candidate in the local elections. She was obviously thinking of the next general election. It seems that O'Leary insisted on putting his picture on the literature and making a statement, but Miss Bowler would not accept this and resigned. She knew by then that she was not wanted. O'Leary refused to let her form some Labour branches as he did not want any more opposition from her which could deprive him of his *Dáil* seat.

During the count at Bolton Street school during the general election of 1965, it was touch and go between them for my seat. Some of O'Leary's crowd, comprised mostly of college students, were present. They were heard bickering: 'That bitch! If she wins, there will be a big row in the Labour party!' A Labour monthly, *The Irish Militant,* published just before the local election of 1967, had an article headed 'If you knew Susy'. The article was obviously inspired by the Labour party. It stated that her main campaign weapons were free sweets for the kids, free tea for the parents, her pregnancy, her fortune-teller and her campaign's Alfie-istic shades, accredited to Alfie Byrne. They referred to her as a 'Solicitor, Housewife and Slum-landlord'. They admitted that they had accepted her into the Labour party because of her large sums of money. A low trick, you must admit, when you consider how they capitalized on her and her money to rob me of my

Dáil seat which resulted in O'Leary's election. I had good reason for attacking her but not the Labour party. When I accused the Labour party of bribery during the general election of 1965, O'Leary in a press statement said:

> No Labour candidate could descend to such a level as to get at people's votes by manipulating their affections for their children in this cynical manner. Our principles would not allow us to deal with people so contemptuously. Public life in Dublin has for so long been poisoned by shabby electioneering.

When you consider the admissions in *The Irish Militant* two years later, you will realize what a deceitful and dishonest business politics is. Not only did Labour bribe and lie in 1965 but their student thugs tore down my election posters and covered others. They also attacked a number of small children including my own son in Bolton Street. He was only 7 years of age. Some of the children went home crying when they took election banners from them. I informed the *Gardai* at Bridewell Station who took statements from the children. I wonder what James Connolly would say if he could speak from the grave?

James Connolly was self-educated. He was the son of an Edinburgh street cleaner and was a cleaner himself. He had no trade or profession. He lived in tenements and was always poor. He was an extreme socialist. A member of his family said that he was, in fact, a communist. No matter what he was, he was sincere and in his day there were good reasons for being extreme. There were no social benefits and 28,000 families lived in unfit dwellings in Dublin. The children of the poor were sent to poor-houses and mental homes and men, mostly unskilled labourers, worked long hours for wages that could only buy one-third of what a worker could now purchase. Connolly was a Labour candidate in the Wood Quay local elections of 1902. He only received 431 votes. He was the victim of large-scale slander, misrepresentation and bribery. Connolly contested the same ward in 1903. In his election address he said:

> Let us remember how the drink sellers of Wood Quay Ward combined with the slum owner and house jobber. Let us remember how the publicans issued free drink to whoever would accept until on the day before Election Day. The scenes of bestiality and drunkenness around the shop were such as brought the blush of shame to every decent man and woman who saw them. Let us remember the threats and bribery, how Mr Byrne of Wood Quay told the surrounding tenants that if Mr Connolly was elected their

rents would be increased. Let us remember how the paid canvassers of the capitalist candidate hired slanderers, gave a different account of Connolly to every section of the electorate. How they said to the Catholics that he was an Orangeman, to the Protestant that he was a *Fenian*, to the Jews that he was an anti-Semite, to others that he was a Jew, to the labourers that he was a journalist on the make and to the tradesman and profession classes that he was an ignorant labourer.

Slander and free drink won the day, Connolly only received 243 votes.[4]

Connolly was a nationalist as well as a socialist. However, he knew enough to know that socialism was not possible until the country gained its freedom as the country was then subject to Britain. He was executed for his part in the Rebellion of 1916. Had he lived, he more than likely would have been expelled from the trade unions and the Labour Party, as up to recent years they were anti-communist, even anti-socialist. In January 1914, the Labour party split. The big unions refused to support Labour because they accepted Big Jim Larkin. They said there were communists in the party and Connolly would have been one of them. Prior to the Rebellion of 1916, Connolly was Secretary of the Irish Transport Union with headquarters at Liberty Hall, Dublin. He was also leader of the Irish Citizens Army, a small but well-armed force. He used Liberty Hall for meetings of this force and for some weeks before the Rebellion he flew the Irish green flag from Liberty Hall. The majority of the union bosses objected to Connolly's association with the Irish Volunteers and told him to cease using the hall and to take down the flag. When he refused, they threatened to expel him. He overcame their objections by disclosing the information that a rebellion was about to break out. Obviously, they were afraid of the consequences if they expelled Connolly. After the Rebellion, there was a union congress in Sligo in August 1916. A member proposed a vote of sympathy for Connolly who was one of those executed. There were strong objections from the leaders. They agreed, however, to accept the vote if the Irish soldiers who died fighting for the British in France were included. This was agreed and the vote was passed.

NOTES

1   See *The Evening Herald*, Tuesday 22 October, 1963, p. 1. It is entitled: 'Dillon says he would abolish that tax'.

2   *Parliamentary Debates, Dáil Éireann*, 'Turnover tax – motion of no confidence', vol 205, 30 October, 1963, cols 644/5.

3   Michael O'Leary was born in Cork, became a trade union official with ITGWU and was elected as a TD for the Labour party in 1965. He served as Minister for

Labour from 1973–77 under Liam Cosgrave. He became leader of the Labour party in 1981 but his short spell as leader was largely unsuccessful. He became *Tánaiste* and Minister for Energy (1981–82) under Dr Garret Fitzgerald. He left the Labour party in 1982, after the party failed to enter into an election pact with *Fine Gael* and was elected as a *Fine Gael* TD in the November 1982 general election. He failed to contest the 1987 and 1989 general elections and failed to be selected as a candidate in Cork North Central in 1992. In 1997, he was appointed a judge of the District Court.

4   The Labour party used the same dirty tactics against Sherwin in 1965.

11

MY WORLD HAD COLLAPSED[1]

There was no chance of my returning to the dance or auction business and I had no other line to turn to. I had had some serious disappointments in life but none as bad as this and, of course, I was getting on in years. I applied for the miserable small pension, but were it not for the help my wife got from our son Christy we would have been the poorest family in Ireland. He was engaged to be married but put it off to help his mother. Nevertheless, things were bad. I had some advantages: I had no car. I never ate out. I spent little on clothes. I had given up drinking and smoking seventeen years before to fight elections. I never reverted to either again. When I was drinking, which was seldom on my own, I would drink a fair amount because I had so much company between politics, the old IRA, the dance business and the auctions. I would meet up with people all day and invariably this led to the pub. I spent a lot of money on drink, largely on other people, and neglected my business. I always remember the night before I gave it up. I met up with a regular associate who repaired my radios, which I bought at the auctions. This man lived for drink and seldom ate. He called up to me at 55 Lower O'Connell Street where I had my school of dance and produced a bottle of *poteen*. I had never drunk the stuff before and agreed to sample it. It tasted like water so I took another. Soon the bottle was emptied and we still felt sober. With that, I stood up to go upstairs to the school when I suddenly got dizzy and my legs went from under me. My friend fell down the stairs. I got myself up and decided to go home, making my way down Lott's Lane. I was falling from one side of the lane to the other and on making it to my home, I fell into the fireplace. My family helped me up to bed. Next day, on being told of the show that I had made of myself, I decided there and then never to drink again. I learned that my friend had been picked up near O'Connell Street, unconscious on the public sidewalk. He spent the night in a cell at College Street *Garda* station. It was difficult to give up drinking. My friends told me that they did not feel at home with me anymore and gradually left my company. I was always ambitious to become a councillor and a member of the *Dáil*. I realized that unless I changed my way of life that it would never happen. I was however by determination to find that I could survive without drink and found myself saving a little money. I sent letters to the newspapers and the rest you know.

Some months after I had given up drinking, I decided to give up smoking. I had been a chain smoker for many years largely due to the state of my nerves. When I came out of jail in 1924, I had bronchitis as well as the other complaints. I got colds regularly and coughed day and night. When I stopped smoking, I stopped coughing and seldom got colds. Smoking and drinking in moderation does no harm. Life would be lonely to many without a little social life and pubs are the workers' clubs. However, if you are prone to taking much drink in company, making every day a session, then you will not achieve your ambition if you have one and more than likely make life miserable for your family. After my defeat in 1965, I became more active as an alderman in corporation affairs. It gave me something to do although there was no money in it, as councillors were not paid. I loved the work.[2]

The municipal election was held on the 28 June 1967. I stood as an Independent candidate for North Dublin, area number five. I put my son Christy forward for area number six which I had previously represented as a member of the *Dáil*. My reason for putting him forward was to keep my name alive in the area, as the two areas were combined for a *Dáil* election. This was my big mistake as I divided my resources. While my son and my three daughters were busy in his area, I depended on my wife and a few friends to help me. I had only dozens to help me while other parties had hundreds. I had no cars, no amplifiers and little money. In spite of that, I headed the poll getting 1,762 number one votes. Under proportional representation you need many first preference votes unless you get elected on the first count as you can rapidly slip down the scale as candidates are eliminated, which is what happened to me. I ended up losing my seat by eighty-six votes. My son received 693 number one votes in area number six. Had I concentrated all of my efforts in my own area, I would have won without any doubt, as my own area was only half canvassed. My best canvasser, next to my wife, was my daughter Kathleen. She actually canvassed in both areas from morning until night but as she was six months pregnant and had a threatened miscarriage ten days before the poll, she was confined to bed on doctor's orders.

Miss Bowler, or as she was then, Mrs Susan Bowler Geraghty, received 1,424 number one votes and lost her seat. She did badly when you consider that in the general election of 1965 she had received 2,418 number one votes against my 1,615. She spent a lot of money, had many cars, several with public address systems, and she paid many canvassers.

I could not afford to pay anyone. There were three seats and they were won by three newcomers. *Fianna Fáil* elected an auctioneer. *Fine Gael* elected a publican and Labour elected a person described by a Republican paper as a capitalist and friend of O'Leary's. None of these people would have been elected without party support. In fact, I doubt whether any of them would have got more than 300 votes had they been on their own. It is known that some of my opposition spent a lot of money on drink in order to get votes. Mr Seán Lemass, the former *Taoiseach*, said on television that the average person representing political parties was worth no more than 500 number one votes and then they had to be popular to get that number. Parties brag that in certain areas they could get a walking stick elected. When you consider that I got 1,762 number one votes with all of my handicaps, I certainly represented the people more than the three elected members combined. In addition, I had all the expertise and was invaluable to people in need. I also had time to help people all day every day whereas those elected were green-horns and had little time as they had business to attend to. I hold that political parties should not contest local elections as local councils have no political power and that it is wrong to foster know-nothings and do-nothings on to councils, when real helpers and informed people are necessary.

I continued to go down to corporation departments about once a week as many people still came to me for help. The new City Council consisted of forty-five members. Twenty-four were new members. In other words, the majority were inexperienced and that had a lot to do with the council being abolished twenty months later. A few old members of the council who were also members of the *Dáil* used the corporation for vote purposes in view of the impending general election and influenced the new members to refuse to strike the rate for 1969–70. When the council was warned that it would be abolished if it did not strike the rate and they got time to do so, the opposition hoped that the government members would move the striking of the rate, thus saving face. However, the government members decided to let them stew in their own soup.

Following the local elections of 1967, the opposition had a majority on the Council. They decided to eliminate all the *Fianna Fáil* members from controlling the five committees that decided all corporation business. Some of the *Fianna Fáil* members were experienced and in the interests of the citizens should have received some of the appointments, as the Corporation was not the *Dáil*. It had no political power. Five chairmen and five vice-chairmen were elected. Only one position went to *Fianna Fáil*, the vice-chairmanship of the Finance Committee. The opposition also controlled the election of the Lord

Mayor, the plum job worth several thousand pounds. Also, anyone who was Lord Mayor in an election year would stand to reap a big vote. The Labour party decided to bully the *Fine Gael* party. They said that they wanted the mayoralty that year and the following year. *Fine Gael* said that Labour could have it that year but insisted on getting it the following year. Labour would not agree, so *Fine Gael* out of spite allowed Tom Stafford, an Independent, to become Lord Mayor. The Labour party hated Independents. They never voted for an Independent during the eleven years that I was a member. Stafford wanted to be Lord Mayor and it was Labour's avariciousness that gave him the dream of his life. Labour, realizing their mistake, agreed with *Fine Gael* to divide the remaining four years. Deputy Cluskey, then a parliamentary secretary, became Lord Mayor the following year but near the end of his term, the council was abolished.[3] Fred Mullen of *Fine Gael* was supposed to be Lord Mayor the following year, so he lost out. Fred was a hard worker and a decent fellow. When I spoke to Kevin Boland, Minister for Local Government, some weeks before the council was abolished, he told me that he did not think that *Fine Gael* would be so foolish as to have the council abolished just when Fred Mullen was certain to be Lord Mayor. As I said, the opposition was hoping that *Fianna Fáil* would save face and move the striking of the rate but *Fianna Fáil* knew that they had been vindictively robbed of everything and decided that they were not going to save them.

The opposition make party propaganda out of rising rates every year, but when in power they defend rate increases. A book, *Practical Newspaper Reporting* by G. Harris and D. Spark, gives advice to young journalists as follows:

> At rate meetings quite frequently there is a last minute bid by the opposition to reduce rates, the figure that the finance committee is recommending. In many cases this may be done mainly for the benefit of the press for propaganda purposes, to give the public the impression only the opposition cares about the ratepayer's pocket. It is ironic that an opposition will scream in opposition for certain economies but bloodily announce that they are quite impossible when their party is returned to power. The figure will have been arrived at after many meetings at which the opposition members would have been fully able to put their case for a reduction. As a rule the figure has been set as low as possible, as big rate rises are not good publicity for the Government party.[4]

As already mentioned, after losing my seat on the City Council I continued to call in at the corporation offices once a week to assist people who asked for my help. I was seldom to see any of the new councillors there. On a certain day, I proceeded to the rent office to help people who were threatened with eviction owing to arrears in rent payments. I was to be told by the rent supervisor that he could not help me any more as there had been objections by members of the Housing Committee because I was an ex-councillor. I then proceeded to the Allocation Department on behalf of people looking for dwellings, only to be told by the Allocation Officer that he could not give me any more information and not to come into the Allocation Office again. He said that he was acting on the instructions of the Principal Officer. I immediately located the Principle Officer and asked for an explanation. He said that objections had been made by councillors at the Housing Committee. He added that he told them that it had always been the practice to give information to former councillors.[5] I complained to Des Flanagan, Assistant City Manager, who told me to see him in a few days.[6] I did, and he told me that the question of giving information was a question for the City Manager and not the councillors and that was that. He said that he had instructed the Housing and Rent Departments to show me the usual courtesy. He suggested that I should call in not more than once a week, but that I could phone at any time.

Since the council was abolished, I was never to see any of the abolished councillors in corporation departments trying to help people. In other words, they objected to me trying to do what they could not do. Later, I was to be informed that the person who objected to me was Seán Dunne, Labour TD for Dublin South-West.[7] He was a member of the City Council when I became a councillor in 1955. Shortly thereafter he was declared bankrupt and had to forfeit his seat. He had personality and was about six feet three inches in height, the son of a British police officer. He specialized in contrivance and tear-jerking to get support. He was always talking about Ballyfermot, the area he represented in the *Dáil.* Whenever he was on television, no matter what the discussion was, he would bring in Ballyfermot. He obviously believed that the people living in Ballyfermot were chumps who would fall for any sort of playacting. He never made any constructive proposal. He was always talking about what the poor should get, but he, like all opposition parties, would never agree to vote for the money. The cost question was never mentioned. He did make representations on behalf of individuals but beyond that, nothing constructive. He was always complaining about the policy of inquiring into family means to ascertain income in connection with the differential rent system operating in local authority dwellings. He knew that this would go down well with all those on differential rents.

He was always blaming the government but he knew that the differential rent system was introduced by his own party in 1946 and operated in 1950. It was first recommended by James Larkin, the Labour leader, who was chairman of Dublin Corporation Housing Committee at the time.[8] The scheme was approved by the Labour Minister for Local Government Mr T. Murphy in a communication dated 5 June 1950.[9] The following is a copy of his letter of approval to the City Council:[10]

Custom House,
Dublin.

5 June 1950

I am directed by the Minister for Local Government to refer to Mr Byrne's letter of the 28 April last and previous correspondence on the subject and to state that he has approved of the proposal to fix maximum and minimum rents set out hereunder. I am to add that the minimum rents should be subject to review from time to time having regards to the variations in the municipal rates.

Mise le Meas,
G.H. MEAGHER.[11]

When you consider these facts and considered Mr Dunne's play-acting with reference to the inquiry system into means for differential rents purposes, i.e. his concern for the poor, you can obviously see the duplicity of politicians. When the Housing Bill of 1966 was going through the *Dáil,* Mr Dunne and the rest of the Labour party had their chance to delete the section regarding the inquiry system from the bill.[12] No deputy objected on the committee stage and again no deputy objected on the report stage or any other stage and thus a section which was repealed was again made law with heavier fines. It was not a question of not knowing what was being discussed in the House. All deputies receive copies of every bill, every amendment and copies of *Dáil* reports of everything discussed in the House further. All political parties discuss every section of every bill before it comes before the *Dáil.* Or so they claim.

In 1966, the City Manager and the Minister for Local Government decided to increase all Dublin Corporation tenants' rents with five annual increases of about six shillings a week each year in the case of a four-roomed dwelling and more or less depending on the size of the dwellings. I complained in the newspapers and strongly objected to these increases at corporation meetings. Not only that, I met the chairman of the Tenants' Association, Shay Ronan, and other members of the association regularly and kept them informed and advised them on tactics to defeat the authorities. In fact, without my help they would have failed because the Tenants' Association then was a small organization and they did not know anything about the manager's plans to increase their rents until I told them. I was rapped on the knuckles by Labour councillors for, as they said, stirring up the tenants. When, largely as a result of my help, the tenants organized a big march through the city, Mr Dunne tried to cash in by joining the march.

In the *Dáil* on 8 November 1966, Mr Dunne moved the following motion: 'That *Dáil Éireann* condemns the action of the Minister for Local Government in urging city and county managers to revise local authority rent schemes on an exorbitant scale.' Note the use of the adjective 'exorbitant'. In other words, they were not against rent increases if it was not exorbitant but at corporation meetings where the tenants' representatives were present in the gallery, they said nothing about exorbitant increases. They were against all increases. One face in the *Dáil* and another at corporation meetings! Deputy Dunne in his *Dáil* speech said:

> One of the great disabilities of the system has been the inquiry into the circumstances and the income of individuals. It is not at any time desirable that the income of the ordinary citizen should be subject to scrutiny by outside sources, except in so far as it can be proved to be socially desirable. Here we have a *Fianna Fáil* Deputy who will go right down the line to have the income of the humble Corporation tenant examined in detail and in every particular, and make it legally obligatory on him to report an increase or a decrease in income to, it is to be assumed, Dublin Corporation.'[13]

I stress the ambiguity used by Deputy Dunne to illustrate how popular politicians get the votes. Obviously he is no worse than others, except that Dunne overdid it.

There are three types in the average party. The vote catchers or gimmick men with a sort of dilettante approach to everything. They usually represent a poor working-class constituency, the people who do not reflect on what the politicians say. Then you have the mummies who have no push or go but go around with a 'hail fellow well met' approach. They always back the party machine and kow-tow to the leaders. They do not prevaricate. In fact, they do not do anything. You then have the sophisticated or leader type. They deceive just as much as the gimmick men but more subtly. Proinsias MacAonghusa, who was vice-chairman of the Labour party, was expelled some years ago because he sneered at the poor quality of the Labour *Dáil* representatives, referring to them as 'Mickey Mouse' representatives.[14] Proinsias is now a television commentator. He is an able fellow. Michael Mullan was a Labour councillor and TD. When he spoke in the *Dáil* on the turnover tax, he distorted everything about the tax:[15] 'There is an indication in the Budget that there will be an increase in non-contributory pensions and in unemployment assistance. There is no indication of any increase in the health services.' This was not correct. Both contributory and non-contributory classes got an increase including those who came under the health services: disabled and those with infectious diseases. Deputy Mullan again: 'The increase in the non-contributory pensions means 5d [pence] will go into the differential rent.'[16] Again this was incorrect. As a result of my action in 1957, I proposed a motion at Dublin Corporation that increases in social benefits in the case of old-age, non-contributory pensioners should not be taken into account when calculating differential rents. This motion was carried and accepted by the City Manager.[17] I later included that disabled people be paid from the Health Service. Deputy Mullan again said: 'Take the case of a married man with £8 a week. We are left to assume he will pay 4/- in tax.[18] If he has three children, he will benefit by the children's allowances to the extent of approximately 3/-. He loses a shilling on the deal each week.'[19] This was also wrong. To begin with, the average labourer had £10 a week, not £8. Further, there was no tax on rent, bus fares, insurance, etc. so the tax would be on about £6, assuming that the worker had only £8 weekly and three shillings tax. Now such a person, if he had three children would get two shillings and sixpence extra in children's allowance for the first child and one shilling and one and a half pence for the third child. In other words he got three shillings and seven and a half pence for the loss of three shillings.

Not much I agree, but as Deputy Mullan was trying to make the worker's case look as bad as possible, the truth makes a difference. Deputy Mullan argued that taxation should be on wealth but he did not say on whom. At the time, only 4,500 people paid surtax out of 300,000 on income tax and most of the latter were workers. If all tax was put on so-called wealth, then there would be no wealthy people in the country as all those with money would leave. Those with money would stay out and our whole economy would collapse. One Labour leader suggested an increase in income tax but there were loud protests from workers so the suggestion was dropped. The *Taoiseach* said, speaking on the turnover tax:

Will one member of *Fine Gael* Party [the Opposition] in this debate say what they would do if the Finance Bill were defeated and they came into office as a Government? Would they replace the taxes in these proposals and, if so, with what other taxes? And if they would not substitute these proposals by other taxes, what would they cut of the present Government services? Will one of them answer that question? I shall lay £1 million to 1d that not one of them will say one word.

Nor did they.[20] Deputy Steve Coughlan, another Labour man, a virile type, representing Limerick city said in reference to the turnover tax: 'This is the death-knell of the small shop keeper', but at the same time Mullan, Dunne and many others said that 'the shop-keepers would rob the workers'.[21] How would it be their death-knell if they were going to make money out of 'robbing the workers'? Again, it shows the double-talk at its best. Deputy Coughlan is a controversial individual. It was said that he encouraged people to attack shops where communist literature was sold. He was also accused of encouraging attacks on Jews even though he was always posing as a pillar of the Church. On one occasion in the *Dáil* when I was speaking he interrupted and said, looking at me: '...and where did you come from?' I answered: 'You drink your beer and leave me alone!' I thought he seemed jarred. He interrupted no more. On television, he was seen drinking and singing among a crowd of people in a pub. He was a publican and a bookie. When interviewed he said that he did not believe in telling people what to do. He believed in doing what they wanted him to do and that was why he got the votes. In other words, he was going to run with the crowd even if they were going to harm themselves or the country. He was not going to advise them. In that way he could always escape responsibility and he could never be blamed for any failure as he said nothing or did nothing. Most gimmick men took the same line. Deputy Coughlan, when speaking on the Liquor Bill of 1962, said that he did not like people who did not drink. This reminds me of a saying by the famous American night club queen Texas Guinan who said: 'Suckers should never get a break because people who expected something for nothing were suckers and they should be taken for every penny they have.'[22] The political gimmick men hold the same view as Texas Guinan. They do not do anything for the people, but take everything they have, particularly their votes.

Hilaire, eminent British writer, created a *Knight of the Order of St Gregory the Great*.[23] He was a British Liberal MP in 1904. He was straightforward in his views. He refused to stand for a second term. He concluded that the party system was fraudulent and that corruption was rife. Years later, in about 1940, when he was sick and being visited by an old friend who referred to what was said in the House of Commons the day before, he interjected and said was that bloody business still going on? He also said that politicians were sly and shifty. Yes, I repeat. That bloody business is still going on and will continue. Perhaps Edmund Burke was right when he said that the voters were just as corrupt as the politician and that no reform will ever change their nature. We can only hope that with more education and the advent of television, more people will become more sophisticated and see through the party game. If voters were more honest or more aware you would have more honest politicians, for as they say – the people get the politicians they deserve.

As I said, when the Minister for Local Government and the Dublin City Manager decided to increase corporation tenants' rents by five annual increases in 1966, there was playacting on a grand scale by the politicians. There were 40,000 corporation tenants in Dublin who represented about one-third of the city population. There were only two corporation tenant members of the council, Rory Cowan, son of the late Peadar Cowan to whom I have already referred, and myself. Rory Cowan was co-opted when his father died. He was unemployed and joined or was enticed into the Labour party, who got him employment. He is now a trade union official. As a member of the Labour party, he would have to obey the party whip. I alone was free to fight for the tenants. The parties had no interest in the tenants as they were all house owners and many were businessmen and always held the view that they were subsidizing the tenants. They expressed their hostility many times at housing committee meetings. Of course, some of them, the gimmick men, played both sides. I decided on a campaign to whittle down the rent increases. I wrote letters to the press. I addressed members of the Dublin Tenants' Association and explained that we would have to make some offer as the minister had threatened to cut housing subsidies unless the rents were increased. The City Manager was determined to impose the increase whether the council liked it or not, as he had that power. I put it to the tenants that if we refused to make some offer, then the councillors would lose all control and the minister and the manager would make conditions worse. At all times in the past the manager had tried to meet the councillors half-way. He knew that his job would be made difficult if there was much friction between the councillors and himself. The councillors were indifferent to the tenants' case, but municipal elections were due in a few months so they had to 'box clever'. They wanted the rent increases but they wanted someone else to 'hold the baby', in particular some of their opponents. Of course, they were afraid of me that I would expose their duplicity. Some people may hold the view that the doings of the local councillors are not important but I see it differently.

There is no difference in modifications, in the pursuit of power as between mere local councillors and members of Parliament, members of Cabinets, whether national or international. In fact, most members of Parliament and Cabinets were once mere councillors and that is where they learned to play politics. In 1970, we had the famous 'arms case', when several Cabinet ministers were forced to resign.[24] They were all former councillors. The first president of the state, William T. Cosgrave, was a Dublin alderman, as was President Seán T. O'Kelly.[25] When Machiavelli wrote *The Prince*, he only intended it for the eyes of a few small-time dictators but the politics of these petty dictators was the politics of the world. The world read *The Prince* and learnt how to succeed through corruption.[26] Little has changed since the time of Machiavelli. It was said by his opponents that De Valera studied *The Prince* when a prisoner after the Rebellion of 1916. I am satisfied that Mr De Valera was an honest man but like President Lincoln and President John F. Kennedy. According to their biographers they were ruthless, cunning and adroit and they had to be to survive in the political jungle. I would not say that De Valera was cunning but he was ruthless, or as Dan Breen said, 'a unique dictator'.

At a meeting of the Housing Committee on 16 January 1967, I moved a motion that rent increases should relate to only one year. The minister and the manager wanted five annual increases. The committee agreed to my motion. The manager said that he would accept the terms of my motion. I then moved that the proposed increase be reduced to 10 per cent on standard, fixed-rent dwellings and 7.5 per cent on differential rent dwellings, about half of what the manager wanted. The Labour party did not accept my motion. They moved an amendment that there would be no increases at all. This was a dangerous move as the manager and the minister would then fix all rents without consulting the councillors and bring in their adverse regulations at the same time. In fact, this is what they did. The Labour party's policy was to make the tenants suffer as much as possible. In that way they could pose as their defenders. Labour's amendment was defeated by six votes to three. The *Fine Gael* group voted for my motion which was carried by six votes to three. The three who voted against the motion were one ratepayer and two *Fianna Fáil* members. They wanted the manager's proposal: the full rent increase. Labour did not vote.

In a report to the City Council the decisions of the Housing Committee were submitted.[27] The manager stated that he would accept Alderman Sherwin's motion that the increase would only relate to one year but he said that he could not accept my second motion that the proposed increase be reduced to 10 per cent in the case of fixed-rent dwellings and 7.5 per cent in the case of differential rent dwellings. It was clear that any chance I had of winning, Labour had none. I believed that half a loaf was better than no bread at all, but obviously Labour agreed with Hitler, that no bread would be good for votes. They wanted misery just as they invented misery on the turnover tax issue in 1963. When the Council met on 6 February, the *Fianna Fáil* party moved a motion that the manager's report be noted and that there should be no increase in any rents. The motion was carried. Denis Larkin, on behalf of the Labour party, moved a somewhat similar motion and it was carried. Here were all of the parties, except the ratepayers, 'washing their hands of it in public', but at committee meetings where the press were not present, most of them were voting for increases. I was going to put my motion regarding a small increase so as not to leave the decision to the minister and the manager but *Fianna Fáil's volte face* meant that the majority had voted against any increase, or at least pretended to. At a meeting of the Dublin Health Authority of which I was a member, the week before the council met, I asked Denis Larkin, leader of the Labour party in the corporation, to support my motion for a small increase so as not to let the matter out of the control of the councillors. He answered that the Labour Party would make its own decision.

Arising out of the council's decision on rents, the manager reported to the Minister for Local Government; the minister in reply said that he would accept my motion, that there should be only one increase but approved of the increases proposed by the manager to range from two shillings and nine pence to six shillings and nine pence a week depending on the size of the dwelling.[28] This is where all the tenants were introduced. He also said that his sanction was conditional on other things being done regarding section five of his letter:

All changes in tenancies arising on or after a date in the near future to be decided by the authority – either from vacancies, transfers, inter-transfers, succession cases, or otherwise, should be subject to the new tenant going on the appropriate differential rent scale. In this connection, the Minister has no objection to the application of high rent to new tenancies in dwellings first let on or after 1 January 1954.

In other words, all the fixed-rent tenants, approximately 15,000 in number, would go on the high rent when their parents died, which had not been the case up until then. Furthermore, if the corporation transferred a family from one dwelling to another, they would also go on to high rents.[29] This also included all tenants who arranged an inter-transfer with one another, this being the unkindest cut of all. I tried to avoid all of this and that was why I tried to get the Labour party to agree to a small increase so that the matter would not go to the minister to decide on, but Labour was playing their own game. Misery would get them more votes and they were right. The pushovers fell for it and Labour increased their number of councillors in the Dublin Corporation from five to thirteen at the local elections. These were largely in corporation housing estates.

At the Council meeting on 14 March 1967, I decided to save as many tenants as possible so I moved a motion that no regulations should be made in the case of inter-transfers. The motion was carried. The ratepayers voted against. I then moved that the reconditioned tenements as well as all pre-1932 dwellings be required to pay not more than sixpence a room, where the manager wanted one shilling and sixpence a room. Where any of the above dwellings were required to pay the full rate increase, then they received credit as proposed above in an adjustment in the rent structure. The motion was carried. I then moved another motion: 'That succession cases or transfers subject to new agreements be placed in scheme (A).' The motion was carried.[30] The manager's motion with the amendments as recommended was then put to the council and was carried by nineteen votes to eleven. Supported by the *Fine Gael* party, the *Fianna Fáil* party had earlier voted in council on 6 February 1967 against all rent increases. Now on 14 March 1967, they both voted for the manager's original rent proposal which they had rejected on 6 February, and the rent increases they agreed to on 14 March were made worse because of the minister's additional proposals. The manager could accept or reject my motions as rent increases are a managerial function. However, as I have said, because he was always anxious to go some way towards meeting the councillors, he agreed to accept some of my motions.

At a meeting of the City Council on 1 May 1967, the manager was asked to state his decisions regarding the motions passed by the council on 14 March 1967. The manager replied:

(1) That the scale of increases in the maximum differential rent applying to reconditioned dwellings be – 1 room 9d; 2 rooms 2/-; 3 rooms 3/-; 4 rooms 4/-; and 6d per room per week for those on fixed rent for pre-1932 dwellings and acquired property on fixed rent and the same increase for those on differential rent.

(2) That in the case of a tenant recommended by the Medical Officer on the grounds of overcrowding who is granted a transfer

whether as part of an inter-transfer or otherwise, the rent of the dwelling to which he is being transferred will not be altered by reason of the new tenancy.

He added: 'There is no provision in the approved scheme for succession cases', but the Housing Committee at its meeting on 21 April 1967 asked that this aspect be placed on the agenda for the meeting on 19 May 1967. The proposal to reconsider succession cases was put by me at the Housing Committee on 19 May. The matter was on the agenda.[31] As the manager could not be present, it was agreed to defer the matter until the next meeting and it was agreed to request that the manager be present. No further meetings of the Housing Committee were held as the municipal elections were held on 28 June 1967. It is a rule of standing orders that all motions lapse when municipal elections take place, so I was not there to re-enter the motion and those elected were not interested. In fact, only two of the newly elected councillors were corporation tenants. The net result of my efforts on behalf of the tenants was

(1) Reducing the rent increase to one year instead of five.
(2) Reducing the rent in the case of 7,000 pre-1932 reconditioned and acquired dwellings, easement of the conditions regarding transfers and inter-transfers and a promise of re-consideration of succession cases by the Manager.[32]

At a meeting of the City Council on 1 May 1967, I asked the manager the number of voting members who attended the four committee estimates meetings in order to fix the rates for 1967–68. There were eighteen voting members on each committee.[33] The manager replied: 'Housing Committee: nine; Finance Committee: six; Planning Committee: seven and General Purposes Committee: six.' When the council met in private to reconsider all the committee estimates on 14 March 1967, the meeting commenced at 5.15 p.m. and ended at 7.40 p.m. Only twenty-three members attended out of forty-five. Only eighteen were present when the meeting finished. When the council met in public on 30 March 1967 to strike the rate, only twenty-eight members turned up out of forty-five but five left before the rate was struck. Twenty-three were present. Twenty-two were missing. I moved the following motion on 8 August 1966:

That this Council request The City Manager to publish annually the attendance of members at all meetings. It is most unfair and not encouraging that those who always attend should not get any more credit in the public eye than those who never or seldom attend the Corporation meetings. The Manager is aware that despite the small number needed for a quorum, three out of eighteen, meetings are often delayed and sometimes postponed because of poor attendance.

In the absence of support this motion was dropped, although there were twenty-eight members present. In other words, voters were invited to vote for slackers, at least discerning people would not support those with a good attendance record but the party men and others were afraid of the truth being known. The municipal elections held in Dublin on 28 June 1967 resulted in one Labour man who only attended one committee meeting in 1966, the year before, out of a total of sixty-six, becoming an alderman. Five others were elected councillors who attended less than four committee meetings. In fact, one member elected attended none, nor did he attend any during the previous few years. As I said, I attended sixty-three out of sixty-six and the three that I missed was when I was on official corporation business or ill, but I lost my seat.

NOTES

1   The original chapter title was: 'Back to square one'.
2   When Sherwin lost his corporation seat in 1967, he felt that his world had collapsed.
3   Frank Cluskey, Lord Mayor of Dublin (1968–69).
4   Geoffrey Harris and David Spark, *Practical Newspaper Reporting* (London: Heinemann, 1966).
5   This is the practice in the *Dáil* towards former members and they can enter any part of the *Dáil* at any time.
6   In the *Parliamentary Debates, Seanad Éireann*, vol. 108, 8 May 1985, col. 209, the then *Taoiseach* Garret Fitzgerald (born 9 February 1926, *Taoiseach* 1981–82 and 1982–87) is addressed. The following is declared by the speaker: '... Mr Des Flanagan, who up to recently was an Assistant City Manager in the Corporation, was on that [ad hoc] committee [of the Department of Health] and indeed served on after he retired. He is a man with considerable experience in housing in the city.'
7   John Horgan, Professor of Journalism, School of Communication, Dublin City University, refers to Seán Dunne in an article entitled 'Anti-Communism and Media Surveillance in Ireland (1948–50)'. In this, he refers to Seán MacEntee's correspondence with Peadar Cowan of *Clann na Poblachta* where he accused a number of people of loyalty to the communist cause. Many of them were for many years standard-bearers of the Irish Left such as John de Courcy Ireland, Seán Dunne, Roddy Connolly, James Larkin Jr and Con Lehane.
8   At the City Council meeting of 19 July 1946, James Larkin moved that report number thirty-one be adopted. The report was that a differential rent system be adopted: reference to *Minutes of the Municipal Council of the City of Dublin 1946*, dated 19 July, p.151. It was pointed out by the law agent that the corporation had

no power to force tenants to disclose their income. It was agreed to ask the government to introduce legislation to give the corporation that power including fines.

9   Timothy J. Murphy, Labour Minister for Local Government, was a member of the thirteenth *Dáil* (18 February 1948 to 7 May 1951). This first inter-party government was comprised of *Fine Gael*, Labour, *Clann na Talmhan* and *Clann na Pobhlacta*. Murphy died during term on 29 April 1949. Michael J. Keyes, Labour TD, filled the vacancy of Minister for Local Government following Murphy's death.

10   Notice how the Labour minister asked that the rents of those on the minimum, i.e. the poor people, should be increased every year? Sherwin reversed this practice in 1966.

11   Perhaps G.H. Meagher was a relative of Thomas Francis Meagher, born 3 August 1823. Thomas F. Meagher was an Irish nationalist and later transported convict, escapee, American Civil War general and Governor of Montana. He drowned in July 1865 and his body was never recovered.

12   Section 61 of the Housing Bill of 1966.

13   *Parliamentary Debates, Dáil Éireann,* 'Private Members' Business Local Authority Rent Schemes', vol 225, 8 November 1966, col. 458.

14   Proinsias MacAonghusa, former RTÉ broadcaster and chairman of *Bord na Gaeilge,* was born in Salthill Galway in 1933. His career in broadcasting began in 1952 when he started working for *Radio Éireann.* By the 1960s, he was working in television for RTÉ, UTV and the BBC. He finished his RTÉ career as editor of the long-running current affairs programme, *Féach.* Throughout his career he was a regular contributor to a range of national newspapers and the author of many books on politics and history in both Irish and English. MacAonghusa ran unsuccessfully for the *Dáil* on two occasions: first as Labour party candidate in Louth in 1965 and subsequently as an Independent candidate in Dún Laoghaire-Rathdown in 1969. He was briefly Vice-Chairman of the Labour Party, served as Chairman of *Bord na Gaeilge* and was a member of the Arts Council. Proinsias MacAonghusa died in September 2003 and has been described as 'one of the most significant broadcasters in Irish on both media' and a man who 'set the standard for Irish language broadcasting'.

15   *Parliamentary Debates, Dáil Éireann,* 'Committee on Finance Resolution No. 14 – General', vol 202, 24 April 1963, col. 343.

16   Ibid., col. 343.

17   In 1963 Michael Mullan was a member of Dublin City Council.

18   This is the equavalent of sixpence in the pound.

19   *Parliamentary Debates, Dáil Éireann,* 'Committee on Finance Resolution No. 14 – General', vol 202, 24 April 1963, col. 344.

20   *Parliamentary Debates, Dáil Éireann,* 'Finance Bill 1963, Second Stage (Resumed)', vol 203, 20 June 1963, col. 1395.

21   Stephen Coughlan, Alderman and member of the Labour party who was to cause conflict in 1972 leading to the resignation of fellow party member Jim Kemmy (1936–97). An interesting article written by journalist John Downing appeared in *The Limerick Leader* dated Saturday 18 April 2004. It was entitled 'Politics: Reaping the whirlwind or the fruits of his Labour?' Downing referred to a landmark Labour party conference which was held in Dublin on 24–26 January 1969. Labour pledged to nationalize all banks, credit and insurance companies, encourage group farming, take state control of land sales which would be banned to foreigners and a wide range of free health, education and

welfare services. *The Cork Examiner* described the agenda as 'communistic', *The Irish Independent* said it revealed 'a basic approach so drastic as to be unreal to most Irishmen'. The Federated Union of Employers dismissed it as 'a watered down version of Russian ideas'. Downing stated: 'Non-Dublin TDs such as Steve Coughlan in Limerick were undecidedly uncomfortable with the outcome.'

22   Mary Louise Guinan, saloon keeper, actress and entrepreneur, was born on 12 January 1884 in Waco, Texas. In 1917 'Texas' Guinan made her film début in the silent movie *The Wildcat*. She became the United States' first movie cowgirl nicknamed 'The Queen of the West'. In addition to her film career, she also had a sojourn in France entertaining the troops during the First World War. Upon the introduction of 'prohibition', she opened a 'speakeasy' in New York City called the '300 Club' which became famous for its troupe of forty scantily clad fan dancers but also for Ms Guinan's personality. Her aplomb made her a celebrity but she was arrested several times for serving alcohol. Guinan earned $700,000 in ten months in 1926 while her clubs were being routinely raided. Guinan returned to the screen with two sound pictures playing fictionalized versions of herself as a speakeasy proprietor in *Queen of the Night Clubs* in 1929 and *Broadway through a Keyhole* in 1933. During the Great Depression, Guinan took her show to Europe but was denied entry at every European port she attempted to disembark at. She turned this to her advantage by launching a satirical revue entitled *Too Hot for Paris*. While on the road, she contracted amoebic dysentery in Vancouver, British Columbia, and died there on 5 November 1933. The number 'All that Jazz' in the musical *Chicago* is thought to be a homage to her.

23   Hilaire Belloc, 1870–1953. A debate between Belloc, Bernard Shaw and Gilbert Keith Chesterton and a portfolio of engravings by Edward Handley-Read with a foreword by Belloc is listed in the bibliography.

24   The 'arms case' will be dealt with later.

25   Seán Thomas O'Kelly was born on 25 August 1882 and died on 23 November 1966. O'Kelly was a member of *Dáil Éireann* from 1918 until his election as President. He served as *Ceann Comhairle* of *Dáil Éireann* from 1919–21 and Minister for Irish 1920–21. He was Minister for Local Government from 1932–39, Minister for Finance (1939–45), Vice-President of the Executive Council from 1932 until 1937. He became the first *Tánaiste* from 1937 to 1945 and second President of Ireland from 1945–59.

26   Machiavelli died in 1527. At this time Italy was divided into a number of states.

27   *Reports and Printed Documents of the Corporation of Dublin, January to December 1967*, Report no. 12, p.46.

28   28 February 1967, reference number H. 29/20/15.

29   There were a few exceptions to this.

30   In the differential rent structures there were three scales of rent (A), (B) and (C) where (A) was the lowest and (B) was the highest. There is now a higher scale called '70'.

31   It was numbered item 2258.

32   Mr Molloy, the new Minister for Local Government said that 'The time for pruning the rates is at the estimates' meetings of the committees and not at public meetings of the Council. It is just playacting to the gallery and playing politics.' He continued: 'There is a tendency on the part of certain members not to take the active interest in the affairs of the Council and not to do their homework and when that happens the Council's affairs are not being fully examined.' *The Irish Press*, 18 January 1971, 'Molloy calls for planning review'.

33   *Minutes of the Dublin City Council 1967*, item 18, p.110.

12

I SAVED THE COUNTRY

Shortly before I lost my *Dáil* seat, March 1965, I attended the Savoy Cinema in O'Connell Street, Dublin. The picture was an historic film, *Mise Éire*, illustrating episodes of the fight for Irish freedom. Everyone was there by invitation. They were all notables of one sort or another. When the show was over, I stood in the foyer of the cinema entrance. When Seán T. O'Kelly, the former President of the Republic emerged, he saw me standing with my wife. He came over and put his arm around me and said: 'Frank, I'm proud of you! You saved the country!' This compliment has been paid to me many times even by members of the opposition, but of course, not publicly. They know that in saving the country I also saved the government, thus keeping them in power. That is what politics is all about – power – not 'saving the country'. Mr Kevin Boland, former Minister for Local Government and honorary secretary of the *Fianna Fáil* party, admitted to me that, in not letting the government down on the turnover tax vote, I had prevented a general election at the time, which would have been bad for *Fianna Fáil.*

So I saved the country, and the government, and found myself out of the *Dáil* with no job, no business, no *Dáil* pension, very little money and a wife and four dependent children to keep. I was told by Joe Groome, another honorary secretary of *Fianna Fáil*, that I had been chosen as one of the *Taoiseach*'s eleven senators, as he had the power to appoint them. I was glad of the news in view of my financial position and my dependent family. It had always been the practice to appoint those who had lost their *Dáil* seats as a result of voting for the government and *Fianna Fáil* had been successful in the general election. I had no agreement with the government and I did not join the party. Had I done so, I would have been elected. About a week before the date of the announcement of the new senators, I was told by a leading member of the party that I was not included on the *Taoiseach*'s list. I wrote to Mr Lemass and while admitting that I had no agreement with the government, I nevertheless expected that in view of my financial position and the fact that I had lost my safe seat as a result of voting for the government, he would consider me one of his eleven senators. I received the following reply:

Department of the *Taoiseach.*
8 June 1965.

Dear Frank,
I have received your letter. I fear I cannot hold out much prospect of a senate nomination for you, having regard to all my existing commitments in this connection. I was somewhat surprised to learn that you have no income, as I had assumed that you qualified for a military service or disablement pension. I have asked the Minister for Defence to examine your position in this regard and report to me.

Yours sincerely,
Seán Lemass.

The disablement pension to which he referred was one that I could have had in 1937, twenty-eight years earlier, but I refused to apply for it, thus sacrificing several thousand pounds. The pension amounted to three pounds and five shillings a week. As I have already alluded to elsewhere, a person on public assistance with a wife and four children had four pounds two shillings and sixpence a week, plus free turf and other small benefits. I had a wife and four dependent children and I was expected to be financially secure with less than a man on public assistance. I wonder how would Mr Lemass feel had I written such a letter to him, had he been in my circumstances?

He said that he had commitments to others. As far as *Fianna Fáil* power was concerned, they were all nobodies. Had they never existed, it would not have affected *Fianna Fáil.* Had I let the country go to hell and looked after myself in 1963, then *Fianna Fáil* would have lost twenty *Dáil* seats, especially with the turnover tax as the main issue. They would not have been in power in 1965. Many *Fianna Fáil* leaders were surprised that I was not nominated and several press commentators also expressed surprise. Had I joined *Fianna Fáil* before the election, I am certain that I would have held on to my seat or that I would have been nominated to the senate but I did not apply to join. I had been asked several times to do so but I was always an Independent and did not feel like joining any party. Joe Leneghan, the other Independent who supported the government, joined *Fianna Fáil* but lost his seat. However, he was nominated to the Senate and in the general election of 1969 regained his *Dáil* seat as a *Fianna Fáil* candidate. He was a man in good health. He owned a pub and was a man of means, nevertheless he got the Senate from Mr Lemass in 1965 worth no less than £25 weekly at that time and I was expected to be satisfied with three pounds and five shillings weekly to keep a wife and four children.

Early in November 1968, Senator Miss Margaret Pearse died.[1] A general election was expected in the following June. I realized that if the *Taoiseach* nominated me to the vacant seat in the Senate I would qualify for a *Dáil* pension. I had seven years and four months' service to my credit. I only required eight years' service and I would get about £6 weekly. This small sum plus my disability pension would not even give me a labourer's wage. This pension is paid out of a fund, which deputies and senators contributed to. I paid into it myself. I wrote to the *Taoiseach* and asked for the nomination. I received the following reply:

> Department of the *Taoiseach*.
> 11 November 1968.

Dear Mr Sherwin,

I have received your letter of the 11th instant about the vacancy in the Senate caused by the death of Miss Margaret Pearse. You will, I am sure appreciate that I have not yet considered the question of filling this vacancy and that, when I come to do so, other names will also have to be considered.

In the circumstances, I can only promise no more than that. I will bear your name in mind when the time comes.

> Yours sincerely,
> J. Lynch.

Later the *Taoiseach* nominated a young member of the *Fianna Fáil* party from Leitrim.

About this time, all *Dáil* constituencies were revised and to my dismay, I lost 70 per cent of my North City *Dáil* area. Over 65 per cent of the new constituency called 'Dublin Central' was centred in South Dublin City, where I had little support. All of my political activities during the previous thirteen years were centred in North Dublin. In fact, since I was born! Not only did I lose all the North City area where my son stood as candidate in the local elections of 1967 but a big corporation housing estate, O'Devaney Gardens, and part of Arbour Hill where I always got strong support was put into another area, namely North Dublin West. Further, the new area was much larger. I would not be able to canvass it and, worse still, not only had I De Valera's son as a candidate in the new area but I also had the outgoing

Lord Mayor and another very popular former Lord Mayor. There was also a very active Independent in the field from South City who seemed to have plenty of support and money. I was in two minds as to whether I should go up for Dublin Central or North-West as I knew large numbers in the latter area. In fact, I was an alderman for half of this area and 80 per cent of all voters were corporation tenants. I was advised by many, including Noel Lemass, the former *Taoiseach*'s son, to stand for Dublin North-West, as there were no strong opposition candidates. I decided to take a chance and fight Dublin Central, largely because I lived in the North City part of the constituency and I knew that I would get strong support around the locality in which I lived. I realized that I had made a mistake. Not only was I not elected but I lost my £100 deposit for the first time. Some of my expenses were paid from subscriptions from a number of friends but I came out of it in debt. I received 1,456 number one votes. Poor but not bad when you consider my tremendous difficulties.

I blame, to some extent, the absence of any television coverage for Independents during the general election of 1969 and previous elections. Television, the new media, has a powerful impact on viewers. To many people, if you are not on it (television), you are not in it (elections). Newspapers are not read by everyone and Independents get little publicity during elections. Party machines and personalities crowd them out and many people do not read political news. Many others have little education and do not understand what they read. Many have poor eyesight and read very little but they all watch television and repeat what they hear to others. I wrote to the directors of broadcasting in *Telefís Éireann* and asked for time for Independents and was told in reply that only parties could be accommodated according to the Broadcasting Act of 1960. This was not true. Section eighteen of the Broadcasting Act of 1960 states:

(1) It shall be the duty of the Authority to secure that when it broadcasts any information, news or feature which relates to matters of public controversy, or is the subject of current public debate, the information, news or feature is presented objectively and <u>impartially</u> [Sherwin's emphasis] and without any expressions of the Authority's own views.

(2) Nothing in this section shall prevent the Authority from transmitting political party broadcasts.

There is nothing in this section which states that political parties must get time; it is left to the authority's discretion and there is nothing in this section that states that Independents cannot be accommodated.[2]

During the election, the RTÉ Authority agreed to give the Independents a 'dummy show' on the television. In other words, they could be seen speaking to constituents but no sound was allowed. How could a candidate impart what was in his head, heart or soul by a 'dummy show'? Would we have ever heard of Christ's 'Sermon on the Mount' had He merely opened and closed His mouth, issuing no sound? How could Caruso, the great singer, delight people if there was no sound?[3] How would Abraham Lincoln have fared had his immortal oration at Gettysburg been a silent oration?[4] How could he appeal to the hearts of his audience or of mankind? Just as it has been said that when it comes to votes, 'the moron and the discerning are alike'. People who just open their mouths without emitting any sound are likewise. Some of the Independents were favoured. Three of them, including a television commentator, got an interview on radio. Sheridan, the only Independent who was elected, was interviewed on television, when touring his constituency. On the night before the poll, the other Independent who was competing with me for votes in Dublin Central was shown with a big parade of cars carrying his election literature on television, which was worth hundreds of pounds and hundreds of votes to him. I asked for the same facilities but was denied them. I was in debt as a result of the election and all the more so after losing my £100 deposit.

I continued to go down to the corporation offices once a week, but often I phoned on behalf of people in need. In October 1969, I helped to form a corporation tenants' association in my parish of St Michan's. I was elected chairman and because of my know-how, I was responsible for many improvements of a maintenance nature in the parish. It is our policy not only to attend to individual complaints, but also as part of our annual programme to give an outing to the old-age pensioners, a party for the children, and an outing for the members. The Tenants' Association is affiliated to NATO, the National Association of Tenants' Organisation. Towards the end of 1970, I was elected secretary to the Dublin Regional Council NATO. When the Dublin Corporation estimates were published in April 1972, they included a proposal to increase the rent of 20,000 corporation tenants. As secretary of NATO, I called an emergency meeting and advised the chairman to ask for a rent strike to begin on 1 May, if the increase was included in the rates. The strike began as decided and lasted for fifteen months. Thousands of eviction orders were signed by the court. An attempt to evict the first tenant at Coolock was resisted by hundreds of local tenants and members of the Regional Council and the National Executive. About a hundred policemen were present. A riot developed and several people were injured. The police broke into the dwelling and arrested those inside, including several NATO officers. The scenes made the headlines in all of the newspapers. The tenants decided to resist all further attempts at eviction and the tenant who had been evicted got back into his home that night. I was in court for the possession of my home but I argued a point of law and the case was adjourned. Later I argued another point of law and the case was dismissed, although the corporation issued a new summons. As a general election was called in February 1973, the opposition made promises to everyone in order to get votes. The tenants were promised better conditions so the NATO executive recommended the opposition to the tenant voters. As I did not trust politicians, I proposed a motion that the opposition put their promises in writing, giving specific details, and that the document be signed by the spokesmen for local government of both opposition parties. They duly signed the document and later gave concessions so the strike was called off.

I took no part in the election but I wrote letters to the evening papers asking for support for Independents and Charlie Haughey. I was anxious to help Haughey as he was under fire from all of the anti-national politicians in the south because he is alleged to have helped the nationalists in the north when they were under siege in 1969. He was also a man with heart. As Finance Minister he gave the most spectacular social benefits of all: free travel for all old-age pensioners and IRA veterans, as well as substantial increases in social benefits. Other Finance Ministers refused to grant free travel. Due to my writing this letter, the majority of the Regional Council asked for my resignation as secretary. I refused to resign as I had broken no rule but I decided not to attend further meetings until the next general meeting. Most of those who asked for my resignation were members of opposition parties.

NOTES

1   Senator Margaret Pearse, the sister of Willie and Patrick Henry Pearse, leader of those who took part in the 1916 Rising, was born on 4 August 1878. She was the first woman to be honoured Honorary Freeman of Wexford Town and was conferred on 13 July 1952. She died in November 1968. Margaret Pearse, her mother, was devastated when her sons Willie and Patrick Pearse were executed in May 1916. Patrick or Pádraig Pearse, writer, founder of schools, member of the Supreme Council of the IRB, Commandant-General of the Irish Volunteers and head of the Provisional Government, read the Proclamation of the Irish Republic on the steps of the GPO Dublin. He was executed by firing squad on 3 May 1916. His mother Margaret joined Sinn Féin after the Rising and gave support to candidates during the 1918 Westminster Election. She was elected to *Dáil Éireann* as a TD for Dublin County in the 1921 general election. She strongly opposed the Anglo-Irish Treaty and when it was ratified, she left the *Dáil*. She

supported those who opposed the Treaty during the Civil War and continued to be a member of Sinn Féin until 1926. In that same year, she left the *Ard Fheis* with Éamon De Valera and became a founder member of *Fianna Fáil*. She was elected to the *Dáil* again at the 1933 general election for Dublin but lost her seat in 1937. She was also a senator and involved with the Irish Press. Her son, Pádraig Pearse, is considered the spiritual figurehead of *Fianna Fáil*.

2   During the general election of 1965, Sherwin was a controversial figure. He had kept the government in power for three years and it was his vote that saved the government from defeat on the turnover tax issue. Nevertheless, he never got a chance to give his side of the case on television.

3   Enrico Caruso, born on 25 February 1873 and died on 2 August 1921, was one of the most famous tenors in the history of opera.

4   Abraham Lincoln, the sixteenth President of the United States (1861–65). Lincoln was born on 12 February 1809 in Hodgenville, Hardin County, Kentucky and died on 15 April 1865 the morning after being shot at Ford's Theatre in Washington, DC, by John Wilkes Booth, an actor.

13

MY WORK AS COUNCILLOR AND TD

Some people ask what can an Independent do in politics. They judge an Independent because he is only one vote against many. These people forget that one man can do as much as any minority party. A minority party cannot pass legislation and the governing party always opposes motions proposed by the opposition because to accept such motions would benefit the opposition, just as the opposition will always oppose government motions even when they are good and likely to benefit the country and people in need. An Independent can talk without conditioning his views with bias, as do all party men. He can afford to be honest and because he is only an Independent his views may be accepted by the government because he presents no political threat. This happened with several motions and suggestions made by me in the *Dáil* when they were accepted by the government. In addition, although parties consistently misrepresent one another, they keep mum on matters where they share equal guilt when it would be safer to be silent, which is where the Independent comes in. He has nothing to lose by dragging these skeletons into the open in the interests of the public.

Professor Hogan had this to say in his *Proportional Representation*:

> Something is to be said for at least a few Independents who because they have minds of their own and are not afraid to speak them, can become the medium for expressing unpalatable truths and opinions, however bitter in the mouths of party leaders and however unpopular with large sections of the electorate.[1]

The dictionary's definition of an Independent is as follows: 'Not relying on or supported by or governed by another. Not easily influenced; unbiased; one who in politics, art, literature, etc., acts or thinks for himself.' All the great figures of history were Independents. They were all successful people. Big and small, they were Independents or had the traits of an Independent. There are a number of Independents in every party. They usually dominate or influence them. They are often controversial and in danger of expulsion by party hacks who gang up against them. As a rule, they are not wanted and fixers who control the parties at local level contrive to keep them out. St Paul was not one of the original apostles. He came on to the scene after Christ was crucified. He was a Jew like the others. He had independent views. He held that Christ's Message was for all mankind but other apostles held that only Jews or those who accepted Jewish rites could be members of the New Church. The other apostles tried to expel him. He fought back and was only accepted because he was most successful in his mission. Paul's independent views, his energy and his defiance are typical traits of Independents, great and small. The Pauls of politics are not welcome. They upset the hacks. They endanger the ambitious nonentities, upset the leaders with their outspoken views, and are likely competitors. Shakespeare's *Julius Caesar* spoke only too truly when he asked that he be given fat men around him, they sleep at night. Lean men have a hungry look, they think too much, they are dangerous.[2] Frank Kent is quoted in Kennedy's *Profiles in Courage* stating that probably the most important single accomplishment for the politically ambitious is the fine art of seeming to say something without doing so.[3] George Saunders, the film actor, was quoted in Roderick Mann's column in *The Sunday Express* as saying that he knew a public relations man in Los Angeles, Hal Evry, who specialized in getting people elected for public office.[4] The formula was quite simple. You must on no account ever make a speech. You must stay at home and be seen nowhere. You must say nothing or do nothing. In that way you will offend nobody and get the votes at election time. Of course, the gimmick men like to be seen and heard. Their formula is just as simple: run with the crowd. Disagree with nobody, especially if they represent many votes. Tell pleasant lies and flatter the voters. A friend of mine, known as Steam O'Brien, said that he always 'steamed' everybody.[5] He told me many times that you can't beat the steam.[6] He said that when you steam people they will always be with you and come back for more. Party politicians practise all of these tricks. Independents as a rule are straightforward.

Before I voted for Mr Lemass in 1961, I was always described by reporters as 'the most Independent of all the Independents'. I still am. Even when I voted for the government, I remained Independent in the *Dáil* and corporation. I did not consult with any party or individual as to how I would vote. In spite of all handicaps, an honest Independent can do a lot of work for the country, for certain classes of people and numerous individuals. While he is up against it because of his refusal to lie, he can always hope that enough people will come to see the light. Professor Hogan states in his book, *Proportional Representation*, that people are by nature wholly reasonable and virtuous and if in practice they err and act wrongly, that it is only an accident due to their corrupting surroundings and the wrong kind of education.

When I became a councillor in June 1955, I attended all the meetings, even meetings of committees of which I was not a member. It takes several years to understand corporation work and all activities are considered by committees. If you do not attend regularly, you will never have the know-how. I remember one councillor, now a TD, at the Housing Estimates meeting in 1967, stating that although he was a councillor seven years, he still did not understand housing estimates. An active local authority councillor is considerably more active than a TD because a councillor does a lot of committee work and is in touch with considerably more members of the public.

A TD does little or no committee work. He is not expected to speak in the *Dáil* and is discouraged from doing so. He is only expected to be on hand to vote when the bell rings and even if he is drunk, there are no objections, provided he can make his way to the lobby to cast his vote, and provided that he does not make an exhibition of himself. In fact, if a TD does little local authority work, then he is doing nothing as it is the ministers and the front bench members who do all the work in the *Dáil*. The *Dáil* is usually empty, except when there is a vote or at 'Question Time' or, as I call it, 'Gimmick Hour'. All the ministers are present at 'Question Time' which lasts about an hour. There is a good muster of members, all anxious to see the ministers or start some excitement in order to get into the press the next day. There is seldom anything constructive in the questions. The main purpose is cheap publicity. When 'Question Time' is over, the *Dáil* empties again and many members leave to attend to their private business.

As a member of the *Dáil* I attended every day and spoke often, especially on matters affecting Dublin or those people in need. Of course, I spoke on national and economic matters. I was always anxious to put pressure on ministers where there were obvious injustices. One such case was the treatment of disabled people or those suffering from infectious diseases. These people were paid from the Health Account. The other politicians were always pressing the causes of those under social welfare, thus there were often small increases at budget time but the health cases were forgotten. They received £1 a week in 1954, then nothing for six years. Before the 1960 budget, Deputy Desmond of the Labour Party and I complained about the miserable £1, which these people got.[7] Deputy Desmond and I suffered from physical disability. Perhaps that had much to do with our sympathy for these people. As a result of our intercession, they got the first increase, two shillings and sixpence, in the 1960 budget.

In the *Dáil*, on 29 March 1962, I asked the Minister for Health that welfare benefits be paid to disability claimants by the Dublin Health Authority.[8]

> Mr MacEntee, Minister for Health: '...the regulations prescribe that the maximum rate of allowance shall be twenty-two shillings and sixpence a week...'
> Mr Sherwin: 'Is there any hope that the Minister will increase the benefits?'
> Mr MacEntee: 'Better wait and see.'
> Mr Sherwin: 'We hear a lot of talk about these unfortunate people. A sum of twenty-two shillings and sixpence a week is a miserable form of allowance for a person who cannot earn a button. The others can earn £1 a week but these people cannot.'

When the Health Account was discussed in the *Dáil*, I said: 'In my opinion health cases were the worse cases of all. They are the most pitiful cases. In 1954, £1 a week was granted to chronically disabled persons. This House then forgets all about them. They were the forgotten people, perhaps because the money does not come from the Welfare Account.' Every year there is lobbying for the old-age pensioners and the unemployed but disabled persons are completely forgotten. The proof of that is that the first increase they got was in 1960. So far as I can see, anyone who wants to get anything in this world must kick up a row. A blind man gets thirty-two shillings and sixpence a week. A non-contributory old age pensioner gets thirty-two shillings and sixpence. There is no reason why disabled persons should not get thirty-two shillings a week, except they have been forgotten. In many cases, they are crippled from birth and are bedridden. I am asking the minister next year to consider bridging the gap and making their allowances similar to others.[9]

On 6 November 1962, I put down the following motion in the *Dáil* that *Dáil Éireann* is of the opinion that disabled people in receipt of twenty-four shillings a week, paid by the State and the Health Authority, should receive the same benefits as blind persons and non-contributory old-age pensioners (32/6d).[10] The motion was discussed on 29 January 1964 and again on 5 February, 1964. In reply to the motion Mr MacEntee said: 'I will press for acceptance in principle.' In answer to the Minister's promise, I said: 'I accept the Minister's word and I will withdraw the motion.'[11]

Mr MacEntee said: 'I really intended to indicate why it is in my view considerable weight should be given by the House to any proposition put before it by a man of the independence and integrity of Deputy

Sherwin . . . I was indicating that I felt serious consideration should be given by the Government and the House to the proposition which has been put forward by Deputy Sherwin.'[12] In the 1964 budget the disabled people got a five shilling increase. The others on non-contributory benefits got two shillings and sixpence. Thus my efforts began to bear fruit and, better still, these health cases were transferred to the Welfare Account so that they would not be forgotten in future budgets. In the 1965 budget they got a ten shilling increase, the same as others on social benefits but I lost my seat in the general election which came just before the budget was announced so I was the victim of ignorance and political prejudice.[13]

In the *Dáil,* on 29 October 1963, I moved the following motion: 'That *Dáil Éireann* is of the opinion that following a general increase in wages a proportionate increase (apart from budget increases) should be granted immediately to all those in receipt of social benefits, because a general increase in wages is usually followed by a general increase in the cost of living.'[14] In my opening statement I said:

I have waited a long time to introduce the motion. There ought to be a complete reassessment, and there ought to be an improved scale in relation to what the labourer earns.[15] In the past, whatever benefits were granted, they were granted in a begrudging manner. There are many people who sympathise with this class of people but when they are asked to contribute, they do not want to do so. About fifty years ago we made a start but I am not satisfied that what they now receive is a just amount.[16] A man who has to live on an old age pension ought to receive at least quarter or a third of the amount an employed manual worker earns. A new figure should be reached for all the various classes that I have in mind.

Up until now it has been pot luck. It depends on the government, on the minister, on whether the governments are strong or weak. Nothing is regularized and it ought to be. The fate of the people that I speak for should not have to depend on the whims of any minister. They ought to have the right to receive an increase in proportion to wage increases. If there were a procedure by which those in receipt of social benefits would obtain those benefits as a right, there would be no need for individuals or groups of politicians to cash in on this business. That is the principle behind the motion.

I replied to the debate on 6 November 1963.[17] I was asked by Deputy Coogan, *Fine Gael,* if I would vote against the government.[18] I replied: 'I shall press the motion if that is what you want to know.'[19] Mr Sherwin: 'I moved this motion because . . . I want to tie in not just this government but the Coalition, or any other government...the principle is clear enough. I am asking that they get an increase proportionate to whatever increase occurs in wages. I want no more gaps of twenty-eight years.'[20] Mr S. Collins, *Fine Gael*: 'Are you going to vote for it?' Mr Sherwin: 'Yes'. The government was at that time depending on my vote to stay in power. The question was then put before the House and declared carried. The government accepted the motion. Mr S. Collins: 'Deputy Sherwin is in control. He has taken over the government.'

This motion was the poor people's charter. From then on, they received increases every year, rising from two shillings and sixpence a week to a £1 a week. Their standard of living has doubled since 1963, over and above all increases in the cost of living but it took money to do it and that is why I voted for the small turnover tax. If the money was not voted, they could not get what they got. Most of those people took these increases for granted. They did not even bother to find out who helped them and many were worked up to vote against me in elections. I accept that they erred because of corrupt influences or perhaps I did not get a chance to make my case through the mass media. About 300,000 gained because of the substantial increases in social benefits. At least another 100,000 gained as a result of my efforts in the *Dáil* or corporation. A total of 200,000 people employed by the state benefited because had there been a shortage of money in the exchequer, they would have got less in wage increases as would state pensioners. The country would also have suffered and I mean 'the people' for had the state been short of money, then there would have been less productivity owing to less state investment and grants.

NOTES

1   See James Hogan, *Election and Representation, Part 1: The Experiment of Proportional Representation in Ireland*, Cork and Oxford, 1945.

2   William Shakespeare, actor, poet and playwright, was born on 23 April 1564 in Stratford-Upon-Avon. He died on 23 April 1616 on the day of his 52nd birthday. The edition of *Julius Caesar* read by Sherwin is listed in the bibliography.

3   Sherwin stated 'Frank Kent'. An author of that name penned 'The Good Die First' in *Air Adventure* published by Ziff-Davis in 1939. Frank R. Kent is credited as saying '...the evils of government are directly proportional to the tolerance of the people', which is most likely the correct reference. He published 'The political decline of America' in *Harper's Monthly* in December, 1925; 'Whose business is it anyway' in *The American Magazine* in April 1932 and 'Roosevelt's Big Chance' in *The American Magazine* in March 1937. See J. Anthony Lukas, *Common Ground: A Turbulent Decade in the Lives of Three American Families* (New York: Vintage Books, 1986). Lukas refers to John F. Kennedy and *Profiles in Courage* in ch. 24 'The Editor', pp. 484–85, and to a piece written by Frank R. Kent 'People:

the ordeal of self-government in America' in Chapter 28 'The Mayor', p. 617. Lukas was winner of National Book Award (1985) and National Book Critics Circle Award (1985). Ironically, an actor named Frank Kent Smith, born on 19 March 1907 in New York and died on 23 April 1985 in Woodland Hills, California, had a connection with Kennedy's work. He starred in the TV series *Profiles in Courage* (1964–65), directed by Michael Ritchie and Joseph Anthony. Frank Kent Smith appeared in the episode 'Charles Evans Hughes' on 14 March 1965. He considered this his favourite of all the roles he had done.

4   Hal Evry was arguably the first and best of the political PR campaign managers. He was noted as being one of the most outspoken political media advisors and one who has worked for Canadian and American politicians alike. US Representative Morris Udall quotes Evry as saying: 'Clients who campaign least, win the most votes.' See Morris K. Udall, *The High Cost of Being a Congressman* (HMH Publishing, 1967). An article entitled 'Democracy Incorporated' appeared in the American journal *New International* dated April 1985. Journalist Joyce Nelson uses the following quotation of Evry's: 'It's simply a marketing job. Research is the tool that lets us find out what's in the consumer's mind – in this case, the voter's mind...Party support is a mirage...what has the real effect today is television, not people, get on television and don't say anything but make it sound good, you get three out of four to like what they read into you.'

5   Steam O'Brien was not a politician.

6   O'Brien meant flattering people.

7   Barry Desmond served thirty years in politics from the 1960s to 1990s. He served as politician, member of the Twenty-fourth *Dáil* (12 December 1982 to 21 January 1987), former Minister for Social Welfare, (until 14 February 1986), Minister for Health (resigned on 20 January 1987), former deputy leader of the Labour party and MEP. Desmond has been described as a young upstart in the Labour party. He went on to become a central participant in the party's fortunes in and out of government and a reforming Minister for Health. From opposing his own party's stand on EU membership in the 1970s, he took on the Catholic Church over contraception in the 1980s and played a crucial back-room role in Labour's success in the 1990s. See Barry Desmond, *Finally and In Conclusion: A Political Memoir* (Dundrum: New Island Books, 2000).

8   *Parliamentary Debates, Dáil Éireann,* 'Disablement Allowances', vol 194, 29 March 1962, col. 906/7.

9   Disabled people received another two shillings and sixpence in the budget of 1962, largely as a result of Sherwin's agitation. In fact, they received an increase every year thereafter.

10   *Parliamentary Debates, Dáil Éireann,* 'Committee on Finance Vote 51, Office of the Minister for Social Welfare', vol 197, 6 November 1962, col. 533.

11   *Parliamentary Debates, Dáil Éireann,* 'Payment to Disabled Persons: Motion (Resumed)', vol 207, 5 February 1964, col. 449.

12   *Ibid.,* col. 431/2.

13   Compare this with nothing between 1954 and 1960.

14   *Parliamentary Debates, Dáil Éireann,* 'Increase in Social Welfare Benefits: Motion', vol 205, 29 October 1963, col. 452.

15   This motion had been on the agenda for at least twelve months.

16   Social benefits began in 1910.

17   *Parliamentary Debates, Dáil Éireann,* 'Increase in Social Welfare Benefits: Motion', vol 205, 6 November 1963, col. 1022.

18   *Ibid.,* col. 1024.

19   Sherwin is possibly referring to Fintan Coogan, TD for Galway North and
      member of the Sixteenth *Dáil Éireann* (1957–61). The old-age pensioners had
      17/6 in 1949; 20/- in 1951; 21/6d in 1952; 24/- in 1955; 25/- in 1957; 27/6d in
      1959; 28/6d in 1960; 30/- in 1961; 32/6d in 1962; 35/- in 1963. For twenty-eight
      years, between 1921 and 1949, they got nothing. There were periods in between
      the years that have been mentioned when they got nothing.
20   *Parliamentary Debates, Dáil Éireann*, 'Increase in Social Welfare Benefits: Motion',
      vol 205, 6 November 1963, cols 1027/8. 'Gaps' here refers to years when they got
      nothing.

PART II

REFLECTIONS BY FRANK SHERWIN
ON THE IRELAND OF HIS DAY

14

MENTAL HOSPITALS ARE A SORROWFUL SIGHT[1]

As well as being a member of Dublin Corporation, I was a member of the Dublin Health Authority, which comprised Dublin City Council, Dublin County Council and Dún Laoghaire Borough. The authority was made up of twenty-seven members: fifteen appointed by Dublin Corporation, nine appointed by Dublin County Council and five appointed by Dún Laoghaire Borough. The population of Dublin was about 600,000; County Dublin about 180,000 and Dún Laoghaire 55,000. The rate contribution from each rating authority from 1970–71 was Dublin £5,710,746; County Dublin £1,166,264, and Dún Laoghaire £486,168. In other words, Dublin members represented almost three times as many people as the other two and contributed almost the same percentage in money. These figures are interesting when you consider that for the next seven years, members of the County Council and Dún Laoghaire, with the help of the small *Fine Gael* group, three from Dublin, debated all policy, took over the chairman and vice-chairmanship and monopolized practically all discussion. And this was supposed to be a democratic assembly? As a result of this conspiracy, Dublin ratepayers were disenfranchised. In fact, some of the Dublin members did not bother to turn up to meetings and on several occasions at annual general meetings, members of Dublin City Council left the meeting before the election of chairman and vice-chairman took place because they knew that a caucus meeting of the conspirators had already taken place and decided who was to be chairman and vice-chairman. During the period of seven years, six chairmen and five vice-chairmen were from County Dublin and Dún Laoghaire. The small *Fine Gael* group, three from Dublin, were allowed the chairmanship once and vice-chairmanship twice. In other words, all of the Dublin *Fianna Fáil* members, all of the Dublin Labour members and all of the Dublin Independents and ratepayers' representatives were barred by the conspirators. This is politics in operation and politics is a dirty business.

As the Dublin Health Authority controlled all of the municipal hospitals, homes, etc. there were several inspection committees appointed to inspect all of these institutions from time to time in the interest of the patients. I was a member of the Mental Hospitals Inspection Committee. Mental hospitals are a sorrowful sight. My fellow members were Jimmy O'Keeffe, the late James O'Connor from Dublin City Council and Ned Gannon from County Dublin.[2] They were good men and took a deep interest in the work. In the old days, mental patients were treated like animals. They were often beaten and starved as a punishment because they gave trouble, although the patients could not help it. Many of the patients became worse because the whole atmosphere would cause you to lose your sanity. Many patients were admitted because they suffered from depression although not violent and I am sure many were committed because they were provoked into some minor assault and then kept there because they were not wanted outside. Many patients were old and senile and left in mental homes to die. They were not violent. Their place was in some home for the dying or the aged. I was sad to see some old bed-ridden people in mental institutions, ghost-like as if from another world, where they could only get limited care. I was told that many patients had been there for thirty to fifty years. They were left there to rot and they became so institutionalized that they could not think of leaving.[3]

The whole atmosphere within mental institutions has a depressing effect on the visitor. It is a combination of zoo, haunted house, morgue and waxworks museum. You can imagine the effect such a place has on those who have only a minor problem or who are on the mend. It seems that once you are certified by a member of your family, you cannot be discharged unless the family signs you out. Thus, patients become institutionalized and helpless. Mental patients as a rule never converse with one another. Since the appointment of Dr Ivor Brown, RMS, things have changed for the better. At least patients are encouraged to mix socially and those who are on the mend are allowed out of the hospital within certain hours. The Inspection Committee examine food, bedding, toilets, etc., also laundries, cook-houses or places where patients are employed. When I first became a member of the committee, I complained that patients were used as free labour, getting only a few cigarettes weekly. In some cases they got two shillings and sixpence a week. I advocated that they should get ten shillings and that profits from the shop be used for the benefit of patients' entertainment. New drugs have played a big part in the control of patients. The noisiest and the most violent are sedated regularly and this knocks the fight out of them. Alas, it seems that they must continue taking drugs even after discharge as there is no certain cure.

I was particularly interested in the case of one patient, William O'Reilly, an old IRA man, a life-long friend as well as the best man at my wedding. We joined the *Fianna* and the National Army together. His wife certified him in about 1954. I knew that he suffered from depression. He always had done, but he was never violent and he was not foolish. He married the wrong woman. His wife gave him trouble from the day that they married. I remember the circumstances. His wife was put out of her home by her father because of her escapades and he married her immediately. There was no love in the marriage. Before O'Reilly was certified by his wife, she ran away to England with another man but later came back and he forgave her. She continued to give trouble and patronized singing-pubs on her own. If O'Reilly did have a temporary breakdown, it was no wonder and if he did threaten her, it is no more than any sane person would have done. However, she had him certified and decided to let him rot there for the rest of his life.

I visited him weekly but I was barred on the instructions of his wife. I was not then a councillor. I found him depressed but neither violent nor noisy. When I became a councillor some months later, I saw him regularly. I tried to get him discharged but I was told that only his wife could sign him out. Later, she went to live in England with the same man she previously absconded with and O'Reilly was left to rot. I raised his case in the *Dáil* and I raised it at meetings of the Mental Inspection Committee but I was told that his wife would have to sign him out. I demanded that patients who were not violent and who were behaving normally should have the right to ask for their own discharge.

When Dr Ivor Brown was appointed RMS about 1965, he agreed to give certain approved patients a pass to visit friends outside but they had to be back by a certain hour. O'Reilly visited me several days weekly for some months in 1967. He behaved perfectly. There was nothing wrong with him. In fact, there never had been anything much wrong with him, and to think that he was kept a prisoner in a mental home for thirteen years. I advised him to go to his nephew in Manchester and get a job. He took my advice so I got him a ticket and got him out of St Brendan's on the pretext of visiting me. I rushed him down to the boat and he sailed for England. When he did not return by 8 o'clock, male nurses called to my home to collect him. I made excuses but kept quiet about England. I knew that according to law, if he was at liberty for twenty-one days, he could not be brought back unless he was recertified. I told him not to go near his wife, at least not until after the twenty-one days were up. When he did, she informed St Brendan's and demanded that he be brought back but they did not have the power to do so, and I had already told St Brendan's that he was okay and employed. He told us that the married man who was living with his wife had threatened him so he had no choice but to go elsewhere and work. He finally got a handy job at Llandudno in a hotel. He had a room and saved all of his wages. I visited him in September 1968. He had been in England for fifteen months and he showed me his savings book with over £700 deposited. In June 1970, I toured Scotland with my wife and son. It was a camping holiday. On our return to Liverpool to depart for home we decided to visit O'Reilly but as Llandudno was over 100 miles from our point of departure, we phoned the hotel to make sure that he was still employed there. To our surprise, we were told that he had died suddenly on New Year's Day 1970.

Nobody in Dublin was told of his death. I spoke to his brother and other members of his family in Dublin when we came home and all were surprised. When I asked the hotel who buried him, I was told: 'his wife.' I am aware that he had her address in his wallet. I suppose the hotel management informed her. Therefore the wife who put him into a mental hospital, tried to keep him there for life and tried to have him returned to the mental hospital while she was still living with another man, got possession of about £1,500. He would have had that amount, as he had £700 in September 1968 after fifteen months' employment and sixteen months had elapsed before he died suddenly on 1 January 1970. Of course, as his death was kept secret, there was nobody to object to her possessing a large sum of money that she was not entitled to. The irony of it! I got him out of a mental hospital so that he could earn £1,500 only to give it to the person who certified him and tried to keep him there for life. She got a small fortune because of my efforts and his hard work. How many other cases are there like O'Reilly's where people are certified and allowed to rot because their spouse is living with a member of the other sex or where the person certified has means which other people are spending? There should be an inquiry into the whole sordid business.

NOTES

1   The original chapter title was: 'Mental homes can be prisons'.
2   Presumably Sherwin is referring to James O'Keefe, Alderman, *Fine Gael* TD and Lord Mayor 1962–63 and he has misspelled his surname 'O'Keeffe'. There is a *Fine Gael* TD for Cork South-West named Jim O'Keeffe. He was first elected in 1977 and has retained his seat ever since. He contested the 1979 European elections in Munster without success and was appointed *Fine Gael*'s Spokesperson on Justice in 2004. He was a Minister of State during the Rainbow Coalition's time in office.
3   Sherwin read *The Empty hours: a Study of the Week-end Life of Handicapped Children in Institutions* by Maureen Oswin. See the bibliography for full details.

15

A REFLECTION ON THE HISTORY OF IRELAND[1]

When in jail, I read any books that I could get my hands on. I only read fact, especially history and biography. Fiction never appealed to me. Since I came out of jail, I have devoured books but I never accepted any one historian's view as I am satisfied that all histories are slanted. When you study many histories or books on the same subject, you get nearer the truth. I was always anxious to know what made people tick, those who made history or created things. The history of Ireland is one long state of disorder, disunity and confusion due in the first place to the clan system where clan or county had a king. There was a high king but he was only a figurehead. He had no army capable of controlling the others. When the British or Normans came here in 1169 they met only local opposition. The rest of the country considered it none of their business. When they saw the danger, it was too late and several local kings and chiefs supported the invaders. Any resolute central authority could have thrown the few thousand invaders into the sea.

The 1916 Proclamation, the gospel of many Irishmen, states that six times in the past 300 years the Irish people have asserted their right in arms to freedom. This is not so. The wars of the 1641 period, namely the English Civil War, were wars to keep Charles I on the throne and he also claimed to be King of Ireland. Only a small minority wanted independence. The wars of 1690 onwards were to keep King Charles II on the English throne. He was also King of Ireland. Irish freedom was not the issue.[2] The 1798 period was a series of disjointed fights of utter confusion from beginning to end. It was originally a revolt by Presbyterians who were denied political rights as much as the Catholics. Only Church of Ireland or England Protestants could be public representatives or hold any important office. The Catholics, the real Irish, had publicly stated that they would not look for the right to be public representatives, let alone freedom. They stated that they only wanted to be allowed to practise their religion. Only the Church of Ireland Protestants could be members of the so-called Irish Parliament which sat in Dublin.

Some Church of Ireland members, such as Wolfe Tone, were sincere republicans but in his earlier years he was a loyal supporter of the English king. After all, he was a member of the English ascendancy and had he been employed by the government before this period, he would never have been an Irish patriot. Tone's conversion was genuine. He hoped to influence the Presbyterians and had several meetings with their leaders in Belfast. Some of those who had pledged support were informers and openly fought against those who revolted in 1798. The revolt in the North of Ireland was confined to two small towns. There was no revolt in Belfast. Only a few thousand actively took part, led largely by Presbyterian ministers who were the chief victims of the Church of Ireland government. Their aim was not the freedom of Ireland but civil rights for Presbyterians. The Catholic bishops instructed all Catholics to support the English government and the majority of soldiers used against the rebels were Irishmen.

In Wexford, because of the tyranny of soldiers and the burning of Catholic churches, the local people revolted, led by Father John Murphy. There were few United Irishmen in Wexford.[3] This was not a fight for freedom. In fact, they murdered many Protestants. There was little fighting elsewhere. The real leader of the United Irishmen was Lord Edward Fitzgerald, the son and brother of two English dukes.[4] He was arrested on the eve of the revolt. Many of his associates were informers. There was very little support among this class for Irish freedom. Wolfe Tone has been described as the father of republicanism but he was out of the country throughout the revolt. In fact, in order to avoid arrest he left four and a half years before Lord Edward Fitzgerald and other leaders were arrested.

In an interview with the French Minister for War, he said that he was interested in the freedom of Ireland but did not care what form of government operated. He said that he would not object to a monarchy and when asked who would be king, he said: 'Some Duke or Lord.'[5] There was no unity of purpose throughout the revolt, which you can judge from the table of events. There was no overall accepted leader, as was the case with republicans when the Civil War broke out in Dublin in 1922. A French army arrived at Bantry Bay, Cork, in December 1796 but departed because there were no Irish there to meet them. Wolfe Tone was on board. The revolt broke out in two towns in the north in May 1798 but the fight was over in one before the other began. There was no revolt in Belfast. A small French army landed on the west coast on 22 August 1798. After a few gallant fights the French were captured. There was no organized Irish force to help them. Wolfe Tone arrived at Lough Swilly, Donegal, again on the west coast, when all other fighting was over on 12 October. He and a small

French force were captured after a short fight. Wolfe Tone's last entry in his diary before he left France states that having read a French newspaper, the militia as well as the yeomanry supported the enemy, comprised largely of Irish. He explained that in all this business he did not see one syllable about the north and recalled what Diggis had said to Russell and himself about five years earlier.[6] Diggis maintained that if ever the south were roused, he would rather have one southerner than twenty northerners.[7] I have always maintained that with the exception of a few, the Presbyterians were exploiting the Catholics and Wolfe Tone in order to drive a good bargain with the British. When the 1798 Rebellion was over and the Irish or rather the British Parliament in Dublin was abolished in 1800, the Presbyterians got what they wanted and then became the worst enemies of the Catholics and Irish freedom.

The so-called revolt in 1848 was only an incident. Historians have described it a 'cabbage-patch revolt'. In 1867, there was a series of small incidents. There was no rising of the Irish at any time during the period described in the 1916 Proclamation. Robert Emmet's revolt was only a Dublin incident in 1803.[8] The 1916 revolt was not a rising of the Irish people. Only about 1,000 took part. In fact, all of the evidence indicates that the vast majority of the people were opposed to the rebellion. When the fight was over, there was some sympathy for the cause because of the executions but the real swing to the Republican side only took place because the British decided to conscript the Irish and it was to save their own skins that they supported the Republicans. The first real fight for freedom took place between 1918 and 1921 when it could be said that the Irish people were fighting for their freedom and it was the real Irish who led the revolt.

Dan O'Connell was probably the greatest national leader this country has had for many centuries.[9] At least he succeeded in dragging the Irish from their knees and made them unite to protest against their servitude. He was not a physically forceful man but force could not have succeeded at that time. He won Catholic emancipation and did away with the Test Act which enabled the Irish to sit in Parliament. He made Parnell's success easier.

Parnell was a cold unusual individual.[10] He made his name fighting for Home Rule for Ireland in the British House of Commons. He was condemned because of his love affair with Mrs O'Shea.[11] I do not condemn him for that, as it is a weakness of men big and small, but he was weak to allow this affair to endanger national success and the care of his party. Wolfe Tone had many love affairs, so had O'Connell and I am told that Michael Collins had love affairs, but they did not allow these affairs to interfere with their national work. Wolfe Tone was not a great national leader. He is noted for his statement that we should have the common name of Irishman and not Catholic, Protestant or Dissenter. He was also responsible for influencing the French to send armed help although nothing came of it.

The 1916 leaders were martyrs rather than national leaders. James Connolly was a great socialist writer. James Larkin, who was in America in 1916, was a great leader of sorts. He was a trade union leader, neither a nationalist nor a social theorist. He was independent by nature and a supreme agitator. De Valera was a great national leader, not so much during the War of Independence, but he became great in the years after he founded *Fianna Fáil*. He was a great moral force. Michael Collins was a great guerrilla-war leader. Few would have accepted his responsibilities. He was ruthless and had the expertise. It has been said by many that the Civil War would have ended much earlier had he lived and there would have been less of the dirty work that was to leave a scar on the Irish psyche for years to come. As I said at the beginning of this chapter, I was a keen student of history and biography, especially of leadership on the international scene. Napoleon is the great success story of history but in my opinion, Hitler's success was greater. He was an uneducated pauper and became chancellor of intellectual Germany. I am not excusing his mass terror but, speaking of terror, communism was founded and sustained by terror worse than Hitler's. Some of our popular religions were also founded and sustained by mass terror. In fact, all party politics are campaigns of terror. There is mass character assassination, large-scale lying, bribery, slander and occasional blood spilling. The Watergate scandal in the United States is proof beyond question.

American history has always fascinated me. I suppose my favourite hero is Abraham Lincoln. I always admire poor men who succeed and Lincoln was poor and had little education. He first stood as an Independent for his home county, Sangamon. In his election appeal he said: 'I am humble Abe Lincoln. If elected, I will be thankful. If not, it will be all the same.' Later, when he was chosen by the Republicans, he said that had he not made himself known and popular, they would never have wanted him: 'I was not good enough for them.' They selected him because of his obvious honesty and the publicity he received in his debates on slavery and the saving of the union with Senator Douglas, his competitor as presidential candidate.[12] To the Washington snobs, he was an animal or an ape. After he was elected, they tried to use him for their own ends but they did not succeed. They plotted against him throughout his two terms and many of them were delighted when he was assassinated.

Franklin Roosevelt was a great president.[13] He introduced the 'New

Deal' to help the ordinary people. In my opinion, it was Roosevelt more than anyone else who defeated Hitler. Churchill was a great figure, brave, independent and defiant, but it would all have been in vain had Roosevelt not been there to help him. It is to Roosevelt's credit that he succeeded in spite of the fact that he was crippled, with no power in both legs. Kennedy was a romantic figure but not a great president. Irishmen were with him because he was a descendant of an Irishman and his difficulty as a Catholic. I doubt that he was much interested in Ireland except from a vote point of view. He would never have been a senator, let alone president, were it not for his father's millions. His two brothers became senators. Again, this was due to the president's glamour and their father's money. We were sympathetic because of his Irish connections but we should not lose our sense of proportion.

The partition of Ireland is the curse of Ireland. In other words, six counties were set up as a separate state by force of British arms in 1920. Of course, they had been there for the previous 300 years because the British forced the inhabitants to flee to the west. British, especially Scottish, settlers were planted. Were it not for the difference in religion, they may have become as Irish as the rest of us but they only married their own so the same British strain is there as was put there at the beginning. Were these people as far away from Britain as were the colonists of America, there would be much less of a problem but they are only a short distance from their original homeland so they remain British even though born in Ireland. It might not be a bad exchange were all of the Irish in Britain to come home and all of the people in the north who considered themselves British to go back to Britain. Many hope that this cancer in the nation will be solved by peaceful means but I don't think that it will as any so-called solution which threatens to give us some sort of nominal recognition in exchange for us compromising on principals would be no solution. Force is not a popular word, especially in peacetime. I don't suggest that it should be considered at any time, unless there was a reasonable chance of success but as I see it, it is the only real solution. I do not agree that a solution by force would cause greater disunity. That is nonsense; practically all nations were unified and consolidated by force. The great United States was saved by force. If the southern states were allowed to secede, there would now be two nations, competing, perhaps often at war, where there is now one powerful nation. Had the north not used force and saved the union, they would not be able to apply 'The Monroe Doctrine' and the American continent would often have a blood-bath like Europe has had, twice in this century.[14] America would not have been strong enough to save Europe twice in the same century. If partition was solved by force, perhaps some thousands of die-hards would get out and it would be good riddance. The rest of the northern Protestants, realizing that we were not ogres and intent on treating them the same as the rest of the Irish people, would soon forget and work for the good of the country with one government and with closer co-operation with Britain.

History has to be pushed. It does not change itself. Let us consider Stalin.[15] Stalin told H.G. Wells that in all history no class ever gave way to another class voluntarily, and this is so.[16] Of course, talk about force is bad for votes. Even if you are convinced that force, or the threat of it, is the only solution. You must deceive the people on this issue. In fact, it seems to be necessary to deceive them practically all of the time if you are to succeed in public life. Machiavelli said that the majority of citizens have no interest in the common good and if they seem to contribute to the common good, they do so only because they are compelled to do so by legislation or other means and that is why lying, even violent lying, is necessary for survival in politics. Citizens tend to destroy one another and responsible people have to take risks with their political future to save the people from themselves. Machiavelli is symbolized as representing all that is evil in politics but he only put into words what has always been practised by politicians since the beginning of time

NOTES

1   The original chapter title was: 'History'.
2   His father Charles I had been executed in 1649, following the English Civil War. The monarchy was then abolished and the kingdom of England and the kingdom of Scotland became a republic under Oliver Cromwell, the Lord Protector. In 1660, shortly after Cromwell's death, the monarchy was restored under Charles II.
3   Wolfe Tone's forces were called United Irishmen.
4   Lord Edward Fitzgerald, united Irishman and active as leader of the movement for Irish independence until his tragic death in May 1798. Lord Edward, son of a duke, heir to estates and influence, died in a Dublin gaol, a rebel and a traitor. Born in 1763, he joined the British Army as a teenager and fought the American War of Independence. He was elected to the Irish Parliament in 1783. He later became a disciple of the Republican Thomas Paine. He visited France and then joined the Irish underground in the 1790s. While plotting Irish independence from Britain, Lord Edward was captured and, as Tillyard phrased it, '... died, raving and wounded as the bloody rebellion raged around him'. See Stella Tillyard, *Citizen Lord: Edward Fitzgerald, 1763–1798* (London: Chatto & Windus, 1997).
5   A reference to Wolfe Tone's diary.
6   Thomas Russell was born in Drumahane, County Cork, on 21 November 1767. He was among the founders and a leading member of the United Irishmen. In July 1790 he befriended Wolfe Tone, having met him in the Irish House of Commons. An Anglican, Russell was a vocal advocate of Catholic Emancipation.

On 18 October 1791, the inaugural meeting of the Society of United Irishmen took place and by 1796, Russell became commander of the United Irishmen in County Down. Russell was arrested that year and lodged in Dublin's Newgate Prison and as a consequence, took no part in the Rising of 1798. In March 1799, he was transferred as a political prisoner to Fort George, an extensive fortress some miles north of Inverness. He was released in June 1802 and transported to Hamburg. He made his way to Paris, met Robert Emmet and returned to Ireland to organize an insurrection in the north. Russell was captured on his way to rescue Emmett. He was brought to Downpatrick Jail and tried for high treason. He was hanged and then beheaded at the gate of the jail on 21 October 1803.

7   Diggis was one of Russell's associates in Belfast and doubted that the Presbyterians would help to free the Catholic Irish.

8   Robert Emmet was born in Dublin on 3 March 1778 and was executed on 20 September 1803 as a result of his ill-organized Rising on 23 July of that year. Emmet was pursued by the authorities when the Chief Justice, Lord Kilwarden, was found brutally murdered in his coach. Emmet was captured at a house in Harold's Cross and sent to Kilmainham Jail. He was tried by Chief Justice Lord Norbury on 19 September at Green Street Courthouse, which is still in use as the Special Criminal Court. Emmet was found guilty of high treason and was hung, drawn and quartered on 20 September 1803 opposite St Catherine's Church, Meath Street, Dublin.

9   Daniel O'Connell was born near Cahirciveen in County Kerry on 6 August 1775. At the time of the 1801 Act of Union, O'Connell was a fierce critic of the binding together of Ireland and England under the one parliament. Although opposed to violence and violent methods, O'Connell killed a political opponent in 1815 after he was challenged to a duel. In 1823 O'Connell formed the Catholic Association and in 1824 introduced the 'Catholic rent' which helped the peasantry become members of the association at the cost of a penny a month. O'Connell wanted Catholic Emancipation for Irish Catholics and the Association quickly became the first mass political movement in Ireland. However, even though the first Irish nationalists were Protestant, Irish nationalism became an exclusively Catholic tradition. O'Connell won the 1828 Clare by-election and the following year the Westminster government conceded Catholic Emancipation. During O'Connell's time in Parliament, he sided with the Whig Party – the 1835 Lichfield House Compact – and was able to make reforms in Ireland. O'Connell's main political aim was the Repeal of the Union. In the 1840s, O'Connell got mass support in the Loyal National Repeal Association. After 1844, O'Connell began to lose ground to the more militant 'young Irelanders'. In that same year, he was found guilty of creating discontent and disaffection. He was in prison for three months before the House of Lords reversed the judgement. Daniel O'Connell died on his way to Rome on 15 May 1847.

10 Charles Stewart Parnell, 'the uncrowned King of Ireland', was a Protestant landlord who resided at Avondale, County Wicklow. He was first elected to Parliament in the Meath by-election of April 1875 and joined the Home Rule Party led by Isaac Butt. On 21 October 1879, Michael Davitt founded the Irish National Land League in Dublin with Parnell as President; their main objective was to provide tenants with a fair rent, fixed tenure and free sale. Gladstone became Prime Minister for the second time in April 1880 and hoped to pass an emergency Land Bill through Parliament that summer. When he was defeated in the House of Lords, the Land League took the law into its own hands. Parnell

became the accepted leader of the Irish Nationalist Movement during the years 1880–82. He channelled the funding he had secured from America into the Irish Parliamentary Party. Parnell and the other leaders were arrested in October 1881 after the British passed a new Coercion Act and the League was put down. While Parnell was in Kilmainham Jail, Gladstone came to terms with him in March 1882 with the Kilmainham Treaty. Following Parnell's release, Lord Frederick Cavendish and his under-secretary T.H. Burke, who was sent to Ireland as Chief Secretary, were murdered in the Phoenix Park by members of a secret society called the Invincibles. That December, the suppressed Land League Act was replaced by the Irish National League. By 1884 Parnell had managed to unite the party, overcoming one of Isaac Butt's greatest difficulties. The general election of 1885 was a huge success for Parnell and Gladstone gave the Home Rule Movement his support for the rest of his career. The Home Rule Bill of 1886 met with fierce opposition from the Conservatives who saw it as a betrayal of empire and of the loyalist and Protestant elements of Ireland. Gladstone lost office in the general election of 1886, the first in Britain to be fought on the Home Rule question. A meeting of the Irish Parliamentary Party was held during the first week of 1890 to discuss the scandal surrounding the O'Shea divorce case which involved Parnell. The party split with forty-five members siding with the Vice-Chairman Justin McCarthy who remained in favour of the alliance with the Liberals while twenty-seven sided with Parnell. Parnell lost the leadership of the Parliamentary Party. He refused to accept the verdict given against him, and throughout 1891 fought three by-elections, during which Parnell's candidate was defeated. Parnell considered it 'a war to the death' although he suffered a lot of indignity such as mud-throwing and personal abuse. Charles Stewart Parnell died in Brighton on 6 October 1891.

11   In December 1889, Captain O'Shea filed for divorce from his wife and Charles Stewart Parnell was named in the proceedings. He and English woman Mrs Katherine O'Shea had fallen in love when they first met in 1880. By that time, her marriage to Captain O'Shea was breaking down. From 1886, Parnell and Katherine O'Shea lived together. There is no doubt Captain O'Shea had been aware of Parnell's relationship with his wife. Parnell had had O'Shea elected as an unpledged Home Ruler to the Galway City seat in February 1886, despite opposition from his party. It is not clear why O'Shea delayed until December 1889 before seeking a divorce. Before this, he had attempted to blackmail his wife for £20,000 but she refused to pay. The divorce case caused a sensation in England and Ireland. In June 1891, Charles Stewart Parnell married Katherine O'Shea but refused to retire from public life.

12   Stephen A. Douglas, US Representative, Senator and founder of the original University of Chicago. He was born in Brandon, Vermont on 23 April 1813 and died in Chicago on 3 June 1861. Douglas was a key political figure in the years leading up to the American Civil War. Despite the growing political turmoil of the 1850s, Douglas attempted to orchestrate sectional compromise. The four-way presidential election was to propel a less established rival of Douglas, namely Abraham Lincoln, into the White House.

13   Franklin D. Roosevelt, the thirty-second President of the United States (1933–45). Roosevelt was born on 30 January 1882 in Hyde Park, New York, and died on 12 April 1945 in Warm Springs, Georgia.

14   James Monroe, fifth President of the United States (1817–25), was born on 28 April 1758 in Westmoreland County, Virginia, and died on 4 July 1831 in New York. 'The Monroe Doctrine' was expressed during President Monroe's seventh

annual message to Congress on 2 December 1823.

15   Joseph Stalin was born on 21 December 1879. His father was a cobbler. At the age of 15, Stalin became connected with certain underground groups of Russian Marxists then living in Transcaucasia. Stalin was expelled from school as a result of his revolutionary activities. He imbibed socialist doctrines and studied Karl Marx. He became a leader of the secret Marxist band at Tiflis Theological Seminary where he was enrolled. By 1903, he had turned to Bolshevism. Between 1908 and 1917, Stalin was imprisoned for revolutionary activities. With the success of the Bolshevik revolution, Stalin assumed editorship of the Bolshevik newspaper *Pravda*. Stalin and Trotsky had mutual political rivalry and fought for succession while Lenin was alive. Stalin held two ministerial posts in the Bolshevik government and was Secretary General of the party's Central Committee from 1922 until his death. He was also a member of the powerful Politburo. In 1925, Stalin renamed the city of Tsaritsyn to Stalingrad and expelled Trotsky from the Soviet Union in 1929. Germany attacked the Soviet Union on 22 June 1941 and Stalin appointed himself Commander in Chief. The Battle of Stalingrad (1942) and the Battle of Kursk (1943) were won by the Soviet Union under Stalin. In 1949, Russia became the world's second nuclear power. Stalin died in Moscow on 5 March 1953.

16   H.G. Wells was born on 21 September 1866 in Bromley, Kent, and died on 13 August 1946 in London. He was an English novelist, journalist, socialist and historian and was famous for his works of science fiction. Wells' best-known books are *The Time Machine* (1895), *The Invisible Man* (1897) and *The War of the Worlds* (1898).

16

THE PARTITION OF IRELAND

I have already referred to the partition of Ireland. It was created by force and is maintained by force and as I have said, only force will solve it satisfactorily. Of course, reforms will come as a result of the combined action of the IRA, the civil rights organizations and the south. The British will press for reform because they would like to be rid of the nightmare but the unity of Ireland is as far away as ever. I can never see the Orange Order, who influence 90 per cent of the northern Protestants, agreeing to unity under any circumstances and that is why I say that only force will solve the problem. We are not in a position to use combined force and public opinion is against it but then public opinion is usually against any action that involves risk or loss. Public opinion never supported any action to achieve our independence. Public opinion is faint-hearted and believes in peace at any price. The reason political parties in the south have betrayed the nationalists of the north is because public opinion in the south couldn't care less about the north. Anyhow, most of the party men are careerists and have no nationalist tradition behind them.

Since I began writing this book, extraordinary events occurred in the summer of 1970. Three Cabinet ministers were compelled to resign from the government by Mr Jack Lynch, the then *Taoiseach*. Another minister, a parliamentary secretary, resigned in protest and accused Mr Lynch of felon-setting and treachery. Mr Jack Lynch was always a quiet and aloof person when I was in the *Dáil*. He had a good image and was therefore good for votes but I thought that he acted rather harshly in dismissing Charlie Haughey, Minister for Finance and Neil Blaney, Minister for Agriculture. They were accused of conspiring to import arms into the south for use in Northern Ireland. They were tried in court, but the case was dismissed against them. Nevertheless, the *Taoiseach* and others believed that they were involved. Before the ministers were dismissed, Mr Cosgrave, then leader of the opposition in the *Dáil*, informed the *Taoiseach* that he was aware of the ministers' involvement. It appears that he received confidential information from some intelligence force, some say the

British. The fact that Cosgrave had the information was enough to force Mr Lynch's hand against the ministers. Politics is a dirty game and the opposition would not hesitate to stab the Northern nationalists in the back if it would gain them political advantage in the south. My own opinion is that even if the ministers were involved, they had nothing to be ashamed about. They were doing something to help Irish nationalists who were under siege in the north. They were not doing anything for their own benefit.[1]

The Orange Order is a secret society and controls the Unionist Party. They have about 100,000 guns licensed and unlicensed. The members swear an oath that they will maintain the British connection and no Catholics can join. The order was founded in 1795. Their long-term policy is to reduce or prevent the nationalist population from increasing. In this way they expect to hold political power forever. Their tactic is not to employ Catholics, thus forcing them to migrate to the south or to Britain. To expedite this migration, they use violence from time to time in order to frighten Catholics out of the north. They invoke religious prejudice to keep the ignorant lower-class Protestants always on the warpath. These people do most of the killing and the burning of Catholic homes. The more sophisticated Protestants keep out of it, but nevertheless they support the mobs because it ensures better jobs for themselves as well as political power. They vote the Orange card always.

On 14 August 1969, the Orange mobs attacked the Catholic areas. Five hundred homes were destroyed and many Catholics murdered. The mobs were accompanied by the armed Special Police, all Orangemen, who fired into Catholic homes. All public houses in the area were burned out. They were owned by Catholics. I visited Belfast a few days after this attack. I entered the Protestant area and there was no damage but all adjoining homes were burned out or devastated. There was one street off Divis Street/Dover Street which divides the Protestant and Catholic areas. One side of the street was annihilated. These were the Catholic homes and the other side was undamaged. This was the Protestant side. I asked people on the Falls Road, the Catholic area, where the IRA had been on 14 August and I was told that there was no IRA in Belfast; at least they took no action to defend the nationalists.[2] I was told that a few men had appeared with guns on 15 August but compared to the fire-power of the Orangemen, they were like pea-shooters. It was this lack of support by the IRA, which was controlled from Dublin, that led to the split in the IRA when the North of Ireland defenders formed a North of Ireland IRA, now known as the Provisionals. The policy of the IRA in the past was to make war on the British army in the north and war on the northern police.[3] This policy failed because they were too weak and had little popular support, north or south. The Provisionals' policy seems to be one of defence. They are satisfied to let the nationalist parties fight their political battles but having learned the bitter lesson of 14 and 15 August 1969, they are determined to fight with guns to defend the nationalists from further arson and massacre. Although the British army is keeping both sides apart, they are concentrating on disarming the nationalists while turning a blind eye to the armed and fanatical Orange order. They are waiting for the opportunity to attack again as the British army will not always be on the streets and not always there in strength. This one-sided disarming makes the nationalists bitter and this leads to incidents and shootings. As admitted by the former North of Ireland Prime Minister, James Chichester-Clark: 'The Provisionals have the ordinary people behind them.'[4] That was not the case with the IRA in the past and this makes this new force formidable and a natural answer to the redoubtable Orange force. The battle is now engaged and what's going to happen in the future is anybody's guess.

The Poles solved this problem by expelling all Germans from East Prussia. The Algerians did the same with the million French colonists. We don't want to do this, but at present we have not the power. If at any time in the future the British were forced to withdraw their army from the north, especially if war occurred with Russia, where the European continent was over-run, under these circumstances we would obviously march north supported by the northern nationalists. We do not want this situation. We would rather that the country was united allowing the north to have their own government and all reasonable guarantees. We don't want England's defeat. Times have changed. We want to be friendly with Britain. We want to see Britain prosper but we also want our country united and Britain can bring this about because without Britain's support, the Orange dictatorship would not survive.

Britain is the key. The Conservative government would like the old set-up to continue because the North of Ireland MPs elected as Unionists support the Conservative government at Westminster. The Conservative government is anxious for some reforms because of all the adverse North of Ireland publicity resulting from the revolutionary protests of Irish nationalists and the southern government. The British Labour party would be likely to support a United Ireland because the Unionist North is Anti-Labour but I would say that both parties would insist on the retention of bases for use in time of war. So far, we have been bending over backwards trying to induce the Unionists to talk about a United Ireland but they will never budge unless they are forced to do so by the British. The reforms that have been promised were due to the pressure of successive British governments. We should assure Britain regarding the bases because whether we like it or not, if ever there is dialogue about ending partition, bases will be a matter of priority with Britain. It is significant that the reforms promised by the British only came after large-scale riots, killings, burnings and barricades. This goes to show that you achieve nothing through normal channels. You must shock or frighten others to get justice and to ensure that justice is seen to be done; you must be prepared to fight again. The battle must always be joined if you are to get your fair share. Nobody gives away anything worthwhile voluntarily. You must fight or threaten to fight for it. This, then, is the background against which southern ministers are alleged to have conspired to send arms to Northern Ireland. As I said, they have nothing to be ashamed of, but at the same time, I can understand Mr Lynch's position. He as *Taoiseach* had conventional obligations to other states including the northern government and Britain, while southern opposition were prepared to stab the country in the back to gain a party advantage.

There are, of course, ample precedents for patriots acting without their leaders' approval. The 1916 leaders were guilty of mutiny. They plotted the Rising without consulting the Volunteers' Executive. They deceived their chief of staff, Professor Eoin MacNeill.[5] They also deceived the elected leader of the Irish people, John Redmond.[6] They even acted without the approval of the Irish Republican Brotherhood Executive.[7] They were a small caucus within the national movement and don't forget Dan Breen and Seán Treacy who commenced the Irish War of Independence without the approval of the *Dáil* or their superiors.[8] John Brown, the anti-slavery leader in America, invaded the slave state of Virginia in October 1859.[9] He had neither the approval of the Republican party nor of other anti-slave organizations. He was captured and hanged. Most people, including the anti-slave parties, said that he was mad and deserved to be hanged. They said the same here about the 1916 leaders when they were shot.

Lincoln was elected president in November 1860 and the Civil War began in April 1861. Eighteen months after John Brown was hanged, the northern troops marched south to end slavery and preserve the unity of the country singing: 'John Brown's body lies a-mouldering in the grave but his soul goes marching on.'

Italy is another case. It became a nation as we know it in 1861 when Cavour, Prime Minister of Sardinia, declared Victor Emmanuel King of Italy.[10] Giuseppe Garibaldi, a revolutionary leader, illegally invaded southern Italy and Sicily, which was controlled by the Bourbon kings.[11] Cavour publicly repudiated Garibaldi.[12] He was afraid of France and Austria, just as we are afraid of Britain, but secretly he encouraged

Garibaldi. Had Garibaldi failed, he might have been hanged by Cavour to save face with France and Austria but he succeeded, so Sardinian troops marched south. Thus the kingdom of Italy was born and Garibaldi became a hero. The City of Rome remained under the control of the Pope. This may have been necessary in the past because of the threats to the Vatican but this state of affairs could not continue. France guaranteed the continuity of the Vatican–Rome state and had an army stationed in Rome. Cavour knew that, if he invaded Rome, the new Italian state would be in danger of collapse. Garibaldi tried twice to invade Rome but was attacked by Italian troops, was wounded and arrested but later released. This 'Jekyll and Hyde' policy was pursued by the Italian government until 1870 when France was defeated by the Germans so the Italian troops took the City of Rome. Garibaldi was like the IRA here. Had he failed in southern Italy, he would have been treated like John Brown or, if you like, Blaney and Haughey here. That is why I say that they have nothing to be ashamed of. Let me repeat that I can understand Mr Lynch's position, just as I can understand Cavour's position when Garibaldi attacked Rome with the danger of attack from France. It is significant that before Garibaldi defeated the Bourbon forces in southern Italy, Cavour offered France, Nice and Savoy as a bribe. This would ensure support against Austria and her neutrality when he decided to proclaim the kingdom of Italy which included other independent Italian states: Parma, Modena and Tuscany. That is why I say that Britain is the key to solving the partition problem. Bases for Britain is the answer.

NOTES

1   In 1969, when conflict broke out in Northern Ireland, Neil Blaney expressed extremely strong nationalist views which contradicted government policy. These views were in support of north-eastern nationalists. In 1970 he became embroiled in the Arms Crisis, a scandal in which he was accused of importing arms into the country. On 5 May 1969 he was dismissed from the government along with Charles Haughey. In the trial which followed, all the accused were acquitted. Blaney was expelled from *Fianna Fáil* in 1971.

2   The IRA refers here to armed Republicans.

3   The Northern police are an armed force.

4   James Chichester-Clark, Baron Moyola of Castledawson and fifth Prime Minister of Northern Ireland (1969–71). Chichester-Clark was born on 12 February 1923 and died on 17 May 2002.

5   Professor Eoin MacNeill, Irish historian, patriot and professor of early Irish history, 1908–45 at University College Dublin, was born on 15 May 1867 in Glenarm, County Antrim. He joined with Douglas Hyde and others in the founding of the *Gaelic League* in 1893 to revive the declining Irish language. In 1913, he set up and led the Irish Volunteers in response to the setting up of the Ulster Volunteer Force in Ulster. It was through the *Gaelic League* that MacNeill

met the leaders of Sinn Féin and he was elected chairman of the council that formed the Irish Volunteers in 1913, later becoming chief-of-staff. MacNeill was opposed to fighting for Britain in the First World War. As a result, the Irish Volunteers split, with the minority led by MacNeill. He was also against the armed Rising of 24 April 1916, seeing little hope of success. He was arrested with hundreds of others and interned on 29 April but was released in 1917 under general amnesty. MacNeil helped to reorganize Sinn Féin and in the 1918 Westminster elections he was elected for the National University of Ireland and for Londonderry city. He was one of those present at the first meeting of the abstentionist parliament *Dáil Éireann* on 21 January 1921. At the 1921 general election, he was elected for the same constituencies, winning a seat in both the southern Ireland and northern Ireland House of Commons. He became a member of the Cabinet of the Second *Dáil.* He supported the Anglo-Irish Treaty in 1921 and became Minister for Education in the first Executive Council of the Irish Free State. When the Boundary Commission was set up in 1924, MacNeill was nominated as a delegate to represent the Free State government but resigned rather than accept the commission's verdict. MacNeill lost his seat in the June 1927 general election. He became chairman of the Irish Manuscripts Commission that year and retired from politics to devote himself to scholarship. His major works include *Phases of Irish History* (1919) and the more formal works *Celtic Ireland* (1921) and *Early Irish Laws and Institutions* (1935). He died in Dublin on 15 October 1945.

6   John Redmond, Irish nationalist leader, was born in Waterford in 1856. He was elected to the British Parliament as Home Rule Member in 1881. He led the faction supporting Charles Steward Parnell and became chairman of the United Irish party in 1900. Having supported the 3rd Home Rule Bill, he was stunned by the Easter Rising of 1916. His influence later declined and he was opposed by the revolutionary Sinn Féin. At the beginning of the Great War in 1914, Ireland was part of the United Kingdom governed from Westminster. Ireland was represented in the Parliament by 105 MPs, one-third of whom were Unionists and generally supported the Conservative Party. The majority of Irish MPs were members of the Home Rule party which had been campaigning for nearly forty years for the right to have their own Parliament in Dublin to take care of domestic affairs but still maintain the link with Britain. The leader of this party was John Redmond and when war broke out in August of that year, he was to be influential in urging Irishmen to support the British war effort. By October 1915 over 100,000 Irishmen were fighting on the side of Britain in the Great War. Redmond died in 1918.

7   The Irish Republican Brotherhood (IRB) was a secret society.

8   Seán Treacy was involved in the first IRA action of the War of Independence in January 1919 when an explosives convoy was ambushed on its way to a quarry. Two policemen were killed. Treacy later became one of the prominent flying-column commanders in the War of Independence. He was killed in October 1920 in Talbot Street, Dublin.

9   John Brown (1800–59). Brown led twenty-one men on a raid of the federal arsenal at Harpers Ferry, Virginia. His plan was to arm slaves with the weapons he and his men seized from the arsenal. His plan was thwarted, however, by local farmers, militiamen and marines led by Robert E. Lee. Within thirty-six hours of the attack, most of Brown's men had been killed or captured.

10   Count Camillo Benso di Cavour (1810–61), was a statesman who was a leading figure in the movement toward Italian unification and the first Prime Minister

of the new kingdom of Italy.

11   Piedmont is part of Italy. This process only came about after several years.

12   Giuseppe Garibaldi, born 4 July 1807, died 2 June 1888. In 1860, Italian unification leader, Garibaldi, proclaimed Victor Emmanuel king of Italy. In 1861, Victor Emmanuel II of the House of Savoy was crowned king. From 1870 until 1922, Italy was a constitutional monarchy with a parliament elected under limited suffrage.

17

TRAVELS ABROAD

I have travelled a little and would like to recount some of my impressions. My first trip to Europe was to Paris on my honeymoon. This was in 1937. I did not know a word of the language and had to make my way around by pointing and making hand signs. As I was in the dance business, I decided to attend an afternoon dance to see what it was like. The admission fee was two shillings and sixpence each.[1] There was no ladies' cloakroom, but gentlemen had to hand over their coats and hats. This was all part of a plan to get as much money as possible out of you. I had no coat, only a hat so I was charged a further two shillings and sixpence for parking the hat. That was a lot of money in those days. There was nowhere else to sit so we had to take a table. We were then approached by a waiter and he asked what we were having. I replied that we were not staying long. He then told us that we could not sit at a table unless we ordered something. I ordered two soft drinks for which I was charged five shillings. This was my first experience of being taken for a ride, but not my last. I visited all of the historic places, Napoleon's Tomb, etc. and of course you paid everywhere.

As I have said, I went to the United States in June 1930 to seek a cure for my disability and to make my fortune. This was a bad time. It was not long after the Wall Street Crash and unemployment was rife. Well-dressed men could be seen at street corners selling apples at five cents each. This was part of the mayor's effort to ease the unemployment problem as there were few or no social benefits in the United States in 1930. Although I lived at Woodside, Long Island, some fifteen miles outside Manhattan, New York proper, I was in Manhattan every day. It is an island of avenues and streets, all numbered and easy to navigate. Like every other city, ghetto areas were not far from pretentious areas. You could travel any distance by subway for a small sum so I visited all parts of New York. Wealth and poverty could be seen everywhere. I visited Sixth Avenue regularly: the crossroads of the world, where you met every nationality. Most of them were looking for work, as many of the shops or offices were unofficial employment agencies. They had long lists of jobs displayed on boards outside their premises. To get a job, you had to pay a sum of money and there was no guarantee just how long it would last. I was told that it was a racket. Sixth Avenue was a sort of bazaar. Here and there, you had demonstrations of strength and of course the sale of goods that would make you strong. The old 'you too can have a body like mine' gimmick. There were lectures in shops and stalls on how to escape venereal disease with lurid pictures on the subject showing people affected. Everyone was welcome. There were hot-gospellers of every description and all kinds of cheap snack joints. While I was in New York, I attended an aviation school, passed the ground course and was supplied with a certificate.

When I arrived in the United States, I landed at Boston, Massachusetts, and resided with my brother Joe for some weeks. He had a hard time of it. He left home for work at 6 a.m. six days a week and arrived back at 7 p.m. It was work to bed. He was a former member of the First Battalion IRA. He fought with his company on the week following the attack on the Dublin Four Courts. He was captured and interned at Mountjoy and Newbridge. He undertook a long hunger strike and came out of jail in poor health. As there was no work he emigrated to the wilds of Canada where he got a job on a farm. If the harvest was good you got paid but you got nothing if it failed. After four years he came home. He married a girl he had kept company with before his arrest and left for Boston. He came home about 1944 and died of cancer, believed to have been caused by the hunger strike in jail in 1923. He was 41 years of age when he died.

I became a councillor in 1955. In 1958 I was nominated to attend a housing conference in Vienna, the Austrian capital. There were two sessions daily on housing and planning. The conference lasted ten days. Delegates from all over the world pooled their ideas. This was beneficial to all and kept planners and councillors up to date. Our nights were our own. I remember the night that we arrived. About six of us went to a nightclub. We, of course, spent our own money. The boys had about three bottles of champagne between them and I had two soft drinks. The bill came to two pounds and ten shillings each. One of the councillors dropped his glass and he was charged five shillings.[2] When we were leaving, the doorman refused to let us out unless we all gave him a tip on the grounds that he had done us a service by opening the door to let us in. Vienna is a large city. The official part has the most wonderful architecture but the rest looked very poor and dilapidated. The government was communist, having taken over from the Russian occupation forces some time before. Eating out was expensive. The cheapest dinner was about £2 a head, dear at that time.

The Minister for Local Government in 1964 invited members of the City Council to inspect system building factories in Paris, Stockholm and Copenhagen. System building was unknown in the Irish republic and we had a serious housing problem. The traditional house builders could not build any more than they had on hand, so system-built dwellings would be additional dwellings. The minister had an option on several hundred acres of land in North County Dublin but the whole development cost would be about £11 million. We were asked to inspect factories, dwellings in the course of construction, and dwellings occupied and report back to the minister and the corporation. Our report to invite tenders was adopted so we eventually had Ballymun of 4,000 dwellings and other similar developments.[3] The trip was all work and no play. We travelled hundreds of miles daily, inspecting. There was mud, slush and puddles everywhere. We had to climb to the top of flats in the course of erection, as the lifts were not in order. We usually came back to our hotel at 6 or 7 p.m. worn out.

However, on the night that we arrived in Paris, we went to a nightclub. There were six of us. The others had about three bottles of champagne between them. This is cheap in France. When we got the bill we nearly sank through the floor. We were being asked for £30. Some of the councillors decided not to pay it but the staff were mobilized and, of course, they had our hats and coats. They also threatened to send for the police who were probably in on the racket. The boys decided to pay, vowing that it would never happen again.

In 1964, I attended a housing conference in Jerusalem. Some of the councillors, including councillors from County Dublin, decided to visit the holy places in Jordan. It was then believed that Jordan would not allow anyone to enter their territory from Israel. As the conference work was on from 10 a.m. to 4.30 p.m. except on a Saturday and Sunday, some of us decided to enter Jordan on a Saturday and we had no trouble because we were Irish. At that time, most of the holy places, including most of Jerusalem, were under Jordanian control. One of the hottest places in Jordan is Jericho. We inspected the famous walls of Jericho which were said to have been blown down by the sound of trumpets. From my observations, the walls were composed of mud. As with all the other holy places, commercialism had taken over. When the boys entered a shop in Bethlehem, the attendants rushed over and offered us coffee and soft drinks. They refused to take no for an answer. A drink was shoved into my hand. This was part of a racket. It was expected that once you had taken the coffee or soft drinks, you were obliged to buy religious souvenirs. I had already bought a supply elsewhere and I had no intention of buying any more. The other councillors bought goods while I waited but an attendant kept pestering me to buy. I walked to the entrance door to await my companions but the attendant followed me and when I walked up the road he followed me. When I entered other shops, I refused point blank to take any drink. This or similar rackets went on everywhere. One Dublin TD bought about £20-worth of religious medals or trinkets to give out to voters when he got home. Getting votes is never far from the politician's mind!

Calvary, where Christ was crucified, was in Jerusalem, now Israel.[4] Arabs were everywhere, selling religious goods. They followed you and it was difficult to shake them off. The area surrounding Calvary and in particular the Via Dolorosa, venerated as the street along which Jesus carried His cross, was more like a bazaar or market-place, a sort of honky-tonk and slum area. You had the contrast of two worlds. Arabs were indifferent to the pilgrims praying on their way to the Church but pressing the sale of Christian religious goods or going about their business. It is a pity that the churches or religious do not purchase the surrounding area and give it a religious or quiet atmosphere instead of the squalor and bedlam, which is a regular feature of the area. I suppose that the Jordanian government did not want to start a local war with their countrymen as this area was and always will be a gold-mine. What the Israelis will do, now that they are in possession of it, is open to conjecture, but I am sure the Arabs will fight to retain their sites or pitches. I would much rather see the poor Arabs make the money than the millionaire-types who have taken over Lourdes, Fatima, etc.

Speaking of Lourdes, my son Francis invited his mother, his brother Éamon and myself to tour Spain, Portugal and part of France in 1968. We camped out as Francis had all the usual equipment. It worked out cheaply as we cooked our own meals. I remember seeing a picture of Robert Kennedy on the front page of a Portuguese newspaper.[5] At the time, he was contesting the California primary. He was the democratic candidate for the presidential election. I asked a Portuguese what was the news of Kennedy as I was anxious to know if he had won or lost. The Portuguese put his finger to his head and tapped it. I thought from that gesture that he had lost as it is a saying when you lose that you got the bullet. I was far from expecting the truth that in fact what the Portuguese was trying to convey to me was that he had been shot.

Everything was cheap in Portugal. We drove to Gibraltar, several hundred miles away. It was a small town astride a rock. There are 20,000 people residing there and things were cheap. We went straight through Spain and detoured towards Lourdes in France, near the Spanish frontier. Spain, especially the rural area and small towns, looked very poor to me. The standard of living is about half that in these islands. This is one of the points made by the people of Gibraltar against joining up with Spain. In Spain, we camped on sites with all of the amenities for as little as seven shillings and sixpence a night. When we entered France, this cost doubled and most things trebled.

Lourdes looks like a rich town, and so it should be. According to a report that I read in 1972, over £30 million is spent annually by pilgrims. Shops and stalls are laden with religious goods or trinkets and everyone buys, some on a large scale, to distribute on their return home. There must be more millionaires in Lourdes than in any town on earth. It is a disgrace that this commercialism should be allowed. We are told that Christ whipped the money changers out of the temple because He objected to a religious place being used for profit, making one wonder what He would think of Lourdes and similar places where religion is used to make huge profits. It makes many visitors cynical of the whole set-up. I know that many people receive a tremendous spiritual uplift, but I do not propose to question whether invalids are cured. However, I think that those who are in a bad state of health should not be brought such a distance, as in many cases they return in a worse condition and in some cases die of the effort. When I was there, I met a woman who had arrived a few days earlier. She knew me as she was from Dublin. She was heartbroken as her husband, who was in bad health and who had accompanied her, had died in Lourdes that day. People should remember that God is not only in Lourdes, He is everywhere.

People should be on their guard against false claims. Some time ago two people appeared on *The Late Late Show*.[6] One was blind and did most of the talking on the prompting of his manager. He was advocating the cause of some mountain area in Spain where apparitions were supposed to have occurred. When asked who got the money that they were collecting in all of the towns and cities that they visited, as they held lectures in local hotels regarding the authenticity of the apparitions, they said that they got the money and that it was used to pay for their travelling and hotel expenses. The blind man was obviously used for the sympathy vote. In India and other countries, professional beggars mutilate themselves to look more pitiful to those who are a soft touch. Recently, I read that bishops in Spain condemned the claim of those who said that they had seen the Blessed Virgin Mary, but people continue to visit the area. Hundreds of thousands visited it when the claim was first made and all the local sites were bought up by would-be millionaires or perhaps the millionaires from other similar areas.

In this country, many dupes believe in fairies, banshees, ghosts, faith-healers and spirits of all sorts. A well-known entertainment artist absconded with a married woman and her children to the United

States. He was to entertain at a Cork play-house, where 2,000 people turned up, paying as much as £1. He did not appear. When interviewed in America, he is alleged to have said that he had been fooling the Irish for twenty years. He had claimed some special power but he admitted that he had no such power. Judging by the number of political frauds who head the polls at election time, and the people I have referred to above, it seems to me that honest people have little chance of survival and I can understand honest politicians being tempted to come to terms with these victims, seeing that they are so numerous.

The good Lord made us selfish. He also gave us a mind to think. He gave us free will. Either we are aware or we are not. It all depends on whether we labour to find out the truth. Most people do not want to struggle so they are likely to have an uninformed opinion. Furthermore, selfishness may condition our thoughts and actions so the dilemma remains. Again, on RTÉ's *Late Late Show*, a young fellow and a manager claimed to be faith-healers. He just rubbed the affected part with his fingers and said a short prayer. Thousands from all over Ireland and some from abroad have visited his abode in county Cavan and he is making plenty of money. He admitted that he had bought an expensive car, property and had just come back from a holiday in the West Indies. Doctors said that there was no proof. In no case did a person produce a medical certificate showing that they had a specific disease before an alleged cure. Nevertheless, they keep coming. As Barnum said: 'There's one born every minute.'[7]

I revisited New York and Boston again in 1971, accompanied by my wife and sister Mary. We went for three weeks by chartered plane. The cost was about £30 less than the normal fare in each case. New York looked much the same but there were more skyscrapers and others were in the course of being built. The 6th Avenue that I had known from my earlier days had disappeared. The Mecca of show-biz, Times Square and the 42nd Street area were much the same except that New York seems to have gone sex-mad, especially the above area. All cinemas were showing sex films and there were scores in this area including peep shows. Posters showed naked men and women and claimed that their show was more revealing and sadistic than the opposition. Bookshops were everywhere showing the most disgusting sex pictures you could think of. It was said that no woman was safe in New York at night unless accompanied by a male companion. In fact, they are not safe in the daytime either. When I was there, a boy and his girlfriend were attacked in Central Park, Manhattan, during the day. The boy was shot and the girl was raped. Again, near Grand Central Station in Manhattan, a beggar stabbed six people because he was not getting any money. Manhattan is full of weirdos of all colours, many of whom were drug-addicts. We stayed with friends about twenty miles outside Manhattan. Most people told me that they would not live in Manhattan.

Boston has changed little. It is a nice quiet city like Dublin. Several relations emigrated to Boston fifty or sixty years ago. Their children are married with children. When they first emigrated, they lived in a poor area in east Boston but thanks to the education system, all children received a good education so it was up to them to make the grade. They all now own or reside in bungalows outside Boston. They all have cars, phones and good jobs. My Aunt Lena was a Ford and her husband Jim was a Sherwin. In other words, two sisters married two brothers. Six of their children were in the army during the last war.[8] A picture of the six in uniform appeared in local Boston papers as an inspiration to others. Some of them rose to the rank of officers. One became a colonel. They all gave us a royal time for the week we were there. All of the clan met in each other's dwellings each night for dinner, which was followed by a party. Americans seldom drink in bars. They have their own and always have a good stock in. There are many unusual characters in the United States and much crime. Nevertheless, the vast majority are decent, hardworking people. They have a serious racial problem at present and it will get worse. It seems that the white and coloured people will not mix. At least they will not live in the same areas and every trick in the book is used to prevent the coloured people from obtaining power or position. With their voting strength they have captured many towns, cities and one State. Some of them are advocating a separate black state and it may lead to another civil war as the United States will never agree to that. Perhaps America will understand why we in Ireland object to a minority of Scot planters setting up a separate state in Ireland. To sum up, America is no place for Irish workers to have a holiday as the £1 is worth about eight shillings unless you have friends or relations to go to. A bed for one night will cost £5 and no breakfast. There are no cheap bed and breakfast abodes as we have here.[9]

NOTES

1   This is the equivalent of about ten shillings each at time of writing, 1972.
2   Its value was nine pence.
3   Ballymun is a tower block flat complex, situated some four miles north of Dublin.
4   Many writers say that Christ was crucified outside the old wall but the site of the Church of the Holy Sepulchre is inside the wall.
5   Robert Francis Kennedy, brother of President John F Kennedy, was born on 20 November 1925 in Boston, Suffolk County, Massachusetts. He served in the United States Navy Reserve from 1944 to 1946. He was elected as a Democrat

from New York to the United States Senate and served from 3 January 1965 until his death in 1968. Robert F. Kennedy was killed by an assassin's bullet in Los Angeles, California, on 6 June 1968, while campaigning for the Democratic presidential nomination.

6   *The Late Late Show.*

7   Phineas Taylor Barnum (1810–91), a consummate showman and entrepreneur, was one of the most colourful and best-known personalities in American history. Barnum was famous for bringing both high and low culture to all of America. Barnum's oddities, spectacles, galas, extravaganzas and events tickled the fancies, hearts, minds and imaginations of Americans of all ages.

8   This refers to the Second World War.

9   This refers to the time of writing: 1971.

18

THE AUCTION BUSINESS

Earlier I referred to the auctions. It is a fascinating business and can be an interesting pastime and profitable at times. There are, however, dangers, such as getting a bad buy or accumulating a lot of junk, but if you are shrewd, observant and examine goods before the auction commences, you can sometimes make a good buy. It must be remembered, however, that auctions are dumping grounds for defective goods. But as I said, if you are experienced you can do well on the rounds. There are public and private auctions. The latter are usually of legal necessity but the former are used to get rid of defective articles, especially wood-wormed furniture. It would be safe to say that one-third of all goods sold at public auctions are defective. There are auctions that specialize in art, antiques or property but I have little or no experience of these matters. My experience has to do with ordinary household goods. It is more of a pastime, during which I make an odd buy, usually portable goods as I have no place of business or transport. I sell these goods from time to time through the newspapers. I make a few pounds, which augments my small pension. My experience goes back thirty years. I bought a sewing machine at an auction for £1.50 on Bachelors Walk where there are about six auctions rooms. When things got bad the following year, I sold it for £3. Apart from auction, thousands of people purchase second-hand goods from second-hand shops, market stalls or privately through newspapers. These goods come largely from public or private auctions so my experience may help such people.

As I have said, I began attending auctions in about 1945, just before the war ended. Having made a thirty-shilling profit on my sewing machine, I decided to buy another one and I went on buying them. I was taken in a few times with defective machines but I soon learned all about them. As the saying goes: practice makes perfect! I bought other goods, especially electrical goods, as I soon learned that people are afraid to buy anything electrical at auctions unless they are guaranteed as perfect. Some electrical goods are returned to the auctioneer because they are defective although working. Many auctioneers on this account will not guarantee electrical goods so such goods go cheap and very often they are in perfect condition. Every dealer could tell you of his or her best buy and the worst. In my case, I bought a full-sized fish and chip pan, like those you see in the fish and chip shops, for a £1. I sold it one week later for £50. The circumstances were as follows. About 1950, I attended Scannell's auction at Bachelors Walk. The late Jim Scannell was the auctioneer. I found him a fussy, unpredictable individual. It is the rule at auctions that you must clear your goods from the auction room not later than the following week but they are often left well beyond that time. On one occasion I bought a bicycle for fifteen shillings. I did not take it away by the following week. When Scannell saw it, he ordered it to be re-sold. He opened the bidding at five pence and sold it on the first bid. However, owing to his erratic nature I made my best buy. This involved the chip pan. It had lain in the corner of the auction room for the previous two years. The owner had put a reserve of £100 on it so it ended up lying there unsold and just as he had sold my bicycle he ordered the pan sold. As it had not been advertised, there was nobody at the auction who would have been particularly interested in such a large article. He asked for £1 so I put up my hand and as there was no other bidder, I got it for £1. I had no place to put it but luckily for me, I knew the manager of a local second-hand shop so he took it in on a commission basis. It was sold the following week for £50 so I made £45 after paying £5 commission. My worst buy was an old motor car from Scannell's shortly after I returned from America in 1932. I knew nothing about cars and could not drive. It cost me £16. My cousin, the late Joe Grogan, tried to drive it. The car was a crock so I dropped it into a garage on Brunswick Street and did not bother about it for the following six months. When I got my bill from the garage owner, I suggested that he could keep the car in lieu of payment and he agreed. Just before I went to America, I bought a motorcycle for £10. I rode it to the Naul and back. Just before I reached home, it packed up because I had forgotten to put oil into it. I left it in the yard of my home on leaving for America. On my return, I found it all rusted, so I sent it to the scrapyard for seven and a half pence. Such was my experience of motor vehicles.

Woodworm is a common defect in furniture, especially modern furniture, because of the amount of plywood used – plywood to woodworm is like cheese to a mouse. It is possible to make a good buy if the furniture is declared as having been treated for woodworm, as it is usually sold at half or even quarter of the normal price especially if there is only a small trace of it. It could be a bad buy unless you have examined it carefully before the auction, as it could be crawling with worm. Old furniture could also have woodworm holes but they may be dead. A bad sign is fresh holes or powder. It is as well to avoid wormed furniture, as it is as difficult to cure as cancer in the human body. Woodworm is usually found in the lower parts or at the rear or, as I have said, wherever there is plywood or under the seat of chairs, especially in the blocks.

Electrical goods could have a minor or a major defect but to the layperson, one is as good as the other. If it has to be serviced it could cost many pounds because you are usually told to send the goods in for repair so you will not know whether it was a big or a small job. If the goods are mechanical and seem to work, remember that there could be an internal problem: the bearings could be worn so never judge mechanical goods by their exterior. You could buy well if you use your head but if you have no knowledge, then keep out of auction rooms. Delph or china may be chipped or cracked so examine it well. If the goods are in a box, there may be a few good pieces on the top but the rest could be defective. Antique furniture is sold at most auctions. It is usually good stuff but it costs. All sorts of goods turn up at auctions and that is what makes it so interesting. There is occasionally a sheriff's sale. These goods are usually sound and as everything must be sold you may get a real bargain, but an army of dealers usually turn up to a sheriff's sale making for stiff opposition. The auctioneer may own much of the furniture. It usually comes from Britain so the auctioneer may bid on his own stuff. Dealers also send in goods and they may bid on their goods in order to boost the prices so make up your mind to bid so much and no more. Some people bid more than it could be bought for in the shop. Two people who are together may, in their anxiety to get an article, bid against one another thus increasing the cost of the article. The auctioneer will sometimes ask the two bidders if they are together and inform them of their mistake. There are many mock auctions and people are usually taken in. The auctions on Bachelors Walk are genuine but it is their job to get as much as possible for the article as they get commission not only from the buyer but two or three times as much from the seller or person who sent the goods in to be sold.

In my opinion, most modern goods are rubbishy. They are all spit and polish but are without substance. They are intended to have a limited life, making it necessary for you to repeat the purchase. In the old days they were made to last. I have seen modern Chesterfield suites at auctions which were falling apart. They could not have been in use for more than a few years. They must have cost between £50 and £100 but sell at the auction for about £5. The seats had collapsed because the so-called webbing that supports the seat had broken in several places and the upholstery was torn at the seams and on the arms. Most other things in the furniture line go loose in the joints after little use. Pots, etc. are wafer-thin and other goods, such as vacuum cleaners, tape recorders, radios, etc., have a Bakelite covering that cracks or breaks into pieces if it is dropped or is handled roughly. It pays to buy good old stuff at auctions if you use your head.

POSTSCRIPT

I began the draft of this autobiography in Bricin's Military Hospital during my periodic check-up related to my disability pension. I had been formulating the idea for some time but could never make up my mind to get going. I worked out a rough draft with outlines of main subjects. When I came out of hospital I got down to details. It took about eighteen months as I had to study notes, old newspapers, *Dáil* reports, histories and biographies. I wrote to the Department of Defence regarding papers in connection with evidence submitted by former IRA men. There was much chopping and changing. I had no previous writing experience, except for the odd letter to newspapers, so it was not easy. I began in January 1971 and finished about July 1972. However, because I submitted the draft to two friends and a publisher, more than a year was to pass before there was any decision regarding publication. I was obliged to write a Postscript on matters which I referred to in my original draft as many relevant changes had taken place. I have made minor revisions in the draft.

Stormont, the seat of government of Northern Ireland, was abolished in the summer of 1972. The civil rights campaign, and particularly the ferocious military campaign of the Provisional IRA, which inflicted heavy casualties on the British forces and threatened a breakdown in the northern economy, forced the British government to change their previous policy of maintaining the supremacy of the Orangemen in the government of the north. The Orangemen were prepared to fight to the last British pound but the British were fed-up, knowing that they would have to pay the full cost. Furthermore, they knew that the Provisional IRA, backed by thousands of women and children, were going to fight to the last. The nationalists had decided that they would no longer be enslaved.

The British issued a White Paper on the future of Northern Ireland and enacted legislation to operate it. Although they made many concessions, it was not enough. The Orangemen resisted the implementation of the White Paper knowing that they would lose much of their ill-gotten ground and power. The government of the south assisted the British in putting down the IRA because they believed that the voters in the south were indifferent to the northern struggle and they were afraid of the British. I can understand their problem but did they have to rub it in? Did they have to jail men who were believed to be IRA men from the north, even though they had not broken the law in the south? I am afraid history will have something harsh to say about the south in this struggle.

Shortly before Stormont was abolished, British Prime Minister Edward Heath asked parties and individuals to let him have suggestions regarding the future of Northern Ireland.[1] I wrote and expressed my views. I told him that I was anxious for peace in the north. I stated that I was a former Independent member of *Dáil Éireann*, that I was anxious for the unity of Ireland and that I was not a member of any party or organiszation. I asked that proportional representation be adopted for local and parliamentary elections. I asked that one-third of all jobs go to Catholics in state and semi-state bodies; that it be made an offence to discriminate against any person in the matter of jobs and housing in the private sector; that a proportion of Cabinet seats be allocated to nationalists; that all obstacles be removed for Republicans advocating unity by peaceful means; that internment be ended and that all persons convicted of political offences be released. I accepted that unity was a matter for the long term, and then only by the consent of the majority.

I received an acknowledgement from Mr Heath. I then sent a copy of my letter to Mr Whitelaw, British Minister for Northern Ireland and received the following reply from Mr Miller, his private secretary.[2]

> Northern Ireland Office,
> Stormont Castle,
> Belfast. BT4 357.
> 7 September 1972.

Dear Mr Sherwin,

The Secretary of State has asked me to thank you for the copy of the letter originally sent to Mr Heath in response to his recent request for the views of all political parties and individuals on the future arrangements for the governing of Northern Ireland and to assure you that your views will be taken into account.

> Yours,
> R. Miller, (Private Secretary)

Most of what I suggested was covered in the White Paper but obstacles to Republicans advocating unity remained, including internment. There is no assurance that convicted political prisoners will be released pending a return to normality in northern politics.

A general election was held in the south in February 1973 which resulted in a coalition government between *Fine Gael* and Labour. A small majority elected them. *Fianna Fáil* had been in power for sixteen years and there was a feeling that a change was necessary. The split in the party helped to defeat *Fianna Fáil.* The opposition offered a statement of intent, which seemed attractive. They decided, among other things, to abolish the health and housing charges in the rates over a period of four years. *Fianna Fáil* had already stated their policy, the main attraction of which was a substantial increase in social benefits. After the coalition's statement of intent was published, *Fianna Fáil* decided to abolish all rates on dwellings. The public took the view that *Fianna Fáil* was trying to be too smart too late, although the *Fianna Fáil* offer helped to prevent a worse defeat for them. Actually the *Fianna Fáil* offer on the rates had been my idea. I had been pressing this matter for almost ten years. At the Dublin City Council meeting on 4 July 1966, I not only asked by motion, which was passed, that those on low incomes should get relief, but that there should be a differential between rates on business and dwellings. In fact, a week before *Fianna Fáil* made this offer, I had a letter in *The Evening Press* advocating relief for dwellings but not for business because, as I have said, it would cost the taxpayer too much.[3] The new government were to improve some conditions and have shown some gratitude towards those who helped them, but they have included people with money. This is a waste of revenue which will land them in trouble later. They had already increased taxation by £22 million and budgeted for a huge deficit, which is not good business unless it is for capital purposes. The new government is lucky. They had the benefit of £30 million saved by joining the EEC. They also had the benefit of economic growth, which makes revenue buoyant. They can thank the government, especially the late Mr Seán Lemass, for this growth. I helped a good part in supporting Mr Lemass so that he could continue in his job. When I became a member of the *Dáil* in 1957, there was no economic growth. There was nothing in the kitty to help the poor. They were lucky to get an extra shilling or one shilling and sixpence in a budget.

In May 1973, a major scandal broke in the United States – known as the Watergate scandal. There were many disclosures of corruption and several of President Nixon's Cabinet ministers were involved.[4] Even the president was suspect. But then, all political parties are corrupt – it is only a question of being found out. Imagine responsible Cabinet ministers! Men who moralised and sermonized others on the high standards to be followed, not only bugging their opponents' headquarters but conspiring to trap innocent girls who attended the party at Martha's Vineyard with Senator Ted Kennedy and Mary Jo Kopechne.[5] The night of the unfortunate accident when Miss Kopechne was drowned, they were to be drugged, stripped naked and photographed in compromising situations so that they could be black-mailed into making damaging statements against Ted Kennedy which could be used against him if he became a presidential candidate. Even President Nixon was suspect and every trick in the book was used to silence those who were arrested, by promises of large sums of money and presidential clemency later. Those men, in such places of trust, stooping to the level of petty gangsters and the mafia proves my point that party politicians have a 'Jekyll and Hyde' existence and live in a sort of hell.

In regard to the north, I would have liked to see the Sunningdale package arising from the British White Paper getting a chance, as little more progress can be expected at this stage. Some sort of understanding must be established with the Provisional IRA because these people must be lived with and they cannot be expected to disappear as if nothing ever happened, as if they never fought and suffered. They believe that they are supported by thousands in the south, that they brought down Stormont and compelled the British to stand up to the Orangemen. They are entitled to a guarantee that they can contest elections under the name of Sinn Féin or any other name that they choose without any contrived obstacles being placed in their way. They are also entitled to guarantees that internment will end and that all prisoners convicted in the north and in Britain, as a result of the political trouble in the north, will be released within a reasonable period after a cessation of hostilities.

When I voted for Mr Lemass as *Taoiseach* in 1961 so that the country would have a stable government, I then stated that I was not concerned with the party game and that I was not voting for *Fianna Fáil*. I stated that we should be concerned with the problem of the Common Market and unemployment, with partition and the boys in the Congo. The same problems remain, except that we now have inflation arising out of joining the Common Market. Arising out of the Sunningdale Agreement, a power-sharing executive was established in Northern Ireland but the extremists on both sides refused to support the new executive. A general election was declared in Britain. As twelve members of the British Parliament are elected in the north, the executive Orangemen supported by most Protestants won eleven seats, largely because their opposition was divided.

They made the Sunningdale Agreement the main issue so they were able to claim that the majority was against it. They demanded a general election for Northern Ireland but as this was not forthcoming, they engineered a general strike, which they enforced with terror tactics. Some people were shot and business premises were obliterated. The strike lasted for fifteen days until the British capitulated. They abolished the Northern executive and later decided to elect a constitutional convention to allow all sides to consider some form of power-sharing executive. I hold that no satisfactory agreement is possible and that war or a state of war will continue. The Orangemen have monopolized all positions of place and power. It is not in their nature to compromise for to do so would amount to handing over many key jobs. It is their long-term policy to wear down the Catholics so that they will migrate to Britain or to the south thus ensuring their continued supremacy.

The Orangemen are more than a match for the northern nationalists and the south combined, because the British army in Northern Ireland is their shield against the south coming to the assistance of those under attack from the Orangemen. The solution to the northern problem is for the British army to get out. When this shield is removed, the Orangemen will know that the game is up as they would not last a week against the northern nationalists supported by the southern government. If the Orangemen did fight, it could be a good thing in the long run as it would cleanse the northern area of foreign bigots. The defeatist and 'peace at any price' policy of certain coalition politicians in the south encourages the Orange fiends to sustain their terror as they have learned from experience that everything is to be gained in this life by the use of force. Their success in partitioning this country and their success resulting from three general strikes prove that. The defeatist politicians in the south have robbed the people of the will to resist aggression and correspondingly have strengthened the Orangemen's will to engage in more aggression. An American authority once said: 'Nice guys usually finish last. Low down rotten bastards win!' That is the case at all times in the northern arena.

In May 1974, the Minister for Local Government fixed the date for the local elections: 18 June. There had been no local elections for the previous seven years. He also changed the constituencies in such a way that I lost half of my old local area. All of Cabra was included for the first time. I knew many old-timers living in Cabra but I was seriously handicapped, especially as I had been out of the public eye for those seven years. I had little money, no car and only my family to help me, but I was determined to win. It was now or never. I had been preparing for this election for some time. I still had a lot of literature, including 500 posters. I also had a copier so I started my campaign two weeks before the opposition. I canvassed no voters in person as I did not have the time, but I put literature into 20,000 dwellings three times before polling day. I worked from 7 a.m. until 2 p.m. every day. I walked about twenty miles a day as there was a bus strike in Dublin over the campaign period. In fact, I was in a virtual state of collapse many times, but I decided to die in the attempt. You can judge the amount of walking that I did from the fact that I wore out a pair of shoes during the period of the campaign. I won a seat by a margin of seventeen votes. It was a great victory when you consider all the difficulties. Many outgoing personalities with means had fought for a seat and failed. It was some consolation for the let-downs in the past. During the counting of the votes I was certain that I had lost. I could not take any more and left for home, not a little dejected, having given up all hope. I returned just before the finish and to my surprise I was to win a seat on the last count. I was the only Independent elected to Dublin Corporation out of forty-five councillors. So never say die! I remain independent and unrepentant in the hope that my past actions will be understood and accepted by a more enlightened public.

Frank Sherwin

NOTES

1   The Right Honourable Sir Edward Heath, KG, MBE (9 July 1916–17 July 2005), soldier and politician, was Prime Minister of the United Kingdom from 1970–74 and leader of the Conservative Party from 1965–75. His spell in office represented a transition between the traditional 'squirearchical' leadership of the party rotating among senior figures such as Harold Macmillan and that of later self-consciously meritocratic figures starting with Margaret Thatcher.

2   William Whitelaw was a Conservative MP when appointed the first Secretary of State for Northern Ireland (March 1972–November 1973). Whitelaw was born on 28 June 1918 in Nairn, north-east Scotland. Apart from holding the seat of Penrith-the Borders from 1955 until Thatcher dispatched him to the Lords after the 1983 election, Whitelaw served as Lord President of the Council (1970–72), Leader of the House of Commons (1970–72), Secretary of State for Northern Ireland (1972–73), Secretary of State for Employment (1973–74), Home Secretary (1979–83), Lord President of the Council (1983–88) and Leader of the House of Lords (1983–88). Whitelaw died on 1 July 1999.

3   The following articles may be of interest. All were published in *The Evening Press*. The first was dated Tuesday 14 June 1966, p. 9, 'Open spaces in Cabra West'. Another was dated Thursday 16 June 1966, p. 10, 'Corporation rents system is unfair'. Also Tuesday 21 June 1966, p. 3, 'To fight rents: tenants engage Council'; Monday 27 June 1966, 'Area "unfit" for housing', inquiry told'. See also article entitled: 'Protest at rise in prices of houses', Wednesday 29 June

1966, p. 8, and 'Plan for 9,600 houses', Saturday 2 July 1966.

4 Richard M. Nixon, thirty-seventh President of the United States (1969–74). Nixon was born on 9 January 1913 in Yorba Linda, California and died on 22 April 1994 in New York.

5 Mary Jo Kopechne was born in the village of Forty Fort, Pennsylvania, on 26 July 1940. After graduating from Caldwell College for Women in New Jersey, she moved to Washington where she worked as a secretary for George Smathers and Robert F. Kennedy. On 17 July 1969, Kopechne joined several other women who had worked for the Kennedy family at the Edgartown Regatta. On 18 July, they were joined by Edward Kennedy at a party at Lawrence Cottage. Kennedy offered to take Kopechne back to her hotel, so they left the party at 11.15 p.m. While travelling, Kennedy lost control of the car. It went off the side of a bridge, turned over and sank into the water. Kennedy managed to free himself from the car and swam to safety. He returned to the party leaving Kopechne behind. Kopechne's corpse was found at the scene. Edward Kennedy was found guilty of leaving the scene of an accident and received a suspended two-month jail sentence and one year driving ban. However, there were doubts about the way Kopechne died. Dr Donald Mills of Edgartown wrote on the death certificate 'death by drowning', but Gene Frieh, the undertaker, told reporters that 'death was due to suffocation rather than drowning'. John Farrar, the diver who removed Kopechne from the car, claimed she was 'too buoyant to be full of water'. It is assumed she died from drowning, although her parents filed a petition preventing an autopsy.

AFTERWORD

I suspect it is more the custom than the rule that we get to know someone when they are in our midst rather than after they have taken their final departure. In my case, I would have to say that this did not apply. When alive, my father did not speak too much of his earlier years. I got to really know him in a roundabout way through certain experiences, etc. I am not going to go into these encounters at this stage and not merely for the want of space. They and other issues have been dealt with in detail in an as yet unpublished venture of my own entitled *A Legacy*. Suffice it to say that were it not for these encounters, you would not now be reading this autobiography of my father. It would have ended up in that place of forgotten things, indeed scattered to the four winds. Dipping into *A Legacy*, I unearth an old memory: my father's election to the *Dáil* and his efforts to interest me in the political scene.[1]

As I sat alone by my father's deathbed on the night of 7 November 1981 watching the last hours of his life tick away, my mind drifted back to earlier times to that day in 1957 when I had never seen him so happy. He had beaten all of the odds and got himself elected to *Dáil Éireann*. I know that getting elected to the *Dáil* today has somehow become a little hackneyed, a mere formula, in fact it is something of a joke among the major parties that they could get a walking stick elected, giving rise in many quarters to a 'so what' shrug of the shoulders. This elation was to be matched equally in despondency on losing that lifelong achievement in 1965.

I recall him trying to interest me in the political life equally to no avail. 'Would you like to go into politics?' he asked. A certain voice in my head cautioned me to say no. I had my own dream and goal in life, which is another long story and I think that I hurt his feelings by declining this offer. Nevertheless, I recall him one afternoon, taking me with him along Parliament Street to the council chamber of Dublin's City Hall hoping maybe that I would change my mind and 'catch the bug'. I soon found myself sitting in a seat on the balcony, from where I could observe the proceedings. In fact, I could have had any seat on the balcony, as I was the only one there.

While I waited for things to happen, I gazed around this room from my elevated vantage point. The chamber is a very imposing room from which I could pick up a sense of history, which seemed to me at any rate to hang about in the air of the place. One often picks up this sensation on entering historical places of note such as famous cathedrals like Canterbury or Notre Dame, especially when they are empty and quiet, for these sensations are subtle and can be drowned out by footsteps and other general noise. The general noise will insist on being heard and talks much louder than that subtle influence, but I found this room whispering to me of its past.[2]

Soon the room seemed to come to life with bodies appearing and taking to their seats. I do not recall what business was entered into on that occasion. My interest was taken up with mere visual observations and impressions. I was to notice that the seating arrangement was dominated by the presence of one ornately carved box affair in which was seated one dapper-looking, moustached figure in his robes of office. Taking in the rest of the august chamber I was to notice that the ornate carving did not end with the carved box affair but ranged lavishly throughout the chamber. The whole room seemed to be made of wood of a rich hue as so many of these establishments are. It was plain to see that no expense had been spared. Turning my attention back to the 'carved box affair' with its robed figure with the funny mustachio, who could only be one Alfie Byrne, Lord Mayor of Dublin, also known as 'the shaking hand of Dublin', I somehow recalled the same figure in even earlier times pushing a penny into my hand as I made my way home from school and almost insisting that I 'go home and tell your mammy that Alfie Byrne gave you that'.[3] I dutifully clutched my bribe and continued on my homeward journey.

I could see that here in this place was where my father's heart was, with its walls and extensive wooden furnishings that soaked in that history of earlier days. However, if my father had hoped that this visit would ignite some hidden yearning for the political scene on my part, I am afraid I was to prove something of a disappointment to him. He told me that I would have nothing to do, that he would take care of everything but I could not live with that. However, in spite of this opposition to the notion and with little help from me, I was to find myself on the ballot paper as a candidate for the municipal elections in 1960, missing a seat by a handful of votes, which came as a relief to me. Apart from a second visit many years later with a work colleague in connection with the job that I was engaged in at that time, this was to be the one and only time I was to set foot inside the chamber.

Frank Sherwin Jr

NOTES

1   *A Legacy*, an unpublished work by Frank Sherwin Jr, is comprised of two parts. Part I is entitled 'Memories of Life' and Part II, 'Some further thoughts on this life and otherwise'.

2   The building known today as Dublin City Hall was built in the latter half of the eighteenth century and was originally called the Royal Exchange until Dublin Corporation took it over in 1851. It was to have an early history unbecoming of its present status, especially during the Rebellion of 1798 where it was used for, amongst other things, a torture chamber.

3   The chair of the Lord Mayor brings me to the second and last time that I was to enter the chamber, many years after my first visit, as part of the job that I was engaged in at that time. My colleague, Andy Fitzpatrick, and I found ourselves inside the chamber where we were to set up a television and recorder for a viewing by the councillors of some programme most probably intended to be broadcast. On arriving there, we found the chamber empty, and after setting up our equipment and with some time on our hands, Andy took advantage of the situation to make his way to the famous seat of power, and suitably seated, issued a dictate: 'Off with his head!' Andy had tasted his two minutes of glory.

APPENDIX I

'IFS' IN IRISH HISTORY

An essay written by Frank Sherwin in 1944

If we would see the future we must first examine the past. The future is shaped by our earnestness, foresight and imagination and the past is made what it is by the use of the above or by the lack of it. I often wonder what our present political status would be if we had not been conquered by the Anglo-Normans. Would we have been the hub of the Empire with Britain as an appendage? Would the fleet that claims to rule the waves be the Irish fleet? Would Ireland now be inhabited by 30 or 40 million people? Thinking like this must seem like imagination running riot; nevertheless, it could have been.

Small nations have dominated world history. Some failed to maintain that domination because they lacked island security. We are an island. We could have dominated and maintained that domination as Britain did by the use of naval power. Some people may choose to differ, holding that we would not try to dominate others, but with this point of view I disagree. We are not different from other people. We are no better or no worse. We brag in our history of the exploits of Niall of the nine hostages and King Daithi. These gentlemen did not roam the continent for the good of their health. They were kidnapping and plundering and we gloried in their deeds. It must be remembered that St Patrick was kidnapped and brought here as a child. Conquest then was the order of the day and if we were later beaten by the Anglo-Normans, our fate was deserved. If we failed to gain our freedom until 1921 it was because we did not deserve to win as we did not make any real effort to free ourselves due to the rotten clan and provincial king system. This was a system of every man for himself coupled with the lack of national leadership, the nation being nobody's business except perhaps that of the invaders.

We boast that the Romans feared to invade us and gloat over our defeat of the Danes at Clontarf. The Romans never planned to invade our country. Had they wished to do so they could have walked through because of their superior military science and armament. In fact it was the decided policy of the Romans not to extend their empire beyond Britain on this side and the Rhine on the continent. It was perhaps our greatest misfortune that the Romans did not come, as they would have destroyed the clan and king system, which was the cancer of our political life at that time. They might have set up a uniform political control, which would have passed into our hands on the collapse of the Roman Empire, as happened in Britain. They would have built military roads, introduced what at that time was the last word in modern armament, and modernized our civilization. It was due to the Roman occupation, coupled with the Norman fusion at a later date, that England became a strong political unit and, incidentally, our conquerors.

It was also a misfortune that the Danes were not the victors at Clontarf. Like the Romans they might have organized a single control with one dynasty as was the case with the Normans in England. The Danes were a bold, seafaring race. They might have destroyed the English fleet, then in its infancy, and invaded and defeated Britain. At least they would have hurled back into the sea the handful of Anglo-Norman invaders who landed in Wexford in 1169. The Danes would have become Irish nationals, as the northern countries were too far away to influence our political affairs for any considerable period. Had a Talleyrand existed in our affairs at the time of the Anglo-Norman invasion, it might have been possible to offer Strongbow the crown of Ireland independent of England. Strongbow was an adventurer, a soldier of fortune. He would have grasped the opportunity, and Ireland's independence might have been preserved.

Dermott MacMurrogh has been blamed as the person on whose invitation the invaders came. They would have come eventually, invited or otherwise. Our only security lay in naval power and our defeat of the Danes destroyed all hope of that security.

It has been stated that Hugh O'Neill was unlucky in his efforts to free Ireland. O'Neill was unconsciously the 'first northern partitionist', he cared only for Ulster. He did not care two hoots for the remainder of the country, being always willing to compromise with England provided he remained undisturbed in the north. In fact he assisted the foreigners to defeat other Irish chiefs. However, all revolts were futile after the defeat of the Spanish Armada. While England controlled the seas she could prevent men and supplies reaching this country to assist in its liberation, while at the same time pouring in her own forces *ad infinitum*, and eventually destroy us in spite of any temporary success on our part.

During the Civil War in England between King and Parliament we had a marvellous opportunity to put up a gallant show, nevertheless 1641 was a hopeless fiasco. Throughout our history we lacked leaders who combined military and political capacity. Owen Roe O'Neill was only a good second-rate general. It is indeed remarkable that when Cromwell landed in Ireland, the taking of the relatively unimportant town of Drogheda ended all our hopes in spite of eight years of *carte blanche* opportunity. In a letter to the English Parliament Cromwell boasted that he had bestowed a favour on Ireland by putting a couple of thousand people to the sword, as otherwise he would have been compelled to give battle throughout the country. This would have entailed loss of possibly hundreds of thousands of Irish lives. As he said: 'I was saved that task by the wholesale surrenders and retreats following the massacre at Drogheda.' The wars of 1641 and 1690 were, in the main, fought to establish English kings on their thrones, the Irish interests were religious concessions. It is significant that Cromwell's ruthless but also successful methods were answered in his own country by Collins in 1920–21 by this equally ruthless determination to annihilate the spy system which was responsible for the failure of our attempts for the last couple of hundred years.

If Henry VIII had not wished to marry a second time while his first wife was still living, the Catholic religion might still be the religion of England. In that case Ireland would be politically joined to England like Scotland and Wales, and the Republican party in Ireland would probably be as unimportant as the separatist parties of Scotland and Wales. Extreme principles are only possessed by the few, the bulk of the people are indifferent. They are only influenced by suffering or sympathy. The interference of the English in religious practice and the martyrs created by such interference gained the separatist cause an impetus at all times.

Had England remained Catholic there would have been no Partition, as religion was the origin and is today the nurturer of that problem. If both professed the same religion the rank and file of Planter and native Irish would have intermarried, thus no problem would have been visible, and the plantation would have been mild in comparison to what it actually was. Religion divided the Planter from the Irish and perpetuated the cultural differences of both, particularly in the north because of the homogeneity of the Protestant element.

The Insurrection of 1798 was a complete debacle due to the action of spies and the indifference of the people in the main. The only spectacular fighting took place in Wexford and it was inspired by religious fervour. In any event, whatever happened, the whole attempt was futile as long as England controlled the seas.

Had Nelson been cashiered for acting without orders at Cape St Vincent, the naval battle at Trafalgar might never have been fought successfully for Britain as the victory was due to Nelson's vigilance and rare qualities.

Had Napoleon or French officialdom been as 'secret weapon minded' as some of the world statesmen of the present time, they would have accepted and developed the submarine or the steam-propelled ship offered by the inventor, Fulton. England might have suffered several Pearl Harbors, which would have given France naval supremacy. Indeed, two years had elapsed between Fulton's offer and the French defeat at Trafalgar. Nelson's victory or rather Napoleon's lack of imagination in this matter decided our destiny, as French naval supremacy could have assured Ireland's liberation.

Wolfe Tone was the father of the physical force separatist movement, while O'Connell's method was constitutional propaganda. Each in his way made an important contribution to our political future.

Had Britain offered Home Rule to Parnell or the Redmondites it would have been accepted and we would, like the other dominions, have fought on the side of Britain in the Great Wars of 1914–18 and 1939–45. Neither the Rising of 1916 nor the 'Tan' War of some years later would have taken place. The events of 1916 gained much sympathy for the revolutionists but it was the British threat of conscription that drew the clergy and the moderates into the arms of Sinn Féin. Many people fancied the king or his money, but fancied the safety of their own skins a great deal more, hence the victory of Sinn Féin in 1918. Had the conscription threat never been made in 1918, Sinn Féin might not have been successful in the election of that year and so the IRA would have lost the moral backing that was essential to success.

Our success in 1921 was, in the main, due to the advance of democracy and the popular press rather than physical force. England had been toying with the idea of Irish autonomy for some years. It was, however, necessary to exert pressure in order to induce her to grant sovereignty, thus the need for the 'Tan' War. We never beat England in the field, but we taxed her morale to the limit. In earlier times she would have applied many times the terror actually used in 1921 and we might have been beaten again. Luckily, propaganda saved us from that. It was impossible for England to speak pious words at Geneva, and subsequently belie them in the eyes of the watching world by overdoing the pressure on this country.

Had De Valera been born in Ireland, he would very probably have been shot in 1916. In that case, Griffith would have been president and this would have had significant and far-reaching effects at a later period.

If Collins had not gained supremacy in the physical force movement of his time, the IRB and in particular, control of the Intelligence Department, the 'Tan' War might have ended in our defeat, as Collins was the only man capable of occupying such an important position. A guerrilla army is at the mercy of spies. The ruthlessness of Collins combined with his capacity to mix with all types of people, and added to these characteristics his vast understanding of human nature, made him ideal for such a task as faced him. Had Collins not been Director of Intelligence, the IRA would have been subject to mass arrests. Their headquarters and communications would have been destroyed, the 'Tan' War would have been prolonged and we would have been physically beaten, perhaps even morally defeated. The moderates would have been willing to accept less favourable terms than were gained by the Treaty. Collins disorganized and finally destroyed the enemy spy system, thus preserving our communications and the nucleus of our fighting organization. De Valera's services as a propagandist in America were invaluable, the combined operations of Collins in Ireland and De Valera in the United States compelled Britain to make a more substantial offer than would have been made had these men failed in their missions. In that case and with the prolonging of the struggle, a general election might have been fought resulting in the defeat of Sinn Féin, as the moderates always come to the fore when morale is on the wane in the physical effort.

Collins' supremacy in the movement was probably due to the mass arrest of the leaders in 1917. Had these leaders not been arrested, we might have lost the 'Tan' War. Some leaders no matter how sincere or hardworking can be done without but the right men are indispensable. The personnel of popular movements are a many-headed multitude. In spite of their common purpose, they retain their snobbish tendencies as individuals. They usually support only those of their own social sphere, often to the detriment of the cause they espouse. Collins, to many of the leaders, was a hard boiled uncultivated individual. The gentlemen 'of the pen' would not have supported him. Perhaps it was fortunate for Ireland that they were swept out of the way. The gentlemen 'of the pen' too have their moments but their weapon is hardly the type for use in the jungle. The 'Tan' War was a jungle. Collins was the man to fight it. He fought it to the end and he won it.

All through our history, we find martyrs by the thousand but the realists with political capacity do not fill its pages. They are few in number though their deeds were glorious. The outstanding figures in order of their appearance on our political horizon include the following. They are figures who will be remembered as long as Ireland's people read the pages on which their names and achievements are recorded. They include: Wolfe Tone, because of his grand conceptions; O'Connell, because he raised the people from their knees and due to his initiation of the Constitutional Propaganda movement. This alone made progress in his day. Collins will be remembered for his ruthlessness, his realism and his destruction of the things that had destroyed us in the past and could continue to weaken us. De Valera will be remembered because he embodied all that was idealistic without losing his sense of realism. He, more than any other, could impress the outside world, particularly America, with the justice of our cause.

Frank Sherwin

APPENDIX II

LOST OPPORTUNITIES

An essay written by Frank Sherwin c. 1950

This essay was written by Frank Sherwin c. 1950. Here, Sherwin assesses the aftermath of the Civil War and the political climate of the time. His advice serves as a remedy for a better future following opportunities lost to the past.

When struggling for freedom, we envisaged a kind of Heaven on Earth for our people. All Ireland was to be free. The emigrants were to be brought back not only from Britain, but they were expected to return from America with millions of dollars to invest in building up the nation. We had high hopes of our population rising to 8 or 10 million, as it was before the famine. There was to be peace and plenty. We were to be a special kind of Utopia because we believed we were an exceptional kind of people, spiritually and politically an example for the whole world.

All this was wishful thinking. We are no better or no worse than any other people. In fact we are less qualified in putting ourselves forward because we are on the fringe of Europe and are therefore less experienced than those who live near the hub of civilization. Don't forget when our people went to America after the Famine they were looked upon as greenhorns and they got the most menial of jobs. In spite of our lack of experience and political sense we could have made big strides on behalf of our people were it not for the Civil War, which, looking back now, was unnecessary and madness in the extreme. It was not 'the rank and file's' job to reason why. They went their way in good faith. The majority of them destroyed their economic future. Others, who were old enough but never lost a night's sleep for Ireland, stepped in and got most of the jobs that were going because they were educating themselves, while 'the boys' were serving Ireland. The leaders will answer to history. They should have sensed the danger and pulled back, instead they were like beggars on horseback.

Had there been no split over 'the Treaty' we would have begun with a kind of national party dictatorship which would have lasted at least ten or fifteen years as all the popular leaders would have been behind the Irish government. Many major problems would have been overcome, including partition, as the will and the essential unity would have gone a long way towards building up the nation, and people would have gladly loaned any extra money required. The old fighting spirit would have inspired the government in all its efforts. Instead, we had disunity, hatred, disillusionment, financial problems and the whole national effort stifled by moral bankruptcy. Since the Civil War we have had party governments. The principal leaders were active participants in that struggle. It is remarkable that after thirty years the same people dominate affairs. What has happened to all the talent and genius of the past thirty years? Have they all left the country or have they gone to seed as a result of frustration?

Political parties seem to be unable to regenerate themselves. The parties within are tied up by little caucus groups who act as 'hatchet men' and supress new men who show any ability, for fear they might lose control of the party. Some of the party leaders protect those groups because they are 'yes men' and the leaders themselves do not want any bright competition from others. It is only the leaders' families or cronies who are granted a clear passage, regardless of their ability. In fact, some of the 'yes men' resent the leaders' families getting priority for public honours, but they cannot do anything about it. It would be dangerous to object, it would be signing their political death warrants on account of the party system.

It seems to be impossible to overcome any major problem because it is the policy of those parties not in power to make everything difficult for the party in power on the principle that the more mistakes the government makes or appears to make, the quicker their chance will arise to take office. As the solution of major problems entails a certain amount of risk or loss, because it is usual for a big crisis to precede a big change, a party in power will not take chances in trying to solve a big problem for fear that party opposition will bring about their defeat and remove them from office, thus the party system stifles any real progress in the country. That is why I say, had there been no civil war we could have performed miracles for the country. The only solution I see now for the nation is national government for the next five or ten years.

Some people favour a popular dictatorship or corporate system. I do not agree. Outside a few able individuals, the vast majority of those who would rule us would be mediocrities whom we would find it hard to get rid of. In fact, it might be necessary to fight another civil war to do so. Despite all its faults, democracy remains best in the long run. When faced with a national emergency, the British formed a national government. Britain is a well-organized and wealthy nation because she has had world pickings over the centuries. We got our freedom too late. We have to be satisfied with crumbs. Thus even in normal times, our hand is forced by a national emergency, and therefore we must accept a national government from time to time.

A national government could be formed after the next election. The *Dáil* will elect a *Taoiseach*, the latter should invite the best brains from each party including the Independents. There is often better material among the latter because they prove their mettle in getting elected under their own steam. The majority of the party men are worn out, they are only in the *Dáil* because they get the honour served up on a plate. The *Taoiseach* should have power to go outside the *Dáil* and pick at least two people if necessary.

A major policy agenda should include: the ending of partition, the raising of a large loan to build up the maximum industrial potential with a particular eye to creating substitutes to take the place of imports; an up-to-date scientific agricultural policy with a view to optimum production with our sights set on continental markets; and a reorganized and up-to-date tourist policy with a view to encouraging the good-time-tourist as well as the Irish emigrant. The former spend much more money and are more numerous, the latter worked hard to save their money and they know how to hold on to it.

All our plans should be made with a view to optimum employment levels of a lasting nature. There will always be some emigration as this country cannot maintain a large population owing to our limited industrial potential, unless we go back to potatoes and salt, which we are not going to do. But we ought to be able to support at least 5 or 6 million in comfort, and that should be our aim.

Frank Sherwin

APPENDIX III

FRANK SHERWIN – AN APPRECIATION[1]

Frank Sherwin stood in the Rotunda of the City Hall. It was 1971. There was no City Council – they had been removed from office in 1969. He looked around, breathed deeply as if to imbibe every iota of the atmosphere of the place. 'Oh God', he said, 'I'd love to die here.' It was his way of saying how much he missed being a member of the City Council and it was the first image of Frank that came to my mind when I heard of his death. He will be missed by the members of the City Council and by the officials of the Corporation in all he was a member of the City Council for nineteen years. How many stodgy debates did he liven up by his colourful contributions? I remember some of them. When a former Lord Mayor made some criticism of the councillors, Frank silenced him by saying: 'It's all right for you up there in the Mansion House – with your jam and your caviar.' Or, the succinct way he summarized the whole debate when there was a dispute about the costly purchase of a supposedly blank canvas for the Hugh Lane Municipal Gallery: 'It's like going into a restaurant and paying for a meal and being given an empty plate.' There was nothing left to be said for that side of the argument.

Beneath all of the flamboyant expressions, there was an understanding of the problems of the people he represented, which was not equalled by many other councillors. Many of the newer councillors quickly realized that Frank's knowledge of housing matters was such that it was unwise to contradict him in debates. He was chairman of the Housing Committee and at the time of his death chairman of the Inner City Committee. He was a courageous man. He was not prepared to be 'pressurized' to use his own expression, by anybody. He did what he believed to be the right thing based on an objective judgement of the question. In a sense he was the conscience of the City Council, the independent judgement not subject to any party loyalties or requirements. It is for others to write his political obituary but his vote in the *Dáil* on the turnover tax, which probably cost him his seat, was a courageous one.

He was, of course, the essential Dubliner. His devotion to his wife,

Rose, was there for all to see. 'I'm in a hurry', he said to me once. 'This is my night for bringing the mot to the pictures.' Once, during a reception in the Mansion House she was persuaded to sing. In a moment that seems frozen in time, she sang to him: 'For all you mean to me, my thanks to you.' It was as if there was no one else in the room and Frank, bow-tie bedecked – it was his trade mark – sat there as pleased as punch. He would be pleased to have heard the tributes paid to him, but I suspect that he would appreciate even more the fact that for many a long year the archives of the City Hall will contain a record of the participation of one Frank Sherwin in the affairs of the city.

Francis J. Feely

NOTE

1   Frank Feely originally wrote this piece as an obituary on Saturday 7 November 1981 after the City Council meeting had been cancelled as a mark of respect for Sherwin. He sent it to *The Irish Times* and it was published on Friday 13 November 1981 entitled 'Mr Frank Sherwin – An Appreciation'.

BIBLIOGRAPHY

Abbott, Richard. *Police Casualties in Ireland 1919–1922* (Cork: Mercier Press, 2000)

Adler, Mortimer, J. *The Common Sense of Politics* (New York: Holt, Rinehart and Winston, 1971)

Belloc, Hilaire. *Songs of the South Country* (London: G. Duckworth, 1951)

Belloc, Hilaire. *The Church and Socialism* (London: Catholic Truth Society, 1909)

Chase, Harold W. and Lerman, Allen H. *Profiles in Courage* (New York: Harper, c. 1956)

Chase, Harold W. and Lerman, Allen H. *Kennedy and the Press* (New York: Crowell, 1965)

Chesterton, Gilbert Keith. *Do we agree? A Debate between GK Chesterton and Bernard Shaw, with Hilaire Belloc in the Chair* (London: C. Palmer, 1928)

Collis, William Robert Fitzgerald. *A Doctor's Nigeria* (London: Secker and Warburg, 1960)

Dalton, Charles *Charles with the Dublin brigades 1917–21* (London: 1929)

Deasy, Liam. *Towards Ireland Free: The west Cork Brigade in the War of Independence 1917–1921* (Cork: Mercier, 1973)

Desmond, Barry. *Finally and In Conclusion: A Political Memoir* (Dundrum: New Island Books, 2000)

Dinneen, Joseph Francis. *The Kennedy Family* (Boston: Little, Brown and Company, c. 1959)

Fraser, Ian. *Conquest of Disability* (London: Odhams Press, 1956)

Handley-Read, Edward with foreword by Hilaire Belloc. *The British firing line: a portfolio of engravings in colour from drawings made on the western front, 1914–1917* (London: G. Pulman and Sons, 1917)

Harris, Geoffrey and Spark, David. *Practical Newspaper Reporting, produced under the auspices of the National Council for the training of Journalists* (London: Heinemann, 1966)

Hermans, Ferdinand A. *Proportional Representation and Electoral Reform:*

the text of a lecture delivered in Dublin on 1 September 1968, Chairman Professor Basil Chubb (Dublin: Business and Finance, 1968)

Hitler, Adolf. *Mein Kampf* (London: Friends of Europe, 1936)

Hogan, James: *Election and Representation, Part 1: The Experiment of Proportional Representation in Ireland* (Cork and Oxford: Cork University Press and B.H. Blackwell, 1945)

Institute for the Crippled and Disabled. *Do You Want us to Teach You a Trade?* (New York, NY: Red Cross Institute for Crippled and Disabled Men, [1919]

Kennedy, John F. *Kennedy and the Press: the News Conference* (New York: Crowell, c. 1965)

Kennedy, John F. *Profiles in Courage* (New York: HarperCollins, 1957)

Kent, Frank. *Air Adventure* (New York: Ziff-Davis, 1939)

Lasky, Victor. *John Fitzgerald Kennedy: the Man and the Myth* (New York: Trident Press, 1968)

Lee, J. J. *Ireland 1912–1985: Politics and Society* (Cambridge: Cambridge University Press, 1989)

Levin, Murray B. *Kennedy campaigning: the system and the style as practised by Senator Edward Kennedy* (Boston: Beacon Press, 1966)

Lippmann, Walter. *Preface to Politics* (New York: Mitchell Kennerley, 1913); *Public Opinion* (New York: Harcourt Brace and Co., 1922); *The Phantom Public* (New York: Harcourt Brace and Co., 1925)

Lukas, J. Anthony. *Common Ground: A Turbulent Decade in the Lives of Three American Families,* (New York: Vintage Books, 1986)

Macardle, Dorothy. *The Irish Republic* (New York: Wolfhound, 1999)

Macardle, Dorothy. *Tragedies of Kerry 1922–1923* (Dublin: Irish Book Bureau, 1946)

Machiavelli, Niccolo: *The Prince* (Geneva: Pietro Aubert, 1550) *The works of the famous Nicholas Machiavel, citizen and Secretary of Florence written originally in Italian, and from thence newly and faithfully translated into English* (London: Printed by T.W. [=Thomas Wood?] for A. Churchill, R. Bonwick, T. Goodwin, J. Walthoe, M. Wotton [and six others in London], 1720)

MacIver, Robert M, *The Web of Government* (New York: Free Press, Collier Macmillan, 1965)

MacNeill, Eoin. *Celtic Ireland* (Dublin: M Lester Ltd., 1921)

MacNeill, Eoin. *Early Irish Laws and Institutions* (Dublin: Burns Oates and Washbourne Ltd, 1935)

MacNeill, Eoin. *Phases of Irish History* (Dublin: M H Gill, 1919)

Manning, Maurice. *James Dillon: a Biography,* (Dublin: Wolfhound Press, 2000)

Meridith, James Creed. *Proportional Representation in Ireland* (Dublin: E. Ponsonby, 1913)

Nolan, Brian. *On rights-based services for people with disabilities* (Dublin: Economic and Social Research Institute, 2003)

O'Farrell, Mick, *A Walk through Rebel Dublin 1916* (Cork: Mercier Press, 1999)

Oswin, Maureen. *The Empty Hours: a Study of the Week-end Life of Handicapped Children in Institutions* (London: Allen Lane, 1971)

Reynolds, H.T. *Politics and the Common Man: an introduction to political behaviour* (London: Irwin-Dorsey, 1974)

Shakespeare, William. *Julius Caesar* (Dublin: Dublin Educational Company of Ireland, 1971)

Taylor, Rex. *Michael Collins* (London: Hutchinson, 1958)

Tillyard, Stella. *Citizen Lord: Edward Fitzgerald, 1763–1798*, (London: Chatto and Windus, 1997)

Udall, Morris K. *The High Cost of being a Congressman* (Chicago: HMH Publishing: 1967)

Unionist Research Department. *Proportional Representation and the Local Government 1972/73* (Belfast: Unionist Research Department, 1972)

United Irish League. *Proportional Representation: Explanation of the System* (N.P: c.1919)

Vidal, Gore. *The Best Man: a Play about Politics* (Boston: Little Brown, c.1960)

Vidal, Gore. *United States Essays 1952–1992* (Broadway: Amazon, 2001)

Wells, H.G. *The Time Machine: An Invention* (New York: H. Holt and Co., 1895); *The Invisible Man: A Grotesque Romance* (London: C.A. Pearson, 1897); *The War of the Worlds* (Leipzig: Bernhard Tauchnitz, 1898)

Younger, Carlton. *Ireland's Civil War* (London: Muller, 1968)

INDEX

Adler, p. 71, 75, 222
Aiken, Frank; p. 15, 29, 34, 109
America, p. 13, 30, 37, 38, 40, 53, 62, 74, 75,
    163, 164, 176, 177, 180, 185, 194–196, 198,
    215–217
'a still', p. 40
    poteen, p. 40, 134
colonists, p. 177
conventions, p. 62
first citizenship papers, p. 39
indoor golf course, p. 38
    roller, p. 38
sand-walk, p. 38
places in…..,
    Boston, p. 10, 11, 37, 75, 190, 194, 195
Brooklyn Bridge, p. 74
California, p. 74, 75, 164, 192, 196, 207
Central Park, p. 194
42nd Street, p.194
Gettysburg, p. 155
Long Island, p. 189
Los Angeles, p. 159, 196
Manhattan, p. 189, 194, 195
Martha's Vineyard, p. 204
Massachusetts, p. 75, 125, 190, 195
New Jersey Pier, p. 38
New York, p. 37, 38, 53, 55, 74, 76, 87, 107,
    150, 164, 180, 189, 190, 194, 196, 207
    Sangamon, p. 176
    6th Avenue, p. 189, 190, 194
the West Indies, p. 194
23rd Street, p. 39
Washington, p. 157, 176, 207
    Woodside, p. 37, 189
prohibition, p. 40, 150
the Civil War, p. 55, 180
the Monroe Doctrine, p. 177, 180
the United States, p. iv, 30, 37, 39, 43, 52–55,
    63, 75, 76, 107, 125, 150, 157, 176, 180,
    189, 190, 195, 196, 203, 207, 215
    the Senate of…., p. 71, 75, 125
        senators, p. 71, 72, 75, 125
the Wall Street Crash, p. 189
the Watergate Scandal, p. 176, 203
The YMCA, p. xii, 39
Arabs, p. 192
Ashe, Thomas; p. 8

auctions, p. 134, 197, 198, 199, 200
    art, p. 158, 197
    antiques, p. 197
    electrical goods, p. 197–199
furniture, p. 7, 197–200
    plywood, p. 198
    woodworm, p. 198, 199
    property, p. 146, 194, 197
Austria, p. 73, 185, 186
Barnum, Phineas Taylor; p. 194, 196
Belgium, p. 8
places in….
Brussels, p. 79
Belloc, Hilaire; p. 150, 222
Belton,
    friend of Sherwin's…., p. 57
    Jack; p. 61, 64
Bethlehem, p. 191
Black, O/C Tony; p. 16, 18
Blaney, Neil T; p. 82, 182, 186
Boland,
    Gerald, p. 23, 32, 45, 54, 104, 110
    Kevin, p. 45, 54, 137, 151
Bolster, Commandant Frank; p. 20, 31, 115
Bonaparte, Napoleon, p. 14, 29, 176, 214
Bonner, Seán; p.47
Bowler, Susan; p. 60, 128–130, 135
Breen, Dan; p.12, 28, 69, 99, 123, 124, 126,
    144
Britain, p. 5, 30, 55, 98, 105, 109, 132, 177,
    178, 180, 184–187, 199, 204, 205, 211–215,
    217, 218
aristocracy, p. 83
ascendancy, p. 83, 174
England's forces, p. 8, 33, 201, 212
Kings of…,
Charles I, p. 62, 65, 173, 178
    Charles II, p. 62, 65, 173, 178
George V, p. 10, 11, 51
MPs, p.105, 206
    liberal, p. 142
    the Conservative Party, p. 76, 110, 185,
    187, 206
places in….
    England, p. 3, 9, 30, 32, 51–53, 55, 56, 61,
    65, 171–173, 178–180, 212–214
    Llandudno, p. 172

London, p. 181
planters, p. 13
Prime Minister of…, p. 55, 89, 202, 206
Scot planters, p. 195
the British, p. 7, 132, 173, 175, 177, 180, 182,
    184, 185, 201, 202, 204, 205, 218
the British Army, p. 7, 13, 33, 53, 178, 183,
    184, 205
the British House of Commons, p. 143, 175,
    206
the British Government, p. 55, 99, 201
the British Parliament, p. 51, 175, 187, 204
the British Parliamentary Party, p. 99
the British Troops, p. 9
the British White Paper, p. 204
the English Civil War, p. 62, 173, 178
'the Oath to the British King', p. 13
    the Sunningdale Agreement, p. 204, 205
Brown,
    Ivor, Dr, RMS; p. 170, 171
    John; p. 185–187
Browne, Noël, *Deputy*; p. 64, 81, 82, 85, 87,
    98, 99, 130
Burke,
    Edmund; p. 48, 55, 143
    P.J; p. 60
Byrne, Alfie, p. 49, 55, 59, 130, 209
Byrne, *Intelligence Officer*; p.16
Campbell, Patrick, *P.C*; p. 96
Canada, p. 50, 190
Carroll, Jim; p. 58, 60, 97
Caruso, Enrico; p. 155, 157
Carton, Victor; p. 100
Casement, Roger; p.9, 55
Castle, Mrs Barbara; p. 83, 89
Cavour, Count Camillo Benso di; p. 185–187
Ceannt, Éamon; p. 9
Chichester-Clark, James; p. 184, 186
Childers, Erskine; p.23, 31
christianity,
    Caesar, p. 90, 159, 163
Calvary, p. 192,
Cardinal Richelieu, p. 55, 99, 108
Christ, p. 49, 90, 99, 107, 130, 159, 192, 193,
    195
Church of the Holy Sepulchre, p. 195
Father Joseph du Tremblay, p. 55
Father John Murphy, p. 43, 54, 174
Father Smith, p. 26
Fatima, p. 192
Heaven, p. 72, 217
Hell, p. vii, xviii, xx, 1, 19, 72, 102, 152
Lourdes, p. 192, 193
nuns, p. 10, 104
parish priests, p.40
pharisees, p.90
Pilate, the Roman Governor; p.99
Presbyterians, p. 173–175, 179
religious souvenirs, p.191
St Michan's Parish, p. 155

St Paul, p. 159
St Paul's (Mount Argus, Dublin), p.26
the Blessed Virgin, p. 193
the Clergy, p.9, 214
    the Gospel, p. 70, 173
the Pope, p. 3, 48, 186
the Rosary, p. 7
the Sermon on the Mount, p. 155
    Via Dolorosa, p. 192
Christie, Bob; p. 47
Churchill, Winston; p. 46, 50, 51, 55, 177
Clarke, James; p. 30, 118, 125
Cluskey, Frank; p. 65, 148
Cole, Seán; p.16
Colley, Alfred; p. 16
Collins,
    Michael; p. 12, 14, 28, 30, 31, 33, 72, 76, 175,
        176
    Mrs, *Sherwin's aunt*; p. 16
    S; p. 163
    Tom; p. 122
Collis, Robert, Dr; p. 71
Coogan,
    Deputy, 162
    Fintan; p. 165
Congo, p. 81, 87, 204
Conlon, Captain Bob; p. 28
Connolly,
    James, p. 40, 52, 91, 106, 107, 130, 131, 176
    John, p. 11, 22, 31
Cooney, Éamonn; p. 46, 55
Copenhagen, p. 191
Corish, Brendan; p. 87, 106
Cosgrave,
    Liam; p. 86, 95, 97, 133
    William T; p. 31, 86, 144
Costello, John A; p. 65, 97
Coughlan Stephen; p. 149
Coughlin, Timothy; p. 32, 36
courts, p. 15, 19 26, 32, 39, 56, 62, 124
crime, p. 48, 99, 195
bank robberies, p. 37
criminals, p. 25, 26, 33, 92
slanderous statements, p. 57
sodomy, p. 25
    the *Gardai*, p. 90, 131
high court judges, p. 62
'wigs', p. 62
legislation, p. x, 59, 62, 73, 80, 99, 149, 158,
    178, 201
monetary reform, p. 103
the Army Pensions Act of 1932, p. 101, 110,
    116
the Army Pension Act of 1962, p. 110, 116
the Broadcasting Act of 1960, p. 154
the Housing Bill of 1966
the Liqueur Bill of 1962, p. 142
the Pension Act of 1937, p. 101
    the Small Dwelling Act, p. 100
the Test Act, p. 175

'the White Paper on the future of Northern Ireland', p. 201, 203, 204
unpopular...., p. 59
the District Court, p. 6, 22, 24, 133
the Central Court, p. 24, 25
the Civil Courts, p. 19
the Four Courts, p. 8, 14, 15, 21, 24, 30, 43, 53, 190
the High Court, p. 62, 88, 111, 112, 124–126
the Supreme Court, p. 124
Cowan, Councillor Rory; p. 61, 143
Peadar, p. 60, 143, 148
Crivon, *SG;* p. 112, 119, 120, 122, 124
Crosby, *a warder,* p. 25
Dalton, Commandant Charles; p. 22, 26, 28, 31, 115, 222
Daly, Michael; p. 29
Daly, P.T, *former labour councillor,* p. 40
dance,
'agents of the devil', p. 40
business, p. 37, 40, 43, 51, 60, 64, 134, 189
diploma, p. 42
dances, p. 3, 35, 39–44, 47, 48, 56
equipment,
amplifier, p. 56
halls, p. 38, 40, 42, 43, 47
'immoral relations', p. 42
Irish, p. 47
'loose women', p. 48
night clubs, p. 43, 142, 150
promoting, p. 38, 43
protection money, p. 41
schools, p. 56, 57
studio, p. 53, 56
the dancing board, p. 42
the theory and technique of dancing, p. 41, 42
world champion dancers, p. 42
Davin, Seamus; p. 46, 55
Deasy, Liam; p. 24, 33
Richard, p. 104, 110
Desmond, Barry; p. 164, 222
DeValera, Éamon; p. 13, 14, 21, 28, 30–32, 34, 48, 51, 65, 79, 80, 82, 85, 104, 109, 110, 144, 157, 176, 214–216
'Chief', p.48
Diggis, *an associate of Thomas Russell,* p. 175, 179
Dillon, Deputy James, *T.D;* p. 81, 82, 86, 94, 103, 106, 127, 132, 223
John, *friend of Frank Sherwin;* p. 37
John, *leader of the Irish Parliamentary Party;* 86
Dockrell, Maurice; p. 101, 109
Dolan, Commandant Joe; p. 15, 20, 21, 26, 28, 30, 32, 115
Donnellan,
Michael; p. 97, 105
P.J; 106
Doody, Mr *of Doody's Dairy;* p. 19
Douglas, Stephen A, *Senator;* p. 176, 180

Dowling, Richard J; p. 119
Doyle, Peadar Seán; p. 62, 65
Doyle, T, *legal team;* p. 112, 121, 122, 126
Dublin, p.ix, xi–xiii, xviii, 3, 5, 7, 8, 11, 14–16, 28–34, 38–40, 52, 55, 58, 59, 62, 65–67, 75–77, 84, 86, 87, 92, 94, 97, 104, 108, 109, 112, 113, 115, 124, 129, 133, 139, 143, 144, 148, 149, 151, 157, 160, 169, 172–175, 178, 179, 183, 186, 187, 195, 206, 209, 223
City Council, p. xi, xviii, xix, 58, 94, 95, 149, 150, 169, 170, 203
aldermen, p. 3, 60, 68, 94, 106, 129, 135, 144, 148, 149, 154, 172
council affairs, p. 60, 62
councillors, p. 60, 62, 63, 67–69, 83, 84, 94, 135, 138, 140, 143–148, 190, 191, 206, 210, 220
council meetings, p. 60, 67
the Council Chair, p. 61
City Hall, p. 8, 16, 63, 120, 208, 210, 220, 221
Corporation, p. 62, 68, 69, 81, 94, 120, 129, 30, 136, 137, 145, 148, 149, 150, 155, 156, 191, 220,
activity, p. 68
committee meetings of..., p. 60, 67–69, 120, 143, 145, 148
administration of..., p. 60, 67
'a quorum', p. 69, 148
expenditure at.., p. 67
housing estimates, p. 160
official records of, p. 68
technical officers at..., p. 67
department, p. 69
officers of..., p. 67, 68
members of.., p. 120
tenants, p. 67, 129, 139, 143, 147, 154, 155
the rates estimates meetings, p. 67
the Tenants Association, p. 140, 155
National Association of Tenants, (NATO), p. xii, 155, 156
Vice-Chairman of Dublin Corporation Committee, p. 68
work, p. xviii, 69, 160
Custom House, p. 13, 139
employment in .....,
auction rooms, p. 198
boot-repair shops, p. 25
building sites, p. 52
grocery stores, p. 17
labourers, p. xii, 52, 92, 132, 141, 162
obsolete trades, p.11
harness maker's apprentice, p. 10
outfitters, p. 21
second-hand shops, p. 57, 198
Health Authority, p. 145, 161, 169
Mansion House, p. 12, 62, 63, 220, 221
mountains, p. 17, 29
place names of...,
Arbour Hill, p. 153

Ashbourne Village, p. 8
Bachelors Walk, p. 197–199
Ballymun, p. 191, 195
Ballytore Road, p. 124
Bank of Ireland Chambers, p. 115
Boland's Mill…., p. 8
Bolton Street, p. 130, 131
Bolton Street School, p. 130
Bray, p. 45
Bridewell Station, p. 131
Broadstone Avenue, p. 5
Brunswick Street, p. 198
Cabra, p. 205, 206
Cartons' Poultry Firm of…., p. 5
Clondalkin, p. 26
Church Street, p. 5
Church Terrace, p. 5
City Centre, p. 17, 77
City University, p. 148
College Street *Garda* Station, p. 134
Coolock, p. 129, 155
Dartry, p. 32, 36
Dáil Éireann, p. vii, 77, 79, 85–87, 95,
    105–112, 121, 122, 132, 140, 149, 150, 156,
    161–165, 187, 202, 208
Doody's Dairy, p. 16–19, 125
Dorset St, Upper; p. 5
Dublin Central, p. 109, 153–155
Dún Laoghaire, p. 41, 169
Dún Laoghaire Borough, p. 169
Dún Laoghaire-Rathdown, p. 149
Exchange Buildings, p. 68
Gardiner Row, p. 45
Gardiner Street, Lower, p. 40, 41, 56
Glasnevin, p. 52
    cemetery, p. 30, 55
Green Street, p. 24, 179
Halston Street, p. 5
Jacob's Biscuit Factory, p. 8, 32
Jervis Street, p. 37, 41, 68
Kildare Street, p. 77
Kilmainham, p. 10, 51, 179, 180
Kingsbridge Station, p. 122
Leeson Park, p. 124
Leinster House, p. xi, 77, 79, 102, 111, 125,
    126
Liberty Hall, p. 52, 132
Linenhall Street, p. 35, 56, 112
Loftus Lane, p. 47
Lord Edward Street, p. 68
Lott's Lane, p. 134
Merrion Square, p. 45
Model Dairy, p. 6
North, p. 3, 135, 153, 191, 195
North City, p. 57, 153, 154
North King Street, p. 7
North West, p. 47, 154
O'Connell Bridge, p. 70, 92
O'Connell Street, p. 9, 21, 36, 45, 52, 56, 95,
    100, 104, 108, 134, 151

O'Devaney Gardens, p. 153
O'Donoghue's of Wood Quay, p. 11
Old Cork Hill, p.8
Oriel House, p. 22, 26
Ormond Quay, p. 30, 112, 113, 115
Parnell Square, p. 11
Peter's Place, p. 16
Phibsborough National School, p. 6
Quays, p. 24, 56
Raheny, p. 16
Rathfarnham, p. 17, 124
Rory O'Connor House, p. 129
Rush, p. 3, 10
Scanlan's, *harness makers*, p. 11
South City, p. 153, 154
South West, p. 3, 4, 138
St Stephen's Green, p. 51, 113, 115
Tallaght, p. 17
the College of Surgeons, p. 8
the Fairyhouse races, p. 6
the Feather Bed Mountain, p. 15
the Labour Exchange, p. 100
the Liffey Junction Railway Station, p. 18
the Metropole Cinema, p. 47
the *Oireachtas*, p. xx, 77
the National, *dance hall* p. 47
the Naul, p. 3, 198
'…the old men's home', Kilmainham, p. 10
the Rotunda Winter Gardens, p. 47
The Savoy Cinema, p. 151
    Werburgh Street, p. 100
    Westmoreland Street, p. 54, 112
    Whitehall, p. 16, 18
    Wood Quay, p. 11, 131
        population of…, p. 169
        the Chief Scout for…., p. 34
        the locals of…., p. 10
Trades Council Hall, p. 40
    Trade Union Council, p. 100
Dunne,
    James, *Senator*, p. 99, 100
    Seán, p. 138, 148
Durocher, Leo Ernest; p. 71, 75
Eason, *Sherwin's driver*, p. 17
East Prussia, p. 184
elections, p. 51, 57, 64, 70, 73, 82, 88, 134,
    154, 163, 204
    by-elections, p. 128, 180
    candidates, p. 46, 58, 62, 63, 66, 70, 72,
    135, 154, 156
    canvassing, p. 45, 50, 63, 65, 80
    circulars, p. 49
    constituencies, p. 32, 43, 47–51, 61, 70, 84,
    87, 95, 96, 105, 108–110, 153–155, 187,
    205
    constituents of…, p. ix, xix, 71, 103, 155
        the Constituency Committee, p. 46,
    47, 57
        the Constituency Council, p. 43
Cork North Central, 133

Cork South-West, p. 172
Donegal North-East, p. 86
Donegal West, p. 86
Dublin Central, p. 109, 153–155
Dublin South, p. 4, 30, 106, 107, 109
Dublin South-West, p. 3, 138
Dublin West, p. 108, 153
Galway North, p. 165
Galway West, p. 105
Laois/Offaly, p. 95, 103
Limerick East, p. 87
Longford/Westmeath, p. 84, 108
Manchester, p. 32, 51, 171
Roscommon, p. 32, 84, 108
the Docks, p. 59
councils, p. 63, 67, 136
'duds', p. 68
local, p. 67, 136
local matters of...., p. 67
Dublin Regional Council, p. 55
Dáil elections, p. 61
delegates, p. 45, 46, 48, 54, 98, 190
democracy, p. xvi, 36, 46, 66, 74, 77, 79, 164,
    214, 218
democratic assemblies, p.66
idealism of..., p. 77, 79
inherent flaw of..., p. 77
symbol of..., p. 77
dictatorship, 34, 66, 184, 217, 218
    dictators, p. 44, 66
        assassination of...., p. 66
        benevolent..., p. 66
progressive, p. 66
revolution against..., p. 66
    tyrants, p. 66
European elections, p. 172
fixing, p. 43, 45, 48
    artful dodgers, p. 70
bribery, p. 72, 104, 130, 131, 176
fixers, p. 49, 70, 72, 159
wangling, p. 45
wire-pulling, p. 45
functions, p. 61, 76
mandates, p. 21
mayoralty elections, p. 61
municipal elections, p. 143, 147, 148, 209
parliamentary elections, p. 202
opponents, p. 57, 68, 88–91, 104, 143, 144,
    204
polling day, p. 50, 206
ballots, p. 46, 209
polling station, p. 50
votes, p. xiii, xv, 30, 32, 45–50, 57–61, 69–74,
    80–83, 100, 105, 128–132, 135, 136, 140,
    142, 144–146, 154–156, 159, 164, 178, 182,
    192, 206, 209
    preference votes, p. 58, 61, 135
voters, p.44, 49, 50, 57, 59, 66, 70, 82, 100,
    128, 129, 143, 148, 154, 159, 192, 202, 206
    tenant, p. 156

women, p. 83
posters, p. 57, 129, 131, 206
presidential elections, p. 62, 73
proportional representation, p. xii, 72, 76,
    135, 202
re-election, p. 69, 94, 125
the electorate, p. 104, 132, 158
    breweries, p. 99
business people, p. 43, 66, 91, 94, 103, 111
Corporation tenants, p. 67, 129, 139, 143,
    147, 154, 155
poor people, p. 5, 59, 129, 149
    publicans, p. 48, 99, 131
    ratepayers, p. 67, 145, 146, 169
'super republicans', p. 57
'the rank and file', p. 58, 213
the unemployed, p. 16, 50, 91, 97, 100, 161
the working class, p. 60, 70, 91, 104
    the lower, p. 70
the General Elections, p. 43, 45, 55, 61, 63,
    91, 92, 96, 102, 105, 108, 128, 130, 133,
    136, 151, 153, 156, 157, 162, 187, 203–205,
    215,
    of 1885, p. 180
    of 1886, p. 180
    of 1918, p. 30, 109
    of 1921, p. 33, 187
    of 1922, p. 30
    of 1923, p. 31, 109
    of 1927, p. 109, 187
    of 1932, p. 43, 106
    of 1933, p. 106, 157
    of 1943, p. 45, 105
    of 1948, p. 64, 65
    of 1951, p. 87
    of 1954, p. 87, 98, 100, 106, 107, 130
    of 1957, p. 32, 61, 63, 87, 106
    of 1961, p. 32, 69, 80, 87
    of 1965, p. 32, 50, 68, 109, 128, 130,131,
        135, 151, 157, 162
    of 1969, p. 49, 50, 82, 109, 152–154
    of 1973, p. 87, 108, 156, 203
    of 1977, p. 108
    of 1982, p. 133
the Local Elections, p. 45, 58, 94, 130, 146,
    205
    of 1967, p. 68, 130, 136, 153
the Wood Quay Local Elections of 1902, p.
    131
    Westminster elections, p. 187
Emmanuel, Victor; p. 185, 188
Emmet, Robert; p. 179
Ennis, Superintendent; p. 37
Everett, James; p. 97, 98, 105
Evry, Hal; p. 159, 164
Fahy, Mr, *legal team*; p. 112, 121
Finucane, *Deputy*; p. 81
Fitzgerald,
Lord Edward, p. 174, 178, 224
Mick; p. 47, 55

Flanagan,
   Des, p. 138, 148
Oliver J.; p. xiii, 73, 95, 100–104 108–111,
   117, 119, 125
Flannery, *prisoner from Galway*; p.27
Ford,
Joe, p. 3, 10
Lena, p. 195
France, p. 9, 29, 55, 62, 75, 99, 108, 132, 150,
   175, 178, 185, 186, 191–193, 214
colonists, p. 184
Paris, p. 51, 55, 74, 87, 89, 150, 179, 189, 191
Prime minister of…, p. 99
'the battle fields in France', p. 9
   the Normans, p. 12
Fraser, Ian, *Sir*, p. 222
Galvin, *Deputy*, p. 127
Gandhi, Indira, Mrs; p. 83, 88
Gannon, Ned; p. 170
Garibaldi, Giuseppe; p. 185, 186, 188
Germany, p. 73, 74, 107, 108, 176, 181
   Germans, p. 9, 10, 105, 108, 184, 186
   The German Consul, p. 105
Griffith, Arthur; p. 29–31, 214
Groome, Joe; p. 151
Guinan, Mary Louise, 'Texas'; p. 142, 150
Guiney, Denis; p. 45, 54
Hales,
Seán, p. 24, 33, 54
   Tom, p. 24, 33
Hamilton, Mr; p. 112
Harris, Geoffrey; p. 137, 148, 222
Harling, Seán; p. 23, 32, 34
Haughey, Charles; p. x, 82, 84, 86, 109, 123,
   156, 182, 186
Hayes & Sons Solicitors, p. 112, 114, 115
Healy, John; p. 111, 119
   Michael, p. 117
   Seán, p. 104
Heath, Sir Edward; p. 202, 206
Heavey, S, *SC*; p. 111, 112, 118–122
Heffernan, Michael; p.97, 106
Hendrick, Tom; p. 21
Heuston, Seán; p. 43, 54
Hitler, Adolf; p. 70, 73, 74, 99, 107, 145, 177,
   223
   German Finance Minister and economic
   expert to…, p. 99
Hogan, *Ceann Comhairle*, p. 128
Dr, p.101
James; p. 76, 158, 159, 163, 223
Mr; p.112, 113, 116
Hollis, Christopher; p. 72, 76
hospitals,
   Bellevue Municipal Hospital, p. 37
Bray Clinic, p. 1
Bricin's Military Hospital, p. 43, 201
Jervis Street Hospital, p. 37, 41
Orthopaedic Clinic, p. 45
mental hospitals, p. 169, 170

the Meath Hospital, p. 45
the Richmond Hospital, p. 45
St Brendan's, p. 171
St Vincent's Hospital, p. 37
Houghton, Surgeon 'Daddy'; p. 45
housing,
   construction, p. 68, 191
   differential rents, p. 59, 138, 139, 141
   dwellings, p.58, 59, 68, 69, 129, 131, 138,
      139, 144–147, 191, 195, 203, 206
      *allocation of…*p. 68
   circumstances, p. 69, 140
   the Allocation Department, p. 138
   the Allocation Office(r), p. 138
   the Principal Officer, p. 138
housing law, p. 68
old people's, p. 58
the housing files, p. 69
the priority system, p. 69
   The Small Dwelling Act, p. 100
housing and rent offices, p. 68
lack of…, p. 58
The Housing Bill of 1966, p. 139, 149
the housing emergency, p. 58
landlords, p. 5
matters…, p. 220
municipal, p. 58
authorities, p. 100
work, p. 62
planning, p. xii, 59, 85, 86, 147, 150, 190,
   meetings around…, p. 60, 66, 67–69, 120,
   143, 145, 147, 148, 150, 156, 160, 169
   the Finance Committee, p. 136, 137
   the General Purposes Committee, p. 147
   the Housing Committee, 58, 100, 138, 144,
      147, 220
      chairman of…, p. 58, 100, 220
      vice-chairman of…, p. 58
   the Housing Planning Committee, p. 59
   the City Manager, p. 68, 138, 139, 141,
      143, 147
   Assistant City Manager, p. 138, 148
function of…, p. 68
tenements, p. 5, 49, 58, 131, 146
Huxley, Aldous; p. 48, 55
India, p. 76, 83, 88, 193
   Prime Minister of…, p. 88
Intelligence,
   officer(s), p. 16, 21, 25, 32, 37, 115
   the Intelligence Office, p. 19, 31, 115, 117
   the Intelligence Room, p. 20, 22, 115, 118
Ireland, p. xii, 36–38, 51–53, 62, 65, 75, 76,
   79, 85–87, 94, 95, 100, 106, 110, 115, 143,
   150, 173–175, 179, 180, 182–184, 187, 194,
   194, 202, 211–217
insurgents of…, p. 9
   partition of, p. 13, 81, 109, 177, 182, 185,
      186, 204, 213, 218, 219
   places in……,
   Arklow; p. 97

Ballinscorney, p. 16–18
Cashel, p. 15
Castlekelly, p. 17
Cavan, p. 194
Clare, p. 26, 28, 55, 179
Cork, p. 8, 12, 15, 28, 29, 33, 55, 62, 65,
76, 84, 97, 103, 110, 129, 132, 133, 150,
172, 174, 178, 194
places in...,
Bantry Bay, p. 174
Mallow, p. 103
Donegal, p. 86, 174
places in....,
Lough Swilly, p. 76, 174
Drogheda, p. 16, 213
Dundalk, p. 15, 16, 33, 108
Galway, p. xii, 27, 53, 55, 105, 149, 165, 180
Kerry, p. 9, 29, 54, 179
Kilbride, p. 44
Kilkenny, p. 40
Lacken, p. 18
Laois, p. 31, 95, 103, 105
Limerick, p. 29, 87, 88, 98, 106, 122, 142,
149, 150
Junction, p. 123
Meath, p. 16, 179
Newgrange, p. 16
Northern Ireland, p. 85, 110, 182, 185–187,
201, 202, 204–206
places in....
Belfast, p. 30, 52, 62, 5, 94, 109,
174, 179, 183, 202
Divis Street, p. 183
Dover Street, p. 183
The Falls Road, p. 183
Prime Minister of...., p. 184, 186
Offaly, p. 95, 103, 105
Sligo, p. 51, 132
Thurles, p. 15
Tipperary, p. 15, 30, 55, 106
Waterford, p. 29, 100, 108, 187
playwrights, p. 63
the clan system, p. 173
the Gaelic League, p. 27, 29, 186
Gaelic football, p. 5
the Irish Citizens Army, p. 52, 132
'the Irish people', p. 48, 112, 173, 175, 178,
185
the Irish Volunteers, p. 28–32, 109, 132, 156,
186, 187
the Irish Transport Union, p. 40, 132
the Northern Police, p. 186
the Orange Order, p. 182, 183
the 1916 Proclamation, p. 173, 175
United Irishmen, p. 75, 174, 178, 179
Israel, p. 83, 89, 191, 192
Prime Minister of..., p.83, 89
Italy, p. 29, 74, 150, 185, 186, 188
places in.....
Modena, p. 186

Parma, p. 186
Rome, p. 186
Sardinia, p.85
Prime Minister of....., p. 185
Sicily, p. 185
Southern, p. 185, 186
Tuscany, p. 186
Vatican-Rome State, p. 186
Prime Minister of...., p. 187
Jericho, p. 191
Jerusalem, p. 90, 107, 191, 192
Jordan, p. 191
Kane, Joseph Nathan; p. 45, 54, 71, 76
Simon; p. 26
Kelly,
James, Captain; p. 94
the man; p. 17
Kennedy,
JFK; p. 45, 54, 70, 74–76, 99, 107, 125, 144,
163, 177, 195
Robert; p. 107, 192, 195, 196, 207
Ted, Senator; p. 117, 125, 204, 205
Kenny, SC; p. 112, 118, 119, 126
Kent, Frank; p. 159, 163, 223
Keyes, Michael J; p. 97, 106, 149
Kinsella, Jack; p. 57
Kopechne, Mary Jo; p. 118, 204, 207,
Lasky, Victor; p. 70, 74, 107, 223
Lemass, Noel; p. 15, 29, 154
Seán, p. ix, x, xviii, xx, 3, 15, 21, 30–32, 64,
69, 73, 80–82, 86, 97, 109, 128, 136,
151–153, 159, 203, 204
Larkin,
Denis; p. 58, 59, 61, 62, 65, 145
James; p. 40, 52, 58, 98, 106, 107, 132, 139,
148, 176
James Jr; 106, 107, 148
Lehane, Con; p. 61, 65, 111, 125, 148
Lehane, a solicitor; 112, 113, 116
Leneghan, Joe; p. 100, 104, 152
Lenihan, Brian; p. 100–102, 108, 109
Leseur, Elizabeth, p. 84, 89
Lincoln, Abraham; p. 144, 155, 157, 176,
180, 185
Lippman, Walter, p. 70, 74, 75
Lindoph, Mr, of Bray Clinic; p. 45
Lynch,
Jack; p. 80, 109, 153, 182
Liam; p. 14, 29
MacAonghusa, Proinsias, p. xi, 65, 141, 149
Machiavelli, Niccolo; p. 70, 74, 104, 144, 150,
178, 223
MacNeill, Professor Eoin; p. 109, 185–187,
223
MacIver, Robert M; p. 71, 76, 223
Mann, Roderick; p. 159
Markiewicz, Constance, Countess; p. xiii, 34,
36, 43, 51, 53, 83
'chairman of the organizing committee', 36
'Madam', p. 34–36, 43

Macardle, Dorothy; p. 29, 33, 223
MacEntee, Seán; Minister for Health; p. 65,
    100, 109, 124, 161
McBrin, Paddy; p. 57, 63
McCabe, Mr, *a delegate*; p. 98
McCann, Jack; p. 63, 65
McCluskey, *a boy called*; p. 6
McDermott, Seán; p. 9
McDonagh, Thomas; p. 9
McGrath, Tom; p. 47
McQuillan, *Deputy*; p. 81, 85, 86
Meagher, G.H.; p. 139, 149
medical,
    conditions,
        gastritis, p. 25
        nerve injuries/problems, p. 37, 119, 123
        palpitations, p. 39
        physical disability, p. 38, 160
        scabies, p. 23, 27
        stroke, p. 37, 40
        'the handicapped', p. 38
    treatments,
        electric, p. 45
        first aid, p. 20, 21
        massage, p. 37–39, 45
        medical aid, p. 39
        medical examinations, p. 43
        physiotherapy, p. 42
        surgical belts, p. 38, 45
        violet-ray, p.37
        x-ray, p. 37
    the Health Account, p. 93, 160, 161
    the Health Service, p. 141
    the Medical Board, p. 101
    the Medical Officer, p. 31, 39, 68, 146
    surgeons, p. 8, 45
Meir, Golda; p. 83, 88, 89
Mellows, Barney; p. 53
Liam; p. 33, 43, 53
Micks, E.C.; p. 125
militant organizations, p. 34
    boy scouts, p. 51
    Chief Scout for….., p. 34
    Deputy Chief Scout, p. 35
    scouts, p. 10, 18, 51
    handbooks, 34
military,
    barracks, 7, 15, 17–22, 26, 28, 29, 31, 44,
        115
        Beggars' Bush Barracks, p. 31
        Collins' Military Barracks, p. 44
        Griffith Military Barracks, p. 26, 29, 115
        Linenhall Barracks, p.7
        Portobello Military Barracks, p. 17, 22, 26,
            28, 31, 115
        Richmond Military Barracks, p.7
        Wellington Barracks, p. 18, 19, 25, 26, 29,
            115, 117, 118
    battalions, p. 10, 11, 22, 28, 34, 44, 56
        B. Company First Battalion, p. 10, 11

        D. Company Second Battalion, p. 10
        Fianna Company O/C/ B.Company, First
            Battalion of 1920, p. 11, 28
        Fianna Company O/C/ D.Company,
            Second Battalion of 1919, p. 28
        The First Battalion IRA Signal Class, p. 11
        The Twenty-Sixth Battalion, p. 56
    camps,
        Newbridge, p. 23, 27, 190
        Tintown Camp, *the Curragh*, p. 15, 23, 27, 30
    court martials, p. 19, 22, 26, 51, 54
    the Military Governor, p. 27
Miller, R; *Private Secretary to William Whitelaw*,
    p. 202
Mitchel, John; p. 54, 55
Moore, *the man*; p. 19
Mullan, Michael; p. 58, 65, 68, 141, 142, 149
Mullen, Fred; p. 58, 65, 137
Murphy,
    Fergus, p. 26,
    Jack; p. 50, 51
    Timothy J; p. 106, 139, 149
W. *Deputy*; p. 81
music,
    concerts, p. 27
    jazz, p. 47, 53, 150
    musicians, p. 40, 53
        songs, p. 7, 53
        *Tramp, Tramp, Tramp, we have the Germans
            on the run*, p. 10
Norton, William; p. 87, 97, 98, 106, 107, 130
nursing homes, p. 80
O'Brien,
    Conor Cruise; p. 82, 87
    Jimmy; p. 42, 60
    Steam; p. 164
O'Connell, Daniel; p. 175, 179
    Catholic Emancipation, p. 175, 178, 179
O'Connor, James; p. 170
    John; p. 55
O'Doherty, Captain; p. 19
O'Higgins,
    Kevin, p. 22, 25, 29, 31
    Thomas F, *Dr*; p. 105
O'Keefe, James; p. 65
    Paidín; p. 27
O'Keeffe, Jimmy; p. 61, 170
O'Kelly, Seán T; p. 3, 150
O'Leary, Michael; p. 129–132
O'Malley, Donagh; p. 82, 87, 88
O'Reilly, Willie, p. 10, 11, 171, 172
O'Riada, Seán; p. 111, 125, 126
O'Shea, *Katherine*, p. 180
parliaments, p. xii, xx, 5, 12 30, 51, 55, 62,
    72, 88, 107, 110, 144, 173, 175, 178, 179,
    187, 188, 204, 208, 212, 213
    members of…, 81, 136, 144, 151, 156, 204
    Parliament of the Republicans, p. 12
    parliamentary secretaries, p. 32, 87, 100, 103,
        105, 109, 137, 182

the Irish Parliament, *abolished 1800*, p. xx, 5, 178
  the *Sanhedrin*, p. 107
Pearse,
  Margaret, p. 153, 156
Mrs, p. 156
Patrick Henry, *Pádraig*, p. 9, 156, 157
philosophy, p. 77, 84
  philosophers, p. 84
politics,
  general, p. 40, 43, 45, 46, 48–51, 57–59, 63, 65, 66, 68, 71, 72, 74, 75, 80, 82-87, 92, 99, 102, 103, 108, 111, 112, 120, 121, 125
  issues, p. 12, 55, 58, 62, 66, 67, 71, 94, 98, 111-113, 145, 152, 157, 173, 178, 205
governments,
  general, p. ix, x, xiii, xvi–xviii, xx, 3, 13–16, 21–24, 27, 30–34, 44, 51, 54, 55, 58–60, 64, 69–72, 75, 76, 79–101, 103–106, 108–111, 116–119, 123–127, 128, 130, 136, 137, 139, 140, 142, 143, 145, 149, 150–152, 156–159, 162–164, 174, 178, 179, 181, 182, 184–187, 190–192, 201, 203–205, 218, 219, 223, 224
  Bavarian, p. 73
  Bolshevik, p. 181
  British, p. 55, 99, 174, 201
  coalition, p. 32, 73, 84, 95, 97, 98
  Dutch, p. 75
  inter-party, p. 60, 64, 86, 87, 105, 106
  local, p. 23, 31, 33, 54, 79, 86, 87, 106, 109, 137, 139, 140, 143, 145, 149–151, 191, 205, 224
  Italian, p. 186
  Janata, p. 88
  Jordanian, p. 192
provisional, p. 13, 14, 31, 33, 89, 156
state, p. 31, 34, 187
  the Church of Ireland Government, p. 174
  Westminster, p. 179
  'headquarters of the political police', p. 22
  the *Ard Fheis*, p. 31, 47, 48, 109, 157
  the Common Market, p. 31, 81, 90, 204
  women councillors, p. 83
  women in...., p. 83, 84, 89
  politicians, p. x, xiii, 23, 57, 66, 67, 70, 72, 78, 79, 85, 89, 90–93, 100, 111, 119, 124, 125, 139, 140, 143, 156, 159, 160, 162, 164, 178, 194, 204, 205
  democratic p. 70
  *misrepresentation of...*p. 129, 131
political parties, p. xiii, 43, 45, 46, 48, 58–60, 66, 70, 136, 138, 154, 182, 202, 203, 218
  campaigns, p. 54, 57, 58, 74, 88, 94, 97, 120, 129, 130, 143, 164, 176, 201, 206
  Clann na Poblachta, p. 57, 64, 65, 80, 87, 148
  Clann na Talmhan, p. 64, 80, 85, 97, 105, 149
  cliques, p. xvii, 43–48, 70
  the National Executive Clique, p. 43

clubs, p. 46, 47, 57, 135
  'paper clubs', p. 43
  the Club Committee, p. 57
  'The Cole and Colley Club', p. 35
  youth clubs, p. 35, 36
committees, p. 62, 136, 150, 160, 169
community associations, p.
  meetings, p.
cumann, p. 31, 33, 36, 43–47, 51, 103, 106
  the Casement Cumann, p. 46
the Father John Murphy Cumann, p. 43
the *Fianna Fáil* Cumann, p. 36, 103
the John Mitchel Cumann, p. 46
conventions, p. 13, 29, 45, 46, 48, 62, 205
deputations, p. 58, 93, 96
  deputies, p. 24, 34, 45, 64, 85, 86, 97, 101, 102, 104, 122, 128, 139, 153
extremists, p. 44, 204
funding, p.
groups, p. xv, 44, 54, 58, 63, 80, 81, 88, 128, 181, 162, 218
  caucus, p. 63, 70, 169, 185, 218
  grass roots, p. 82
  protests, p. 36, 141, 184
  trade union, p. 52, 82, 88, 100, 132, 143, 176
  congress, p. 65, 74, 88, 132, 181
the Provisional United Trade Unions, p.100
leaders of..., p. 33, 51, 82, 84–87, 94, 97, 98, 103, 105–108, 127, 130, 132, 133, 145, 146, 156, 164, 174, 176, 178, 180–182, 185, 187, 206
  opposition, p. xvi, xvii, xviii, 32, 46, 52, 58, 62, 72, 80, 81, 83, 89, 91, 93, 94, 97, 102, 103, 110, 111, 117, 123, 127, 128, 130, 136–138, 142, 151, 154, 156, 158, 173, 180, 182, 183, 185, 194, 199, 203, 204, 206, 209, 218
  organisations, p. xii, 32, 87, 110, 155
party games, p. 80, 143, 204
party politics, p. xiii, 57, 176
party systems, p. xvii, 57, 71, 142, 218
political platforms, p. 67
policies of...., p. 27, 29, 30, 32, 34, 52, 65, 70, 86, 88, 97, 99, 100, 103, 107, 110, 138, 144, 155, 169, 183, 184, 186, 201, 203, 205, 2111, 218, 219
political prizes, p. 70
party machines, p. 67, 129, 140, 154
'hatchet men', p. 72, 99, 218
strategists, p. 63
the *Fianna Fáil* Party, p. x, xvii, xviii, xx, 3, 4, 28, 30–36, 43–45, 47, 49, 51, 54, 55, 57, 60, 61, 63, 65, 80–83, 85–87, 93, 94, 96, 98, 101–103, 105, 106, 108–111, 130, 145, 145, 151, 153
  candidates, p. 60, 61, 98, 152
  deputies, 102, 127, 140
  Director of Elections *for...*, p. 82
  the National Executive of *Fianna Fáil*, p. 44

the *Fine Gael* Party, p. 31–33, 58, 59, 61,
    63–65, 80, 82, 83, 86, 87, 91, 93, 94, 96,
    97, 101, 103, 105, 106, 109, 111, 127,
    133, 136, 137, 142, 144, 146, 149, 162,
    163, 169, 172, 203
        candidates, p. 58
deputies, p. 64, 97, 101
the Independents, p. ix, xvii, 30, 51, 60,
    61, 66, 67, 69, 73, 80, 81, 91, 92, 128,
    137, 154–156, 158, 159, 169, 219
the Labour Party, p. 22, 30, 40, 51, 52, 59,
    60, 61, 63–65, 68, 80–85, 87, 89, 91, 93,
    94, 97–100, 103, 105–107
annual conference; p. 98
councillors, p. 40, 65, 68, 94, 140, 141
chairman of…., p. 141
vice-chairman of…., p. 149
the National Progressive Democrats, p. 80,
    87
the *Sinn Féin* Party, 8, 28, 30, 31, 33–35,
    51, 63, 105, 109, 156, 157, 187, 204,
    214, 215
chairman of…, p. 34
Executive, p. 34
public representatives, p. 43, 66, 68, 173
    public affairs, p. 66
propaganda, p. 36, 52, 93, 137, 214, 215
Portugal, p. 29, 192
Powell Enoch, John; p. 105, 110
presidents,
    Cosgrave, William T; *of Ireland*; p. 26, 34
    Kennedy, John F; *of USA*; p. 45
    Lincoln, Abraham; *of USA*; p. 144
    Nixon, Richard M *of USA.*; p. 204
    O'Kelly, Seán T; *of Ireland*; p.
    Roosevelt, Franklin D *of USA*; p. 176, 180
    Truman, Harry S *of USA*; p. 71, 76
prison,
    Bridewell Prison, p. 22, 26
    Dundalk Prison, p. 15
    Mountjoy Prison, p. 15, 23, 24, 26, 27, 29,
        35
        the political wing of, p. 23
        camp officers, p. 27
        conditions in….,
        diet, p. 27
        cooks, p. 27
        cells, p. 22–24, 26, 27, 53
            'Hut no. 16', p. 23, 24
            recreation, p. 26, 27
    prisoners, p. 19, 20–27, 35, 51, 106, 203,
    204
        ex-, p.106
        female, p. 51
        imbecilic, p. 25
        older, p. 24
        political, p. 24, 26, 27, 203
            remand, p. 27
            young, p. 23
    reformatories, p. 6

'The White Cross', *prisoners' aid society*, 35
    warders, p. 25
    recitations,
    The Story of Easter Week, p. 7
Redmond, John; p. 185, 187
Reid, *a solicitor*; p. 24
Reynolds,
    Albert, p. 78, 84, 85
    Thomas; p. 34
RGDATA; p. xii, 94, 95
Rigley, Patrick; p. 22
Robinson, Major; p. 22
Rochford, Daniel; p. 18
Ronan, Shay; p. 140
Roosevelt, Franklin D; p. 176, 177, 180
Russell, Thomas; p. 75, 175, 178, 179
Ryan, Dr James; p. 23, 31, 32, 100, 109
Sardinia, p. 185
Saunders,
    George; p. 159
    Seán; p. 44, 54
Scannell, Jim; p. 198
Schacht, Hjalmar Dr; p. 99, 103, 107, 108
'Sergeant Instructor', p. 44
Shakespeare, William; p. 163, 224
Sheridan, *Independent TD*; p. 127, 128, 155
Sherwin,
    Alan, p. 65
    Christopher, p. 5
    Christy, p.134, 135
    Éamon, p. 65, 192
    Francis, p. 192
    Jim, p. 195
    Joe, p. 6, 11, 15
    Kathleen, p. 135
    Liam, p. 65
    Marie, *see plate section*
    Mary, p. xviii, 3, 4, 27, 31, 194
    Mary Jane (*née* Ford), p. 3, 5
    Roseleen, p. 129
    Rosie (*née* Kinsella), p. 40–42, 51
    Vincent, p. 65
Slein, *Dr*; p. 119, 123
Spain, Jim; p. 26
Spain, p. 192, 193
    places in ….
        Gibraltar, p. 192, 193
Spark, David; p. 137, 148, 222
Stalin, Joseph; p. 178, 181
Standing, Bordon; p. 122, 123, 126
Stafford, Tom, *Alderman*; p. 94, 95, 137
Stockholm, p. 191
Sylvester, Victor; p. 42, 52, 53
Taylor, Rex; p. 76, 224
taxation, p. 59, 60, 72, 90–92, 97–100, 103,
    127, 141
    increases in…, p. 59, 72, 90, 92, 98, 100,
    203
        public assistance, p. 35, 56, 152
        social benefits, p. 59, 86, 90, 91, 93, 97,

98, 128, 131, 141, 156, 162–164, 189, 203
  disability pension, p. 43, 101, 110, 116–118, 153, 201
  'the dole', p. 56, 57, 64, 102
  the Turnover Tax, p. ix, x, xiii, xviii, xx, 55, 90–94, 100, 102, 104, 111, 112, 116, 127, 141, 142, 145, 151, 152, 157, 220
VAT, p. xviii
theatres,
  La Scala, p. 31, 35, 52
the Burns' Detective Force, p. 38
the continent of Europe, p. 67, 211
  conferences on..., p. 67
the *Dáil*, p. ix, x, xvi, xx, 12, 13, 32, 33, 35, 47, 50–54, 57, 59, 62, 64, 65, 68, 69, 73, 79, 80–84, 86, 87, 90–96, 99, 100–106, 109, 111, 116, 117, 123–126, 128, 129, 135, 136, 138–142, 18, 149, 151, 156–163, 71, 182, 185, 203, 208, 219, 220
  cabinet ministers of...., p. 63, 144, 182
  Ceann Comhairle, p. 64, 128, 150
  chairman of the ...., p. 64, 80
  chamber, p. 86, 101, 127, 128
  hustings, p. 92
  members of..., p. 136
  reports, p. 139, 201
  seats, p. 151, 152
    *loss of...*p. 151
TDs, p. xii, x, xiii, 3, 30–33, 50, 54, 55, 59–61, 64, 65, 68, 69, 86, 87, 94, 95, 97, 98, 100, 103, 105, 106, 108, 109, 111, 119, 123, 125 150
  ex–, p. 69
the *Fianna*, p. ix, 10, 11, 16, 18, 23, 34, 35, 44, 56, 171
  brigade, p. 47
    area commanders, p. 13
  Company O/Cs, p.11, 28
  comrades of..., p.16
  Éireann Executive, 34
    General Headquarters Staff, p. 13, 34
  Non-Commissioned Officer (NCO), p. xii, 54
  recruits, p. 44, 45
  the Active Service Unit, p.20
  the Adjutant General's Staff, p. 11
  the Dublin Brigade, p. 23, 44
    Intelligence Unit, p. 34
  the Old *Fianna*, p. 44
  chairman of..., p. 44
the Irish Free State, p. 28, 29, 31, 33, 62, 106, 187
  Army, p. 28, 33
  authorities, p. 23
  murder gang, p. 16, 22, 28
the National Army, p. 11, 14, 21, 22, 76, 171
the National Movement, p. 64, 185
the Irish Republican Army, *the IRA* p. xii,

7, 9, 11–16, 18, 19, 21–25, 29, 31–36, 44, 47, 51, 53, 55, 85, 86, 94, 100, 104, 112, 114, 116, 134, 156, 171, 182–184, 186, 187, 190, 201, 202, 204, 214, 215
  adjutant general of..., p. 18
  Deputy Chief of Staff of..., p. 24
  intelligence, p. 12, 35
  leadership, p. 24
  pensions, p. 51, 100, 104, 112, 114, 116
  the Director of Intelligence, p. 22
  the old...p. 32, 33, 44, 134
  the Provisional, p. 201, 204
  veterans, p. 47, 86, 156
  the Irish Republican Brotherhood, p. xii, 13, 22, 55, 185, 187
  the Irish Transport and General Workers' Union, p. xii, 52, 58, 65
  the Lord Mayor, p. 12, 55, 58–63, 65, 67, 93, 94, 96, 137, 148, 154, 172, 209, 210, 220
  mayors, p. 62, 63, 106, 164
  mayoralties, p. 61–63, 94, 96, 137
  'the plum job' of..., p. 137
  the Temporary Chief Citizen of Dublin, p. 62
  the Media, p. 63
    newspapers, p. 15, 83, 85, 94, 125, 135, 139, 149, 154, 156, 197, 201
  representatives of...., p. 69
  The Evening Herald, p. 4, 89, 94, 132
  The Evening Mail, p. 64
  The Evening Press, p. 4, 104, 110, 120, 203, 206
  The Irish Independent, p. 4, 65, 85, 95, 103–108
  The Irish Militant, p. 130, 131
  The Irish Press, p. 4, 85, 108, 150, 157
  The Irish Times, p. 3, 4, 30, 31, 57, 81, 91, 99, 102, 103, 108, 110–112 116, 118, 121, 123–127, 221
  The Sunday Express, p. 159
  publicity, p. 34, 45, 61, 63, 66, 67, 137, 154, 160, 176, 184
  radio, p. xii, 56, 65, 66, 73, 92, 94, 107, 149, 155
  comperes, p. 92
  Radio Éireann, p. 65, 92, 94, 149
  television, p. 63, 66, 69, 70, 82, 92–95, 104, 111, 129, 136, 138 141–143, 149, 154 155, 157, 164 196, 210
  personalities, p. 82
  programmes,
    'Hurlers on the Ditch', p. 69, 111
    'Question Time', p. 160
    'The Late Late Show', p. 95, 193, 196
  Radio Telefís Éireann, p.94
  the Pensions Board, p. 2931, 33, 116
  'the Police', p. 8, 10, 12, 26, 41, 155, 191
    agent, p. 34, 36
    spies, p. 36

the Rebellion of 1916, p. 132, 144
'the Rising', p. 7, 8, 28, 30–33, 51–55, 75, 105, 109, 156, 185, 187, 214
   Easter Monday, p. 6, 7
      leaders of..., p. 7, 31, 54
      looting, p. 7
      looters, p. 7
   the Volunteers Executive, p. 185
the Republic of Ireland, p. x, 28, 86, 94
the republicans, p. 12, 14, 27, 28, 102, 111, 175, 176
'the first Irish republican', p. 75
'super republicans', p. 57
the Republican...
   Army, p. 6
   Civil Authorities, p. 14
   Movement, p. 30
   the Staffordshire Regiment, p. 7
'the Treaty', p. 13, 14, 21, 29–31, 33, 74, 82, 109, 157, 215, 217
'the Truce', p. 10–12
Treacy, Seán; p. 28, 30, 185, 187
Trehy, *a publican*; p. 40
Truman, Harry; p. 71, 76
Vidal, Gore; p. 70, 74, 224
warfare, p. 12–14, 30
   tactics
      ambush, p. 28, 33
      barricades, p. 6, 185
      columns, p. 13, 15, 17, 18
      flying columns, p. 13, 16
      the Plunkett Flying Column, p. 16
         convoy, p. 15, 18, 28, 187
      gangs, p. 15, 22, 41
      firing squad, p. 22, 31, 33, 52–54, 156
      gangsters, p. 40, 204
      'gunmen', p. 13, 15, 28
      'Little Caesars', p. 14
      murder gangs, p. 15, 16, 22, 28
      'speakeasies', p. 40
      spies, p. 12, 34, 36, 54, 213, 215
      squads, p. 12, 6, 22, 30, 31, 33, 52–54, 157
      the Four Courts Leaders, p. 24, 43
      'The Hover Gang', p. 41
      thugs, p. 41, 73, 101, 131
      guerrilla *styled*, p. 12–14, 30, 176, 215
      'hit and run', p. 12
      'knocking shops', p. 19
      mutiny, p. 22, 31, 185

patrols, p. 15, 18
sadists, p. 26
signal cabins, p. 18
signal classes, p. 11
telephone wires, p. 18
terrorists, p. 26
war
   the American Civil War, p. 185
   the American War of Independence, p. 178
   the English Civil War, p. 212
   the Emergency (1939–1944), p. 22, 30, 32
   the 'God of Battles', p. 8
   the Great War 1914–1918, p. 10, 187
   'the Germans', p. 9, 10, 186
   the Irish Civil War, p. ix, xiii, 3, 14, 15, 19, 21, 22, 24–30, 32–34, 47, 54, 76, 82, 101, 102, 111, 157, 174, 176, 217, 218
   the War of Independence, p. 12–15, 21, 26, 28, 29, 32, 33, 51, 53, 126, 176, 187, 222
   World War II, p. 76
   weaponry, p. 72, 130, 187, 214, 215
   bayonet scabbards, p. 20
   belts, p. 20
   firearms, p. 22, 51
   miniature rifle range, p. 44
   pellet guns, p. 44
   razor, p.20
   revolver, p. 20, 26, 31, 117
   butts, p. 117
   'Peter the Painter', p. 26
   rifle, p. 9, 20, 26, 44, 94, 115, 119
   bullets, p. 94
   butts, p. 26, 115
   squibs, p. 6
   sticks, p. 20, 119
   wires, p. 18, 20
Walsh, Tom; p. 21
Wells, H G; p. 178, 181, 224
White,
   Alfred, *Fianna* Acting Adjutant General; p. 16, 19, 20, 23, 29, 34, 49, 52
   George, p. 21
Whitelaw, William; p. 202, 206
Wolfe Tone, Theobald; p. 54, 71, 75, 174, 175, 178, 214
Wood, Edward Frederick Lindley; *First Earl of Halifax*; p. 71, 76
Younger, Carlton; p. 33, 224